M000313874

"EXECUTE AGAINST JAPAN"

NUMBER 121

WILLIAMS-FORD TEXAS A&M UNIVERSITY

MILITARY HISTORY SERIES

"EXECUTE AGAINST JAPAN"

The U.S. Decision to Conduct Unrestricted Submarine Warfare

JOEL IRA HOLWITT

Texas A&M University Press
College Station

This paper meets the requirements of ANSI/NISO Z39.48-1992
(Permanence of Paper).
Binding materials have been chosen for durability.

Library of Congress Cataloging-in-Publication Data
Holwitt, Joel Ira, 1981–
  "Execute against Japan" : the U.S. decision to conduct unrestricted submarine warfare / Joel Ira
Holwitt.—1st ed.
      p. cm.—(Williams-Ford Texas A&M University military history series ; #121)
  Includes bibliographical references and index.
  ISBN-13: 978-1-60344-083-7 (cloth : alk. paper)
  ISBN-10: 1-60344-083-6 (cloth : alk. paper)
  1. World War, 1939–1945—Naval operations—Submarine. 2. World War, 1939–1945—Naval
operations, American. 3. World War, 1939–1945—Campaigns—Pacific Ocean. 4. Submarine
warfare—United States—History—20th century. 5. Freedom of the seas. 6. United States.
Navy—Submarine forces—History—20th century. I. Title. II. Series: Williams-Ford Texas A&M
University military history series ; 121.
  D783.H65 2008
  940.54'510973—dc22
                          2008024073

Dedicated to my family:
My mother, Dr. Dara S. Holwitt
My father, Dr. Eric A. Holwitt
And my brother, Greg S. Holwitt

CONTENTS

List of Illustrations   ix
Acknowledgments   xi

Introduction   1

1   Freedom of the Seas, the Submarine, and the First World War   5

2   The U.S. Navy and the Submarine Question   19

3   The Failure of International Law in the Interwar Period   29

4   Legislating Away Freedom of the Seas   48

5   The Accidental Commerce Raider:
       U.S. Submarine Development, Strategy, and Tactics   63

6   Laying the Strategic Groundwork   84

7   Debating Law, Ethics, and Strategy   97

8   "Immediately upon the Outbreak of War"   120

9   Day of Infamy, Day of Decision   139

10   Unrestricted Warfare and the Civilian Chain of Command   150

11   The Victory of Unrestricted Submarine Warfare   162

Conclusion   181

Notes   185
Bibliography   229
Index   237

ILLUSTRATIONS

(following p. 96)

The USS *Covington* sinks after being torpedoed by a German U-boat.

The senior naval leadership of the United States, including some members of the General Board of the Navy, December 1920

The USS *S-44* off Cuba in 1929

The USS *Barb,* one of the most famous fleet submarines

Admiral Harold R. Stark on his first day as the Chief of Naval Operations

Rear Admiral Richmond Kelly Turner

Admiral Edward Kalbfus during the Second World War, presiding as a member of the Naval Court of Inquiry into the Pearl Harbor attack

James Fife as a captain in the Second World War

Admiral Thomas C. Hart, Commander-in-Chief of the U.S. Asiatic Fleet and one of the oldest and most respected submariners in the U.S. Navy

Sailors assigned to the Submarine Base at Pearl Harbor stare at the carnage caused by the Japanese sneak attack on December 7, 1941.

Admiral Harold Stark is decorated by President Franklin D. Roosevelt.

Stark's direct superior, Secretary of the Navy Frank Knox.

The USS *Wahoo* (SS 238) enters Pearl Harbor in February 1943 after the most successful war patrol in the war up until that point.

One of *Wahoo*'s confirmed victims, *Nittsu Maru,* on her way to the bottom in March 1943.

ACKNOWLEDGMENTS

I was very fortunate to have three outstanding scholars on both my dissertation and thesis defense committees: my adviser, Dr. John F. Guilmartin, a soldier-scholar of the highest caliber, who gave me plenty of freedom to pursue my project while still setting high standards; Dr. Allan R. Millett, another distinguished soldier-scholar, who pushed for results and usually got them; and Dr. Kevin Boyle, an extraordinary academic historian, who taught me why academic history is not culturally irrelevant when done right. I am also grateful to Dr. Fred J. DeGraves, professor of veterinary preventive medicine, who served as the outside reader for my dissertation defense.

The professors on my doctoral candidacy committee also held me to a rigorous standard of academic ability and scholarship. In addition to Dr. Guilmartin and Dr. Boyle, I would like to thank the following: Dr. David Stebenne, whose comments and high standards pushed me to work harder, smarter, and better; Dr. Mark Grimsley, who provided a very different but important view on where the scholarship of military history should be going; Dr. James Bartholomew, who took a student largely ignorant of Japan and gave him a crash course in Japanese history from the Meiji Restoration onward; and Dr. Philip Brown, an expert on early modern Japan, who still kept me honest when discussing more recent events in Japanese history. I am also grateful to Dr. Robert Lawson, the graduate school's representative. Finally, I am deeply indebted to Rob Padilla and Evan Dicken, two fellow graduate students who prepared me for the Japanese field of the candidacy exam.

I am also indebted to my other professors at Ohio State University: Dr. Geoffrey Parker, Dr. Matt Goldish, Dr. Warren Van Tine, Dr. Judy Wu, Dr. Randy Roth, and Dr. Alan Beyerchen, all of whom inspired me to become a better historian. I am also grateful to the other graduate students in the military history program at Ohio State: Lieutenant Colonel John Plating, U.S. Air Force; Major Steven Barry, U.S. Army; Major James Doty, U.S. Army; Major Franz Rademacher, U.S. Army; Mark Mulcahey, Leif Torkelsen, Jon Hendrickson, Todd Aoki, Josh Howard, and Jeff Jennings.

No historical work based heavily on archival sources can succeed without the help of the talented archivists at numerous archives around the country. In particular, the following archivists helped me greatly:

Barry Zerby, Archivist, Modern Military Records, National Archives and Records Administration, College Park, Maryland

Rebecca A. Livingston, Archivist, Old Military and Civil Records, National Archives and Records Administration, Washington, D.C.

Dr. Evelyn M. Cherpak, Head, Naval Historical Collection, Naval War College, Newport, Rhode Island

Kathy Lloyd, Head, Operational Archives Branch, Naval Historical Center, Washington, D.C.

Wade Wyckoff, Archivist, Operational Archives Branch, Naval Historical Center, Washington, D.C.

Dr. Regina Akers, Archivist, Operational Archives Branch, Naval Historical Center, Washington, D.C.

Bob Clark, Supervisory Archivist, and Robert H. Parks, Mark A. Renovitch, Alycia J. Vivona, Karen P. Anson, and Virginia H. Lewick, Archivists, Franklin D. Roosevelt Presidential Library, Hyde Park, New York

Dr. Marvin Russell, Dr. Milton Gustafson, Mr. Matthew J. Olsen, and Mr. Louis Holland, Archivists, National Archives and Records Administration, College Park, Maryland

Christine Weideman and Danelle Moon, Archivists, Manuscripts and Archives, Yale University Library, New Haven, Connecticut

In particular, I owe a great debt of thanks to Mrs. Kathy Lloyd, Wade Wyckoff, and Dr. Regina Akers at the U.S. Naval Historical Center, who mentored me when I served two summer internships at that institution in 2001 and 2002. It is because of their education and aid that I was able to navigate the mazes of archival sources as quickly as I did.

My summer internship at the Naval Historical Center in 2001 proved to be special, not only because of my time at the archives, but also because the experience brought me acquaintance with two great submarine captains and their families. I am truly fortunate to have gotten to know the legendary Captain Slade Cutter and his kind wife, Ruth, as well as Captain Lee Moss, his wonderful wife, Holly, and their exuberant daughter, Avery. They inspired and mentored me as I began my journey as a naval officer and a naval historian.

I was also extremely fortunate to receive assistance from a number of outstanding naval and military historians. Dr. Williamson Murray, emeritus professor at Ohio State University, not only insightfully critiqued my manuscript but also gave me some much needed encouragement. Dr. William McBride, U.S. Naval Academy, provided me with inspiration, help, and ideas. Commander Craig Felker, U.S. Naval Academy, courteously sent me relevant sections from his Ph.D. dissertation related to interwar U.S. submarine warfare and training, and then discussed my dissertation with me at length. Dr. Randy Papadopoulos, U.S. Naval Historical Center, talked with me about previous research on this topic and also gave me one of his unpublished papers related to the subject. Dr. Bruce Elleman, U.S. Naval War College, read through and comprehensively critiqued my manuscript. I am also indebted to Justin Accomando, Naval Nuclear Power School roommate, Naval Academy classmate, and Oxford-trained naval historian, for his comments and critique on the manuscript.

I am grateful to a number of people who let me stay at their home while I was doing research for my thesis, including my Naval Academy sponsor family, the Fitzgeralds: Dr. Jeff, Mrs. Lynda, Matt, Danny, and Buddy. Also my close friend and Naval Academy roommate, Peter Buryk, and his wife, Missy; my grandmother, Beverly Holwitt; and my aunt, Elisa Holwitt Duch and her family. In addition, I cannot overstate the unfailing support and encouragement of two other close friends and Naval Academy roommates, Kevin Joyce and Matthew Isenhower, as well as my Naval Academy Senior Enlisted Leader, Chief Aviation Electronics Technician Daniel Williams, who proved that nothing important ever gets done without a Navy chief petty officer.

I cannot thank enough the professional editors who brought my manuscript into print. In particular, I am grateful to Mary Lenn Dixon, editor-in-chief of Texas A&M University Press; Lys Ann Weiss, who copyedited my manuscript into a superior book; Jennifer Gardner Nader, exhibits and special promotions manager; and many others who turned one of my dearest dreams into a reality.

Finally, I would like to thank my immediate family: my brother, Greg Holwitt; my mother, Dr. Dara Holwitt, DDS; and particularly my father, Dr. Eric Holwitt, Ph.D. Dad may be a combat biochemist and a retired U.S. Air Force officer, but he knows enough about naval history to give most naval historians a run for their money. He conceived of this project soon after I graduated from the U.S. Naval Academy, while we sat in a blacked-out restaurant in Maryland during a thunderstorm. He continued to encourage me as I read through secondary literature and then worked my way through numerous archives. He read every major draft of the manuscript, even while serving a tour as a U.S. government weapons inspector in Iraq in the fall of 2004. Dad is exactly what a scholar and an officer should be. I cannot thank him enough.

"EXECUTE AGAINST JAPAN"

Introduction

At 1752 Eastern Standard Time on Sunday, December 7, 1941, about four and a half hours after the initial chaos unleashed by the Japanese attack on Pearl Harbor, the U.S. Navy's Chief of Naval Operations released a simple but dramatic message:

EXECUTE AGAINST JAPAN UNRESTRICTED AIR AND
SUBMARINE WARFARE.[1]

It was 0652 on Monday, December 8, in Manila. It was 1222 on December 7 in Pearl Harbor.[2]

With the orders to conduct unrestricted warfare, all Japanese shipping, from fishing trawlers to freighters to tankers, became valid targets. Because civilian crews manned most of these ships, unrestricted warfare meant that these civilian sailors would be treated like combatants, not innocent noncombatants whose lives were to be spared at all costs. Unrestricted warfare not only directly targeted civilians at sea, it also indirectly targeted millions of civilians in Japan, who suffered starvation and privation. The later U.S. strategic bombing campaign, which would kill numerous Japanese noncombatants, came toward the end of hostilities. The unrestricted war against all maritime shipping, however, started at the very beginning of the war and did not end until Japan's surrender. Thus, well before the United States accepted civilian casualties as collateral damage in the strategic bombing campaigns, U.S. unrestricted warfare struck at Japanese civilians both at sea and on shore.

The decision to conduct unrestricted warfare was a major and dramatic change to the American attitude toward freedom of the seas. From its inception, the United States had strongly stood out for the right of commerce to sail the world's oceans at all times without the threat of attack. Admittedly, the American view toward freedom of the seas evolved from 1776 through 1941, but the United States remained a consistent advocate and protector of noncombatant merchant ships and sailors. The strength of this conviction was demonstrated in 1917, when President Woodrow Wilson placed German unrestricted submarine warfare at the center of the U.S. decision to enter the First World War. Two decades later, President Franklin D. Roosevelt echoed Wilson's views as he assailed German unrestricted submarine warfare as one of the greatest threats to American freedom and security, as well as a crime against humanity.

Unrestricted submarine warfare was specifically and unambiguously illegal. The United States was a signatory to both Article 22 of the London Naval Treaty and the London Submarine Protocol of 1936. The two documents, which were identical, stated that submarines were required to remove a merchant ship's crew to a place of safety before that ship could be sunk. A place of safety, furthermore, was not considered to be a lifeboat on the open sea. It did not matter if the merchant ship belonged to a belligerent nation or a neutral nation. It did not matter if a merchant ship was arguably in the service of a belligerent nation's war machine. Regardless of origin or ownership, merchant ships could not be attacked without warning.

As war became inevitable, however, unrestricted warfare became a far more attractive option to U.S. naval strategists. Well before Pearl Harbor, with no documented approval from the civilian chain of command, the senior naval leadership of the United States decided to commence unrestricted warfare almost immediately upon the inevitable outbreak of hostilities. Although future writers attempted to portray the orders to conduct unrestricted warfare as a spur-of-the-moment decision made in the wake of the Pearl Harbor attack, the orders were really the result of a year of debate and consideration by the U.S. naval leadership.

By abruptly ordering unrestricted warfare in December 1941, the United States effectively turned away from the notion of Wilsonian freedom of the seas and the noncombatant nature of merchant ship sailors. The decision was such a significant about-face that diplomatic historian Samuel Flagg Bemis wrote: "Thus did the United States forswear and throw overboard its ancient birthright, the Freedom of the Seas, for which it went to war with Germany in 1917 and collected adjudicated indemnities, after the victory, for torts against its own citizens by illegal German submarine warfare, 1914–1918."[3] Another

historian, Janet M. Manson, asserted even more dramatically: "no other foreign policy reversal in U.S. history quite matches in magnitude [this] decision."[4] Had unrestricted submarine warfare not been clearly essential to the
U.S. victory over Japan, it might well have become as hotly debated a topic as
the use of the atomic bombs in 1945.

The U.S. decision to conduct unrestricted submarine warfare held dire
consequences for Japan. By the end of the war, Japan's merchant marine and
navy were at the bottom of the Pacific Ocean, due in no small measure to the
U.S. Navy's submarine force. Tens of thousands of Japanese merchant mariners, navy sailors, and army soldiers were dead, and Japanese soldiers and
civilians throughout the former Japanese empire were starving. With all supply lines severed by a scythe of American submarines, Japan's war machine
had collapsed.

Of potentially greater significance, American unrestricted submarine warfare also ended the Wilsonian paradigm of freedom of the seas and ushered in
a new and more pragmatic conceptualization that classified merchant sailors
as combatants and their cargoes as legitimate military targets. With the U.S.
decision to conduct unrestricted submarine warfare on December 7, 1941, the
idealism of Wilson gave way to the brutal reality of twentieth-century warfare.
This study is the story of that transition.

Although many authors and historians have mentioned or discussed the
U.S. decision to conduct unrestricted submarine warfare, often tangentially,
none has comprehensively described the chain of events leading to U.S. unrestricted submarine warfare. Only historians Samuel Flagg Bemis, Janet Manson, and J. E. Talbott have made a deep investigation of the subject. For various
reasons, however, their studies were not comprehensive and contained crucial
errors of detail. This history builds on these previous studies, and clarifies and
revises a number of their conclusions through the extensive use of archival
sources from the National Archives, the Naval Historical Center, the Naval
War College, Yale University, and the Franklin D. Roosevelt Presidential Library, as well as numerous published primary and secondary sources.

This history does not examine in any detail the actions of the maritime
enemies of the United States: Germany and Japan. The German path to unrestricted submarine warfare in both wars has been detailed by a number of
historians, particularly Janet M. Manson, and this study did not need to repeat
their work.[5] Although the warlike actions of Germany and Japan set in motion

the events that led to the American decision to conduct unrestricted warfare, the decision itself and the technological and legal considerations that made it possible all took place within the relatively isolated purview of the United States Navy. Outside influences impinged upon this process only a few times, such as the deliberations of international delegates at the Washington Naval Conference and the London Naval Conference.

This is not a legal history. This is the story of naval officers attempting to reconcile international law and military strategy. Although the officers discussed in this study chose to violate international law in favor of military necessity, they did not make this decision quickly or rashly. They were faced with a difficult and unenviable decision that forced them to weigh the evils of a type of warfare they despised against the terrifying specter of an Axis victory. This is a story of educated naval officers who understood the rules and limitations of international law, while also recognizing the new technological and strategic realities sweeping the world.

CHAPTER 1

Freedom of the Seas, the Submarine, and the First World War

The U.S. decision to conduct unrestricted warfare was intimately tied up with a change in conception regarding a parallel concept—freedom of the seas. Unrestricted warfare deliberately targeted noncombatant merchant ships, leaving survivors of an attack to the mercy of the elements and the sea. This was diametrically opposed to the Wilsonian view of freedom of the seas, which called for the protection of merchant sailors and their passengers. To understand why the U.S. decision to conduct unrestricted warfare was such a monumental change in American policy, one needs to follow the evolution of the concept of freedom of the seas from its inception through the First World War.

FREEDOM OF THE SEAS

Freedom of the seas is an old and important concept that has played a pivotal role in peace and war, particularly in the history of the United States of America. The distinguished American historian Samuel Flagg Bemis called it the "ancient birthright" of the United States.[1] Over time, however, the exact meaning of "freedom of the seas" has changed considerably. At the core of this change has been the conflict between the privileges of belligerent navies and the rights of noncombatant and neutral sailors. This conflict became even more intense in the twentieth century, with the advent of new technologies. Increasingly, the noncombatant status of merchant sailors and their ships came into doubt.

HUGO GROTIUS AND FREEDOM OF THE SEAS

The concept of freedom of the seas is an ancient one, but it was not seriously defined and intellectually defended until the seventeenth century. In 1609 Dutch philosopher Hugo Grotius anonymously published a small but important book, *Mare Liberum,* or "The Free Sea." Grotius's work set the conceptual boundaries of freedom of the seas, starting with the very first paragraph of the first chapter:

> We will lay this certain rule of the law of nations (which they call primary) as the foundation, the reason whereof is clear and immutable: *that it is lawful for any nation to go to any other and to trade with it.*[2]

Grotius asserted that the seas were different from land because while solid land could be owned as property, the ever-shifting liquid seas could not be possessed. Furthermore, while land could be garrisoned and guarded, no nation could ever maintain a permanent presence in one stretch of water. Grotius believed that while a kingdom could rightly tax its own subject sailors and fishermen, it could not extend that control to the ships and sailors of other nations that sailed in waters claimed by that kingdom. In short, because of its fluid nature, "the sea is incomprehensible, no less than the air, [and] it can be added to the goods of no nation."[3]

Understandably, Grotius's ideas drew a great deal of debate and controversy. Because of his detailed denials of the Catholic Church's right to apportion territory or the seas, the Church banned his book. Additionally, a number of scholars wrote detailed critiques, which added important heft and nuance to Grotius's concept, establishing the justification for territorial waters and other caveats to freedom of the seas. Grotius's argument became so thoroughly accepted that he even suffered the ignominy of having his own book used to undermine his negotiating position in a fishing dispute with England in 1613.[4]

Grotius's ideas contributed not only to the concept of freedom of the seas in peacetime but also to a growing debate about the ability to search and seize ships of other nations on the high seas. Grotius's *Mare Liberum* actually served as the twelfth chapter of a much larger philosophical work, not fully published until 1864, *De Jure Praedae Commentaris,* or "Commentary on the Law of Prize and Booty." Within the larger context of *De Jure Praedae Commentaris,* Grotius's explanation dealt with the rights of neutral and belligerent merchant ships in time of war as well as with trade disputes in peacetime.[5]

Grotius confirmed that by natural law, private property was usually inviolable and to seize it was an act of theft. However, the concept of justice demanded that wrongful actions be punished and virtuous actions rewarded. In a just war, therefore, private property could be legitimately seized to recompense the virtuous side while depriving the wicked side of vitally needed supplies. Although Grotius never published the entire *De Jure Praedae,* he often referred to it in other texts and his ideas were in accord with previous "just war" concepts. Consequently, from the beginning, freedom of the seas was implicitly and intricately tied up with the belligerent right of search and seizure on the high seas.[6]

FREEDOM OF THE SEAS IN WARTIME

Transport over water has long proved to be the fastest, most reliable, and most efficient way to transport large numbers of people and quantities of supplies over extended distances. As a result, interdicting supplies at sea is one of the most vital missions of a belligerent navy. Until the twentieth century, the standard method of interdicting supplies at sea was search and seizure, a belligerent right that allowed hostile warships to search almost any ship and confiscate goods. Search and seizure was generally unpleasant for noncombatant merchant sailors, but it rarely cost lives or ships. As with the concept of freedom of the seas, however, the limits and meaning of search and seizure changed over time.

The rules of search and seizure were first codified in the *Consolato del Mare,* a work predating Grotius's *Mare Liberum* by at least a hundred years if not more. Perhaps the first work solely devoted to maritime law, the *Consolato del Mare* was essentially a compendium of legal opinions and precedents regarding the sea. In 1494, an edition of the *Consolato del Mare* included the opinion that enemy cargo could always be seized, but neutral cargo should not be seized, even if found on board an enemy ship. Unfortunately, because the *Consolato del Mare* was only a compendium of opinions and precedents, it was not actually binding upon any nation. Consequently, the French and the British often chose to confiscate any neutral ship carrying even the slightest amount of enemy cargo. Resentment over these actions resulted in a number of nations advocating the "free ships, free goods" concept.[7]

The idea of "free ships, free goods" maintained that a neutral ship's cargo was exempt at all times from seizure. The idea came to prominence in the seventeenth century, and underlay a number of wars between England and Holland. The British wanted to seize neutral ships if enemy cargo of any sort was found on board, while the Dutch wanted to protect their commercial empire. The solution was a compromise: the Dutch were willing to accept that belligerent ships with neutral cargo could be captured, so long as neutral ships were always exempt from capture. Eventually Holland succeeded in wringing

"Free Ships" treaties from France, Spain, and Great Britain, culminating in the Treaties of Utrecht that ended the War of Spanish Succession in 1713. However, the Dutch themselves were not above waiving their own rules in wartime, sometimes attempting to prohibit neutral traffic to an enemy country.[8]

A more practical version of the "free ships, free goods" doctrine admitted that any cargo on board any ship could be confiscated if it was contraband material needed for the war effort and ultimately bound for an enemy country. This, however, required agreement as to what type of material constituted contraband supplies and proof as to whether supplies were ultimately destined for the enemy's war effort. Such an agreement was unlikely. For instance, should clothing, which could possibly be used for uniforms, or wood or rubber, which could be used for ships and vehicles, be prohibited or not? The list of potential contraband could eventually cover every possible item that could be shipped. There was also the problem of "continuous voyage": what if a cargo bound for a neutral country was then shipped overland or by waterway to an enemy nation? Consequently, this concept of "free ships, free goods" was also problematic.[9]

Finally, there was an extreme view that essentially denied the belligerent right of search and seizure: why not simply make all private property on board ships exempt from seizure? In its ultimate form, this doctrine feasibly meant that all civilian merchant ships would be immune from harassment or capture. This concept was first enacted in a 1785 treaty between Prussia and the United States. Although other, more "practical" treaties quickly superseded this treaty, the concept of immunity of private property and the inviolability of civilian merchant ships eventually became a fixture of U.S. foreign policy.[10]

THE UNITED STATES AND THE FIRST ARMED NEUTRALITY

As previously noted, a number of treaties in the seventeenth and early eighteenth centuries called for freedom of the seas and neutral rights. But it was not until the late eighteenth century that a large number of world powers chose to formally codify these principles. In no small measure, this was due to the influence of the newly formed United States of America.[11]

With the beginning of the American Revolution, the Second Continental Congress quickly moved to establish ties with friendly powers. To guide diplomats sent abroad, a congressional committee created what became known as the Plan of 1776. In terms of maritime law, the Plan of 1776 adopted many of the principles of previous treaties:

free ships free goods, freedom of neutrals to trade in non-contraband between port and port of a belligerent . . . , restricted and carefully defined lists of contraband not including foodstuffs or naval stores, and generally liberal and considerate treatment of neutral shipping.[12]

The first diplomatic mission sent to France dutifully followed these instructions and secured these rights in the first Franco-American Treaty of 1778.[13]

Two years and several treaties later, Catherine the Great of Russia took up the initiative of freedom of the seas and neutral rights in response to the seizure of a number of her ships and the lack of an overarching code of maritime law. Catherine used virtually all of the principles in the Plan of 1776 in what became known as the Armed Neutrality of 1780, or the First Armed Neutrality.[14]

The First Armed Neutrality set specifications on close blockade, contraband, and neutral shipping. According to Samuel Flagg Bemis, the five important principles of the First Armed Neutrality were these:

1. That neutral vessels may navigate freely from port to port and along the coasts of nations at war . . .
2. That the effects belonging to subjects of the said Powers at war shall be free on board neutral vessels, with the exception of contraband merchandise . . .
3. That, as to the specification of the above-mentioned merchandise [contraband], the Empress holds to what is enumerated in the 10th and 11th articles of her treaty of commerce [of 1766] with Great Britain, extending her obligations to all the Powers at war . . .
4. That to determine what constitutes a blockaded port, this designation shall apply only to a port where the attacking Power has stationed its vessels sufficiently near and in such a way as to render access thereto clearly dangerous . . .
5. That these principles shall serve as a rule for proceedings and judgments as to the legality of prizes.[15]

The resemblance to the Plan of 1776 was striking, although Catherine was also harkening back to older treaties that contained similar rules. The first principle, as in the Plan of 1776, permitted neutral traffic between belligerent ports. The second principle was a restatement of "free ships, free goods," with a practical proviso allowing for contraband. The third principle set the contraband list to that of the British-Russian commerce treaty of 1766, which excluded naval stores, just like the Plan of 1776. The rules of blockade, embodied in the fourth principle, were also in agreement with the Plan of 1776. Although Catherine and her advisers may have used older treaties for templates, the Armed Neutrality of 1780 was still an enactment of what had become U.S. diplomatic policy.[16]

Although some mocked the Armed Neutrality of 1780 for being a hollow and poorly enforced treaty, many nations agreed to its principles, including the United States, France, Spain, Holland, Denmark, Sweden, Prussia, Portugal, and Naples. Great Britain refused to sign the First Armed Neutrality, but respected many of its principles. The principles of the First Armed Neutrality would become increasingly important over the next seventy years, gaining acceptance and credibility from all world powers. Moreover, the United States had established itself as a nation that placed great priority on the freedom of the seas.[17]

THE UNITED STATES AND THE DECLARATION OF PARIS

The ideas of the First Armed Neutrality gained greater currency during the nineteenth century. During the Napoleonic War, numerous nations discarded the principles of the First Armed Neutrality as they saw fit, including a short-lived Second Armed Neutrality dedicated to excluding British supplies from European ports. By the end of the war, however, most nations ended up returning to the ideas of "free ships, free goods" and other principles expressed by the First Armed Neutrality. After the Napoleonic Wars ended, virtually all treaties dealing with commerce adopted the rules of the First Armed Neutrality.

The watershed moment for the principles of the First Armed Neutrality finally came in the Crimean War (1854–1855). During the war, Great Britain and France both adopted the principles that had been enumerated in the First Armed Neutrality. When the Crimean War ended, these principles were codified in the Declaration of Paris of 1856, including "free ships, free goods," contraband law, blockade law, and an article that abolished privateering. However, even as the Declaration of Paris codified the paradigm of the First Armed Neutrality, a new conception of freedom of the seas was emerging from the United States.[18]

The United States had supported a vigorous concept of freedom of the seas from its inception, as seen in the 1785 treaty with Prussia that attempted to exempt all property from seizure on the high seas. In 1798, in response to predations by French privateers and warships on neutral U.S. merchantmen in the

Caribbean, President John Adams ordered U.S. Navy warships and privateers to retaliate against armed French vessels. Similarly, in 1803 President Thomas Jefferson sent a U.S. Navy squadron to the Mediterranean to end extortion and piracy by the Barbary corsairs located on the North African coast. Jefferson's subsequent trade embargoes and James Madison's War of 1812 were similarly grounded in an attempt to defend the right of American ships to freely and peacefully trade at all times and in all oceans. Many portions of the Declaration of Paris mirrored similar clauses that U.S. negotiators had attempted to place without success in the Treaty of Ghent that ended the War of 1812.[19]

The U.S. president in 1856 was Franklin Pierce, probably one of the strongest American proponents of freedom of the seas. Although most historians have derided Pierce for being incompetent and inept, President Pierce and his administration actively advocated for freedom of the seas and the respect of noncombatant rights at sea. With the vigorous prodding of Secretary of State William L. Marcy, the Pierce administration helped force Denmark to end the extortion of merchant ships coming through the Danish Sound. The Pierce administration also helped to force open for trade the River Plate in South America. Although Secretary Marcy failed to similarly open the Amazon River, his efforts laid the groundwork for the eventual treaty that opened the Amazon for all shipping. The Pierce administration was clearly not a slouch when it came to enforcing and expanding the freedom of the seas.[20]

Unlike previous administrations, which had settled for the principles embodied by the First Armed Neutrality, the Pierce administration adamantly pushed for the immunity of private property on the high seas and the inviolability of civilian merchant ships. Consequently, Pierce and his diplomats refused to sign the Declaration of Paris unless the prohibition of privateering was linked to the immunity of private property, except for war contraband.[21]

The Pierce administration's stance stemmed directly from the weak naval power of the United States and the importance of privateering in commerce warfare. Despite the naval success the U.S. Navy had enjoyed against the Barbary pirates and the famous victories of the War of 1812, the United States remained a relatively weak naval power with regard to naval superpowers like Great Britain. Privateers served as a cheap substitute for a powerful navy. Legitimized by a government-issued letter of marque and manned by well-motivated sailors, privateers sought to capture as much enemy commerce as possible. During both the American Revolution and the War of 1812, American privateers arguably played a far more important role than the U.S. Navy in wrecking the British merchant marine and leading maritime investors to beseech the British government to end the war. Consequently, the United States could always use the threat of privateers to deter naval superpowers from threatening American commerce. The United States was unwilling to throw away its greatest and cheapest maritime deterrent unless the great naval powers promised to enforce rules that would protect American commerce. The other delegations in Paris were reluctant to give up the time-honored practice of commerce interdiction, however, and they refused to add the proposed clause. As a result, although the United States generally abided by the Declaration of Paris, it never signed or ratified the document.[22]

FINAL CHANGES BEFORE THE FIRST WORLD WAR

The U.S. Civil War reinforced the American desire to protect merchant ships. Confederate raiders, such as CSS *Alabama,* decimated the U.S. merchant marine, and caused many American ship-owners to transfer their ships to a foreign registry. Although a small number of ships remained in what had been the U.S. merchant marine to struggle through the rest of the nineteenth century, "for fifty years, until the eve of World War I, the U.S. deep-sea merchant marine was as dead as the [sunk] *Alabama.*"[23] Understandably leery of losing what was left of the U.S. merchant fleet, American diplomats hardened their policy over the inviolability of civilian merchant ships. The U.S. government instructed American diplomats sent to The Hague Conferences of 1899 and 1907 to press for immunity of private property on the high seas. Unfortunately, as in the case of the Declaration of Paris, the great powers refused to countenance the proposal.[24]

The Second Hague Conference did lead diplomats to attempt the creation of an international prize court as well as an international body of maritime law. In 1909 the diplomats met in London, where they attempted to clarify definitions of contraband and issues regarding the ultimate destination of supplies. The Declaration of London hoped to resolve these problems once and for all by creating comprehensive contraband lists and prescribing different treatments for different types of contraband depending on their ultimate destination. In the end, all this effort was for nothing: the British refused to ratify the declaration, and as a result, no other nation ratified the document.[25]

Although the Declaration of London did not go into effect, most powers accepted the broad principles embodied in it—probably the ultimate expression of the principles of the First Armed Neutrality. However, these principles were soon to be challenged by the First World War. Faced with a quagmire on land, both the British and the Germans vied to cut off each other's economic lifelines at sea. The opposing belligerents hoped that without supplies, the massive war industries in the heart of both countries, as well as the entrenched armies in the field, would collapse. This meant that the belligerents would infringe upon each other's rights at sea in order to gain an advantage. The paradigms of the First Armed Neutrality and the inviolability of merchant ships were coming to an end.[26]

FREEDOM OF THE SEAS, THE SUBMARINE, AND THE FIRST WORLD WAR

When the First World War began, the British quickly clamped a massive long-range blockade on Germany. Instead of maintaining ships in a close blockade off the German coast, where they could be sunk by mines or coastal submarines, the British kept their fleet out on the high seas, intercepting any ships bound for Europe and forcing them to detour to British ports for search and potential seizure. The long-range blockade affected many neutral countries, but it was particularly effective against Germany, which rapidly lost most of its imports. The British made no effort to conceal that the point of the long-range blockade was to starve Germany into submission.[27]

In reciprocity for the British starvation blockade, Germany established its own "war zone" around the British Isles. With the German surface fleet effectively blockaded by the Royal Navy, the Germans turned to the fledgling U-boat force instead. The Germans had already recognized the potential effectiveness of the submarine in September 1914, when a small German U-boat sank three British cruisers within one hour. Now, the German Navy intended to use the submarine to its fullest potential. The German government declared that all belligerent merchant ships within the war zone were subject to destruction without warning, and the unrestricted war began in deadly earnest.[28]

During the first three years of the war, the effectiveness of the opposing blockades was largely checked by the influence of the United States. The belligerents recognized that if the United States felt its neutral rights were sufficiently violated to merit war, it could potentially tip the scales of conflict. Consequently, the Germans and the British both attempted to curry favor with the American president, Woodrow Wilson. This turned out to be extremely difficult due to Wilson's principles and idealism. Bred in the relatively recent tradition of the inviolability of merchant ships, Wilson believed that the United States had the right to trade with belligerents at all times, except in the case of a close blockade, the only legally recognized form of blockade, which required a belligerent to maintain ships in active proximity of a port. As a result, Wilson was as offended by the British practice of intercepting American ships on the high seas and detouring them to British ports as he was by the German practice of sinking ships and leaving survivors to their fate. Unfortunately, modern methods of warfare gave the British and the Germans little choice in conducting their maritime campaigns.[29]

The British could not impose a close blockade because their warships would be easy prey for submarines and minefields. By standing out to sea, the British could maintain a modicum of safety while imposing an effective long-range blockade. The Germans were in a similar situation: with their fleet bottled up within the North Sea, the Germans could not hope to contest the British control of the sea with only a few raiders and cruisers. Instead they had to rely on the submarine, which by its very nature could not observe cruiser rules of warfare.[30]

Cruiser rules of warfare were the practical application of the Declarations of Paris and London. They stipulated that a belligerent warship could stop a merchant ship on the high seas and search it for contraband cargo. If some contraband was found, it could be legally seized. If enough cargo was found, the merchant ship itself could be seized. If, under extraordinary circumstances, the warship commander found it necessary to sink the merchant ship, he had to take the crew on board as prisoners.[31]

A submarine, because of its small size, could do none of these things. Certainly, a submarine could stop and search a merchant ship, but it could not take aboard any seized cargo. It could not supply a prize crew to sail off the merchant ship, nor could it take on any more people, particularly as prisoners. Although some termed the German practice of stopping, searching, and sinking merchant ships, leaving crew and passengers to the ocean, as "warfare in accordance with cruiser rules," others justifiably considered the practice to be just as illegal as simply sinking a ship without warning from submergence. In 1915 the sinking of the British passenger liners *Lusitania* and *Arabic,* both with American passengers on board, led to strenuous protests by President Wilson's administration, and caused the German government to act with far more caution regarding passenger liners. The sinking of another unarmed ship carrying Americans, *Sussex,* in March 1916, forced the Germans to suspend submerged unrestricted warfare, in favor of surface warfare "in compliance with cruiser rules of warfare." This was not as great a sacrifice as it might have seemed, since most German submarines usually tried to attack on the surface with their deck gun in order to conserve their few torpedoes and also to prolong their patrol.[32]

The *Sussex* Pledge would not last long, however. There were two reasons: armed merchant ships, and unrestricted submarine warfare's potentially enormous influence on victory. Both reasons would haunt the naval powers long after the First World War.

Armed merchant ships dated from the beginning of the war, when the British Admiralty under Winston S. Churchill armed merchant ships and ordered them to use their armament to sink U-boats or at least fight them off. Although the armed British merchant ships rarely sank German submarines with their small-caliber weapons, they almost always deterred attacks. Moreover, the few cases in which armed merchant ships succeeded in sinking a U-boat were psychologically scarring. In particular, the Germans pointed to the case of *Baralong,* a British Q-ship that shelled and sank a U-boat and then mercilessly murdered the German survivors. Such cases were enough to convince any submarine commander not to risk a surface confrontation with a clearly armed or potentially armed merchant ship.[33]

Even more important than the presence of armed merchant ships was the German belief that unrestricted submarine warfare could bring victory. This belief was encapsulated in a memorandum by Admiral Henning von Holtzendorff, who argued that if the U-boats began unrestricted submarine warfare on February 1, 1917, they could sink enough British shipping to force the British to surrender by July 1, 1917. Although the memorandum's logic and statistics were questionable, the German High Command reached out for this solution like a lifeline. Overriding the concerns of the German chancellor, Theobald von Bethmann Hollweg, the German war leaders resumed unrestricted submarine warfare. Although they believed that the practice of unrestricted submarine warfare might draw the United States into the war, they were convinced that the United States would have neither the time nor the will to make a decisive difference.[34]

It was a costly misjudgment, and one that might have been avoided if the Germans had merely gone with another one of the options that the Holtzendorff memorandum mentioned: unrestricted warfare *only* against armed merchant ships. Despite his ideals, President Wilson pragmatically recognized the problem of armed merchant ships. He even quietly supported a *modus vivendi* by which the British would abolish their armed merchant ships and the Germans would consequently end all submerged unrestricted warfare. However, the British rejected the *modus vivendi,* being unwilling to give up any advantage over the U-boats. It was a wise strategic choice. For all his idealistic indignation, Wilson was not willing to go to war over British armed merchant ships. Yet he recognized that there was a major qualitative difference between the British starvation blockade and the German war zone: the German unrestricted submarine campaign abandoned noncombatants to possible death, while the British starvation blockade did not. Consequently, due to the renewed German unrestricted campaign against all ships—armed and unarmed, neutral and belligerent—as well as the inflammatory Zimmermann telegram, Wilson made his choice to enter the war. Within days of the renewed German campaign, on February 3, 1917, Wilson broke off relations with Germany and sent the German ambassador back home. On April 2, 1917, he went before Congress and asked for a declaration of war.[35]

In his address to Congress on April 2, 1917, Wilson utterly condemned unrestricted submarine warfare as antithetical to the traditional law of the sea that treated merchant ship sailors and passengers as noncombatants:

> International law had its origin in the attempt to set up some law which would be respected and observed upon the seas, where no nation had right of dominion and where lay the free highways of the world . . . I am not now thinking of the loss of property involved, immense and serious as that is, but only of the wanton and wholesale destruction of the lives of noncombatants, men, women, and children, engaged in pursuits which have always, even in the darkest periods of modern history, been deemed innocent and legitimate. Property can be paid for; the lives of peaceful and innocent people cannot be. *The present German submarine warfare against commerce is a warfare against mankind.*[36]

Without doubt, the overriding factor that led to Wilson's condemnation of unrestricted submarine warfare was the deaths of noncombatants, which included merchant ship sailors engaged in their livelihood. For Wilson, however, freedom of the seas entailed the right to travel not only without fear of being attacked, but also without fear of being stopped by a long-range blockade. It was this paradigm of freedom of the seas that would ultimately be enshrined in the second of his Fourteen Points:

> Absolute freedom of navigation upon the seas, outside territorial waters, alike in peace and in war, except as the seas may be closed in whole or in part by international action for the enforcement of international covenants.[37]

In short, Wilson's paradigm was essentially one of absolute freedom of the seas, which could be curtailed only under extraordinary circumstances.

Once the United States had entered the war, Wilson accepted some limits on freedom of the seas in order to win against Germany. For instance, he no longer protested the British blockade, and U.S. naval forces assisted in laying a mine barrage across the northern entrance to the North Sea to stop submarines. The U.S. contraband list expanded to the length of the British contraband list. For the most part, however, Wilson used domestic embargoes, blacklists, and other national coercive measures on U.S. ships and allies to cut off supplies to the Central Powers.[38]

Because the Allied victory hinged so greatly on U.S. intervention, the victory arguably legitimized Wilson's paradigm of freedom of the seas. Consequently, the Paris Peace Conference of 1919 was seen as a great opportunity to enact the Wilsonian paradigm of absolute freedom of the seas, which would deal simultaneously with the problems of long-range blockade and the difficulties posed by the submarine as a commerce raider.

THE BRITISH CHALLENGE TO ABSOLUTE FREEDOM OF THE SEAS

The Wilsonian paradigm of freedom of the seas was the final straw that caused the United States to enter the war on the side of the Allies. But that did not mean the rest of Allies were willing to accept the principle. The British refused to accept Wilson's view of absolute freedom of the seas, since they had no desire to give up the ability to conduct long-range blockades.[39]

The British view on absolute freedom of the seas was summarized in a contemporary pamphlet by Julian S. Corbett, a naval historian who had already left his mark by writing one of the great works on naval strategy, *Some Principles of Maritime Strategy,* published in 1911. In his 1918 pamphlet, *The League of Nations and Freedom of the Seas,* Corbett showed that he was under no illusions regarding Wilson's definition of absolute freedom of the seas:

As used by its most pronounced advocates, Freedom of the Seas denotes the abolition of the right of capturing private property afloat. They would deny to belligerents not only the admitted right to capture neutral property under the law of blockade and contraband, but would also make the trade of the belligerents equally immune, either altogether or in so far as it was not contraband—that is to say, that no matter how fiercely navies contend peaceful merchants and fishermen shall be free to go about their business as though no war were in progress.[40]

Corbett may have been exaggerating how immune belligerent shipping would be in war, but he accurately portrayed President Wilson's position. The Wilsonian paradigm was an evolution of older formulations, but at its core it championed the inviolability of merchant ships, a right that had never been admitted in common international law.

Over the space of ten pages, Corbett proceeded to condemn the paradigm of absolute freedom of the seas as utterly impractical:

It comes then to this—that if Freedom of Seas is pushed to its logical conclusion of forbidding altogether the capture and destruction of private property at sea, it will in practice go far to rob fleets of all power of exerting pressure on an enemy, while armies would be left in full enjoyment of that power . . . the voice of the Naval Powers would sink to a whisper beside that of the Military Powers.[41]

In short, without an ability to coerce enemy commerce, there was simply no point in having a fleet, besides coastal defense. For countries whose power derived from the sea, the ability to enforce their will would completely disappear with absolute freedom of the seas. For Great Britain, that was clearly unacceptable.

Although the British fundamentally disagreed with Wilson's view that all ships should be able to travel the seas freely in time of peace and war, they agreed that sailors and passengers on board merchant ships were noncombatants. So while the British posed an important challenge to the Wilsonian paradigm of freedom of the seas, the submarine posed an even more radical and lethal challenge. Not only were submarines unable to observe the traditional paradigm of freedom of the seas, but also their most effective employment, as unrestricted commerce raiders, directly conflicted with the notion of noncombatant status for merchant ship sailors and passengers. As a result, the submarine problem assumed primary importance in creating a new freedom of the seas.

CHAPTER 2

The U.S. Navy and the Submarine Question

Although it took the First World War to launch submarines to both strategic importance and universal outrage, many nations looked unfavorably upon submarines long before the war began. Even before the U.S. Navy or the Royal Navy had their first commissioned submarines, the issue of banning submarine construction had already been discussed at The Hague Conference of 1899. The nations of Great Britain, Germany, Russia, Japan, Italy, and Denmark all announced their desire to ban submarines, but only if all the attending nations agreed.[1]

THE SUBMARINE QUESTION BEFORE THE FIRST WORLD WAR

Other, weaker naval powers were quick to see the potential of a submarine fleet. Submarines seemed attractive because they could feasibly sink a powerful enemy's navy, while also destroying maritime shipping lanes. Best of all, submarines were cheap and could be built *en masse* by nations in place of massive battle fleets.[2] It was essentially the same rationale that the United States had once used to defend its decision to retain privateers after the Declaration of Paris.

The idea of submarines as a cheap substitute for capital ships enjoyed an early period of intellectual dominance in the late nineteenth century, particularly in France. A group of French naval officers, known as the *Jeune Ecole,* advocated the use of submarines as a cheap deterrent that could sink enemy battleships and, more important, strike directly at an enemy's economic lifelines. The Jeune Ecole presciently called for the use of submarines as unrestricted commerce raiders, claiming that other nations would undoubtedly do the same. By doing so, the Jeune Ecole hoped that submarines, like privateers in the past, would so raise insurance costs and threaten commercial trade that an enemy nation would sue for peace. The Jeune Ecole's high point came in 1886, when its most influential member, Admiral Théophile Aube, became minister of marine and suspended battleship construction in favor of submarine and torpedo boat development. Eventually, however, France resumed construction of battleships and a large battle fleet.[3]

For the most part, naval leaders before the First World War generally ignored the submarine's potential. By the end of the war, however, submarines had not only threatened Great Britain's existence but also helped drag the United States into the conflict. With the end of the war in November 1918, the world's naval leaders and legalists turned once again to the question of the submarine.

DECEMBER 1918: THE LONDON PLANNING SECTION MEMORANDUM

As soon as the First World War ended, numerous nations brought up the call for abolition of the submarine. Having suffered greatly, Great Britain naturally favored abolishing submarines, but other countries, like France and Japan, had different ideas. The idea of abolishing submarines proved controversial within the United States, driving a wedge between American politicians who favored doing so and U.S. naval officers who put their trust in the deterrent value of weaponry, not in treaties.

Of all the major powers, Great Britain was the most vulnerable to submarine warfare. The effectiveness of the German unrestricted campaign had badly shaken the British government, which recognized the danger a future submarine blockade posed. After the First World War, British foreign policy consistently aimed to abolish all submarines.[4]

Great Britain's traditional enemy, France, had everything to gain by building up a submarine fleet. Situated just across the English Channel, the French could easily flank the British trade routes with a fleet of submarines. The French poured money into their submarine force, explaining to their exasperated British neighbors that submarines were "an essential means of preserving [French] independence which [France] could not give up."[5]

Japan was the only other maritime empire with a situation analogous to that of Great Britain (as another island nation dependent on overseas commerce for the economy and national well-being), but Japan's view about the abolition of submarines differed from Great Britain's. Except for the Soviet Union, the Japanese had no close enemies with any naval strength. Although the Japanese recognized that they were just as vulnerable as the British, they favored a strong submarine force because they perceived that their greatest naval nemesis, the United States, would have to make a long Pacific transit before attacking Japan. During such a crossing, the U.S. fleet would be a tempting target for a submarine force.[6]

The position of the United States was not as easily discerned. On the one hand, the United States was not dependent upon maritime trade, so submarine raiding could not harm the United States as it would Great Britain. However, the United States had gone to war for absolute freedom of the seas. Also, it possessed a powerful surface fleet, which it was not willing to lose to submarine attack. On the other hand, against a major maritime enemy like Great Britain or Japan, submarine warfare might be vital. The conflicted American position became clear in a series of memoranda from late 1918 to early 1919 that discussed the potential abolition of the submarine.

After the war ended, the U.S. Naval Forces in Europe Planning Section, based in London, prepared a memorandum calling for the abolition of submarines and for the absolute freedom of the seas. Because of the potential benefits of commerce warfare and the insurmountable problems of conducting cruiser warfare, the Planning Section felt that all countries would eventually choose unrestricted submarine warfare. The planners wrote: "Submarine operations in the present war may be considered as typical of what may be expected in future wars, when success is dependent on the result of a war on commerce."[7]

In view of the deleterious impact of submarine warfare on maritime commerce, the Planning Section felt that most nations had more to lose than to gain from submarine warfare, particularly island empires like Great Britain and Japan. As a result of unrestricted submarine warfare, the world economy had been devastated, with millions of tons of cargo, fuel oil, food, and other important supplies scattered at the bottom of the Atlantic Ocean. The Planning Section believed the world could not afford another such costly war. Like President Wilson, the Planning Section believed that "the destruction of any merchant ships employed as common carriers is contrary to a sound world policy and should be forbidden . . . The loss of cargoes has impoverished the world and subjected many of the neutrals to hardships greater than those endured by some of the belligerents. The tonnage sunk represents a direct economic loss falling upon the people of the whole world, whether belligerent or neutral."[8]

Moreover, the United States did not need submarine warfare. Under absolute freedom of the seas, the only legal uses for U.S. Navy submarines would be naval combat or coastal protection, missions that could already be accomplished by the powerful surface fleet or the U.S. Army's coastal batteries. Other countries might not be as scrupulous, however. If submarines existed, then the United States would suffer from unrestricted submarine warfare waged by unprincipled enemies. The United States, therefore, had nothing to gain from submarines and everything to lose if other countries were allowed to make them.[9]

The Planning Section offered a final reason to abolish submarines and establish absolute freedom of the seas: it would spur international arms reductions. By eliminating submarines, countries would no longer need antisubmarine vessels. Consequently, most small warships could be scrapped, leaving only the capital ships to be dispensed with.[10]

The Planning Section's conclusions were audacious:

1. That an international agreement be concluded to abolish submarine warfare.
2. That to insure against violations of this agreement, all sub-surface vessels of every class whatsoever, now built or building be destroyed; and that none hereafter be constructed.
3. That no merchant vessel shall hereafter be destroyed by belligerent action.
4. That merchant vessels which under present rules would be subject to destruction, may be sent into a neutral port and interned in the same manner as combatant vessels.[11]

At the same time, the Planning Section's conclusions illustrated why absolute freedom of the seas and abolition of the submarine were impossible. The former would mean giving up the ability to coerce enemy trade in time of war, so that a naval power would have essentially no means to coerce a land power. The latter would require an international monitoring and verification agency with the power to intrude upon any country's shipyards and navies at any time—something that few nations would be willing to permit.

Unsurprisingly, Admiral William Sowden Sims, commander of U.S. Naval Forces Operating in European Waters, tersely rejected the Planning Section's conclusions: "The Force Commander does not consider that the arguments put forward by the Planning Section in this paper are logical, nor that they support the conclusions reached. The paper is, therefore, forwarded without approval for consideration by the Department."[12]

JANUARY 1919: THE THREE CAPTAINS

In response to the London Planning Section's memorandum and Sims's dismissive recommendation, three U.S. Navy captains, W. Evans, Harry E. Yarnell, and Thomas C. Hart, studied the memorandum and then issued a rebuttal that agreed with Sims.

The captains came directly to the point. They agreed with the London Planning Section that submarines were susceptible to illegal use, as were a number of weapons. Unlike the Planning Section, however, the captains believed that submarines held a vital role outside of commerce raiding. Additionally, it was ridiculous to assume that weak naval powers would choose to honor a treaty that placed them at a disadvantage by banning submarines. Furthermore, there were a number of locations where submarines could potentially be of great use to the United States. In a point that would later prove unfortunately ironic for Hart, the planners specifically hypothesized that a fleet of submarines could defend the Philippines.[13]

As a warship, the submarine had proven itself as a first-rate weapon. The captains pointed out that U-boats had accounted for almost one-third of the total losses of British surface warships.[14] The captains also credited the U-boat campaign with 12 million gross registered tons of shipping and with killing between 10,000 and 15,000 people. Although the loss of life paled against the losses at the Somme or in the trenches of Verdun, in terms of noncombatants who had been deliberately targeted, it was certainly a staggering cost. Notably, the captains explicitly condemned unrestricted submarine warfare: "The loss of life from the German submarine campaign was partly due to the disregard of elementary principles of humanity, which cannot be too strongly condemned."[15]

Although the captains decried the horrors of unrestricted submarine warfare, they still recognized that commerce warfare would be advantageous to the United States in a war, particularly one with the nation that the captains viewed as their next enemy—Japan. The captains wrote:

(g) On the other hand, sea commerce is vitally necessary to most European countries and to Japan.

(h) It is dangerous to evade the fact that Japan is our most probable enemy at the present time.

(i) In a war between the United States and Japan, the submarine will be an extremely valuable weapon for

(1) defense of the Philippines,

(2) operations against Japanese commerce.

There is no quicker or more effective method of defeating Japan than the cutting of her sea communication.[16]

Although the captains may not have spoken for all naval officers, their memorandum clearly shows that they understood the potential for submarine warfare against Japanese commerce. That one of the writers of this memorandum was Thomas C. Hart, who would be the commander-in-chief of the U.S. Asiatic Fleet in 1941, makes it all the more remarkable. In 1941, as war clouds began to gather, Hart would show that he had not forgotten this 1919 memorandum.

The captains also rebutted legal points in the London Planning Section's memorandum with the aid of George Grafton Wilson, a Harvard University professor and an assistant professor for international law at the U.S. Naval War College. Wilson had played a key role in drafting the U.S. Navy's 1917 *Instructions for the Navy of the United States Governing Maritime Warfare*. He offered a number of legal points that pointed to the shallowness of the London Planning Section's memorandum.[17] In particular, Wilson stressed that the practice of armed merchant ships in the First World War had clearly abused the right of self-defensive noncombatant armament. By prohibiting armed merchant ships, Wilson felt submarines could be legally held to cruiser warfare.[18]

With Wilson's input squarely on their side, the Navy captains concluded with a succinct paragraph that entirely rejected the London Planning Section's memorandum: "In conclusion, the committee strongly recommends that, in view of the great value of the submarine as a legitimate weapon of naval warfare, and its value to us in a future war for coast defense, scouting, and attack on enemy communication, the United States should resist any effort to abolish submarines."[19]

As the three captains were scuttling the London Planning Section's memorandum, Commander Emory S. Land of the U.S. Navy's Naval Construction Corps was forwarding the Royal Navy's views on the subject of banning submarines. One of the senior officers in the Bureau of Construction and Repair, Land had been stationed with the U.S. naval forces in Europe during the war. After the war, he was able to inspect numerous German U-boats to confirm that they were far superior to American submarines.[20] The Royal Navy views that Land reported, as well as his own observations, fully backed up the conclusions of the three captains.

The Royal Navy document that Land forwarded had been prepared by pro-submarine Royal Navy officers to combat a decision by the Admiralty's department heads to prohibit submarine construction. The memorandum apparently had the desired effect, because most of the Admiralty department heads changed their minds and voted to continue submarine construction.[21]

The Royal Navy document had a very simple point: "Prohibition of the building of submarines by International Law is considered impractical."[22] The document's drafters stated that to ensure that no nation was making submarines would require an international agency with the authority to inspect all factories, workshops, and shipyards around the world. The Royal Navy officers, with admirable understatement, commented: "Such a procedure would be resented by all Nations."[23]

The Royal Navy officers listed several more reasons why prohibiting submarine construction would be difficult, if not impossible. For one thing, based upon Germany's success with submarines as commerce raiders, any nation that went to war with Great Britain would immediately start constructing submarines, so prohibiting submarine construction would only be effective for a short time.[24]

The drafters of the document believed the advent of airplanes had made submarines even more vital than before. Given the potential vulnerability of surface ships to aircraft, the Royal Navy needed either to clad its capital ships with far more deck armor to protect against armor-piercing bombs or to invest more money in submarines that could avoid aerial detection. In any event, the writers declared, aircraft might be able to drop more explosives than a submarine torpedo could deliver, which would make prohibiting aircraft far more imperative than abolishing submarines. Since the probability of prohibiting aircraft was minimal, the officers stated: "The development of aircraft, therefore, as an arm of warfare will tend to the increase of the submersible ship."[25]

The problem with submarines had been their illegal use by the German Navy for unrestricted warfare. The answer, the Royal Navy officers decided— like the three U.S. Navy captains and Professor Wilson—was to intelligently regulate submarine warfare. After all, the Royal Navy's submarine force had successfully obeyed the rules of cruiser warfare in the North Sea, the Adriatic Sea, and the Sea of Marmora. The Royal Navy officers concluded: "There appears to be therefore a necessity for the formulation of definite laws and rules to regulate the warlike operations of Submarines rather than the prohibition of their building."[26]

Finally, the Royal Navy officers recognized the potential of the submarine as a strategic deterrent. The writers advocated this role for the submarine: "Any arm of warfare which by its development tends to make war more risky to a likely breaker of the peace, should be encouraged in its development, not prohibited."[27]

In his endorsement, Land agreed with his Royal Navy counterparts. In particular, he reiterated the call for regulating submarine warfare, not prohibiting it, which he felt was doomed to failure. Land remained caustically but pragmatically skeptical that any country would honor such a prohibition: "From the crumbs of information that I have been able to gather from various conferences of the Allies during the past two months, I am forced to admit that the horizons of many of the representatives of the Allies do not appear to have been greatly widened or broadened by the terrible experiences of the last 4½ years. It therefore appears to be folly to believe that the Nations of the World are suddenly going to reach an ideal state of Government for all mankind."[28]

MARCH 1919: THE GENERAL BOARD WEIGHS IN

In March 1919 the General Board of the Navy agreed with the conclusions of the three captains and Naval Constructor Land. The General Board of the Navy held a great deal of importance within the Navy; it usually consisted of several of the Navy's senior admirals, and it was charged with oversight regarding war planning, naval policy, organization, and administration, as well as naval design and construction. Initially, the General Board consisted of the chief of naval operations, the commandant of the Marine Corps, the president of the Naval War College, the director of naval intelligence, and other senior officers of the naval service. As time went on, however, this was not always the case. By the early 1920s the common practice was for most of the work of the board to be carried out by an Executive Committee of officers solely dedicated to the General Board, headed up by the board's "senior member."[29]

In response to a request by Secretary of the Navy Josephus Daniels concerning the changes in maritime warfare during World War I, the General Board wrote a long memorandum with their opinion about what the Navy needed to do in the wake of the changes wrought by the First World War. Although the board felt strongly about the illegality of unrestricted submarine warfare, they also were unwilling to ban submarines.[30]

The General Board's feelings regarding unrestricted submarine warfare were clear: "This phase of submarine warfare . . . presented a backward step in the progress of conducting war humanely amongst civilized nations."[31] Yet the General Board also saw the connection between unrestricted submarine warfare and armed merchant ships: "The simple fact remains that a situation developed, (a), in which defensive batteries of armed merchant vessels were used offensively against submarines, having the effect of making it impossible for them to exercise the right of search; and, (b), in which submarines sank merchant ships without warning and without attempting to use the right of search."[32] Unsurprisingly, the General Board called for changes to international law that would outlaw armed merchant ships, prohibit the use of the *ruse de guerre* of flying false colors by belligerent merchant ships, and order submarines to obey the same rules of visit and search as any surface ship. By accepting such rules, neutral vessels would not be terrorized by unseen submerged enemies or unduly delayed by cumbersome detours to belligerent ports to be inspected for contraband. Instead, for the most part, the routine of visit and search would go on as it had before the war. In short, the changes favored by the General Board would recreate antebellum conditions as nearly as possible while attempting to acknowledge new technologies like the submarine.[33]

With the conclusions of the General Board, the U.S. Navy settled into a position that it would generally repeat for the next twenty years: absolute freedom of the seas was impossible. Unrestricted submarine warfare was morally reprehensible. The solution lay between these two extremes and was only possible through pragmatic rules of cruiser warfare. Submarines should act like surface ships, but for the safety of submarine crews, armed merchant ships had to be prohibited. Although such a turn of events might have seemed as improbable as banning submarines, the Navy obviously seemed to believe it was more practical.

For the next twenty years, however, virtually all naval treaties would focus on the role of the submarine to the exclusion of the armed merchant ship, laying the foundation for unrestricted submarine warfare in the Second World War.

CHAPTER 3

The Failure of International Law in the Interwar Period

Only two decades after the First World War, a new unrestricted submarine war raged in the Mediterranean Sea. Without regard for nationality or destination, unidentified submarines sank belligerent and neutral merchant ships without warning. One submarine even chased a French passenger liner from the Aegean Sea into the Dardanelles Straits. Most of the Mediterranean nations, including the new country of Turkey, were unable to protect their own shipping, let alone foreign shipping. With every sinking, the situation seemed to be slipping further out of control.[1]

HIGH POINT OF A FAILED SYSTEM

It was September 1937. Over a year before, in July 1936, the Spanish Civil War had broken out. Various nations, including France, Great Britain, Turkey, and the United States, had immediately declared their neutrality in the war. The Germans and the Italians, however, aided the Nationalists under General Francisco Franco, while the Soviet Union funneled supplies, including tanks, aircraft, and other weapons, to the leftist Republicans. After the war had dragged on for over a year, General Franco requested that Italy stop Soviet shipping from the Black Sea to the Mediterranean. Italian leader Benito Mussolini agreed, turning Italy's aircraft and navy loose. The month of August 1937 "was marked by indiscriminate attacks upon merchant ships using the Mediterranean as a highway, without warning or inquiry and without regard to the nationality of the vessel attacked, the nature of its cargo, or its port of destination."[2] The attacks ranged from the coast of Spain all the way to the straits leading into the Black Sea. Despite warnings by the French and the British, the number of attacks only increased throughout August. By the beginning of September, it was clear that the great naval powers would have to act if they wanted to protect their shipping.[3]

After informal discussions, the French and the British called for a meeting of the Mediterranean countries, as well as Germany and the Soviet Union. Although Albania, Italy, and Germany refused to attend, the conference still went ahead in Nyon, Switzerland, on September 10, 1937. By the following day the parties reached an agreement, which was signed, after waiting for the approval of all involved governments, on September 14, 1937.[4]

The Nyon Agreement stated that submarine attacks on merchant ships were acts of piracy and would be met with lethal force. Signatories were allowed to destroy any submarines suspected of making attacks. France and Great Britain were authorized to patrol in the Dardanelles Straits and other territorial waters at the request of the signatory powers. The Soviet Union would patrol the Black Sea.[5]

The effect of the Nyon Agreement was almost immediate. Even before British and French ships officially began their patrols, Mussolini ordered his forces to end their attacks. By the end of September, Italy knuckled under to international pressure and joined the Nyon Agreement, patrolling the Adriatic Sea. Ultimately, over sixty ships and aircraft patrolled the Mediterranean. The submarine attacks ended.[6]

"The Nyon Conference," wrote Winston Churchill an eventful decade later, "although an incident, is a proof of how powerful the combined influence of Britain and France, if expressed with conviction and a readiness to use force, would have been upon the mood and policy of the Dictators."[7]

The Nyon Agreement was also the high point of interwar submarine diplomacy, which focused on forcing submarines to abide by the old paradigm of freedom of the seas embodied in the Declarations of Paris and London. Unfortunately, while international pacts like the Nyon Agreement managed to successfully legislate submarine warfare, they failed to address the problem of the armed merchant ship. As a result, without the vigorous enforcement of all parties in a conflict, the interwar submarine treaties were almost certainly doomed to failure.

THE WASHINGTON NAVAL CONFERENCE: THE ROOT TREATY

The Nyon Agreement was the culmination of a number of treaties that ignored the reality of the submarine problem, as well as the thornier issues related to freedom of the seas, starting with the Treaty of Versailles in 1919.

Despite all the attention focused on freedom of the seas and unrestricted submarine warfare during the First World War, the Treaty of Versailles did not address either. Yet these were still major issues. The Americans, after all, had gone to war over absolute freedom of the seas, and both the British and American delegates agreed that the submarine was akin to poison gas and should be eliminated. However, just as the United States had once refused to give up privateers, France and Italy both decided that submarines were a cheap deterrent force and refused to consider abolition. Furthermore, the British refused to give up the ability to conduct long-range blockades.[8]

President Wilson was forced to reckon with this when dealing with the Allies at the Paris Peace Conference of 1919. He tactically retreated from overtly pushing for his paradigm of freedom of the seas.[9] Instead, Wilson hoped that the League of Nations would be able to enforce his vision, as he stated upon his return to the United States:

> One of the principles that I went to Paris most insisting on was the freedom of the seas. Now, the freedom of the seas means the definition of the right of neutrals to use the seas when other nations are at war, but under the League of Nations there are no neutrals, and, therefore, what I have called the practical joke on myself was that by the very thing that I was advocating it became unnecessary to define the freedom of the seas. All nations are engaged to maintain the right, and in that sense no nation can be neutral when the right is invaded, and, all being comrades and partners in a common cause, we all have an equal right to use the seas.[10]

However, the United States never joined the League of Nations, and the concept of freedom of the seas remained open to debate: should freedom of the seas be absolute in times of peace and war, or should international law attempt to restore the principles embodied in the Declarations of London and Paris, while explicitly prohibiting the unrestricted warfare made possible by the new technologies of war? These questions would be addressed, to some extent, at the next major international conference.

At the invitation of Wilson's successor, Warren G. Harding, a number of powerful nations sent representatives to Washington, D.C., for an international conference on arms limitations that began on the third anniversary of the Great War's Armistice, November 11, 1921. To the astonishment of most diplomats, the secretary of state of the United States, Charles Evans Hughes, proposed sweeping naval reductions. The resulting treaty established a 5:5:3:1.75:1.75 ratio of capital ship tonnage among Great Britain, the United States, Japan, France, and Italy, respectively. The treaty set restrictions upon capital ships that caused the wholesale scrapping of numerous warships. Perhaps one of the earliest, most effective, and sweeping arms limitation treaties ever signed and honored, the Washington Naval Treaty, also known as the Five-Power Naval Limitation Treaty, was signed on February 6, 1922, and subsequently ratified by the U.S. Senate. As a result of both the Washington Naval Treaty and the London Naval Treaty of 1930, the United States would not build any new types of battleships until 1936.[11]

The five naval powers also negotiated another treaty, known as the Five-Power Supplemental Treaty or the Washington Submarine Treaty, which set out to emasculate the submarine as a viable warship. The treaty originated from Elihu Root, an American statesman who had served as secretary of war for President McKinley and secretary of state under President Theodore Roosevelt. Even though he was seventy-six years old when he attended the Washington Naval Conference, Root was still one of the premier American jurists regarding international law, and his opinion carried great weight not only with his own countrymen but also with other countries.[12]

Root's suggestions stemmed from Great Britain's initial attempts to abolish submarines at the conference. The British delegates claimed that submarines were truly useful only against commerce shipping, and had limited utility as a defensive weapon. They dramatically described the submarine as "a weapon of murder and piracy, involving the drowning of noncombatants," and pressed for immediate abolition. The other four naval powers were unwilling to accede to the British request. Instead, Root delivered a counter-proposal, aimed at ensuring that the practices of the First World War would not be repeated.[13] His proposal, however, was ultimately meant to "achieve the objective which the British had in mind . . . since no British subject had a more ardent horror for the German method of submarine warfare or condemned it on grounds of law and morals more heartily than he."[14] Unlike the British, however, who tried to eliminate the submarine entirely, Root believed that he could effectively eliminate the submarine as a viable warship by imposing criminal sanctions on submarine commanders who sank merchant ships.[15]

Root proposed a resolution that had at least three important parts, which became Articles I, III, and IV of the eventual Five-Power Supplemental Treaty. Article I reiterated the rules of cruiser warfare for submarines. All warships, including submarines, had to first stop and search a merchant ship before declaring it or its cargo to be contraband. Submarines would not be allowed to attack any merchant ships unless they refused to stop for visit and search. Finally, a submarine could not sink any merchant ship unless the ship's crew and passengers were off the ship and "in safety."[16] As Root noted, this part of the resolution merely repeated existing law, but it stated the rules so clearly and succinctly that there could be no question in future conflicts.[17]

Article III of the treaty carried the enforcement policy for Root's proposals. "[A]ny person in the service of any Power who shall violate any of these rules, whether or not such person is under orders of a governmental superior, shall be deemed to have violated the laws of war and shall be liable to trial and punishment *as if for an act of piracy* and may be brought to trial before the civil or military authorities of any Power within the jurisdiction of which he may be found."[18] Unwritten was the normal penalty for piracy: hanging. Article III was a major leap for an international treaty regarding war, because it essentially surrendered a nation's right to try its own military personnel for possible war crimes. Furthermore, it placed the interpretation and enforcement of the treaty in the hands of an aggrieved neutral or belligerent, a situation that would hardly have pleased any submarine commander taken prisoner.

The third relevant portion of the treaty, Article IV, stated that all signatories would "recognize the practical impossibility of using submarines as commerce destroyers without violating, as they were violated in the recent war of 1914–1918, the requirements universally accepted by civilized nations for the protection of the lives of neutrals and noncombatants, and to the end that the prohibition of the use of submarines as commerce destroyers shall be universally accepted as part of the law of nations they now accept that prohibition as henceforth binding as between themselves and they invite all other nations to adhere thereto."[19] At this point, Root's treaty became very confusing. While the first article laid out rules that would allow submarines to capture or sink commerce, the fourth article would have prohibited submarines to sink any commerce at any time. Root probably meant to prohibit only unrestricted submarine warfare, but if he did, then the first part of his resolution should have been sufficient for that purpose. Naval jurists would subsequently harp upon the ambiguous meaning of Root's treaty.

Root's treaty reaffirmed cruiser rules of warfare while outlawing unrestricted submarine warfare with the harshest possible penalty. Any submarine commander ordered to conduct unrestricted warfare surely would have thought twice about such orders, given the threat of hanging. But the ulterior motive behind Root's treaty was also clear. The resolution would serve as the first stage toward abolishing the submarine itself. It also represented an unprecedented encroachment on a naval service's jurisdiction over its personnel.

The other nations' delegates generally agreed with the treaty, but they pointed out problems with the ambiguous wording and the uncertain intent of portions of the treaty, particularly the part that outlawed the "use of submarines as commerce destroyers." The delegates could not decide whether that phrase meant unrestricted submarine warfare or the destruction of all merchant ships under any circumstances, which would have contradicted the first part of Root's treaty. Apparently impatient, Root told the delegates that whatever the flaws in his resolution, its meaning was clear to the people of the world. Instead of agreeing to a treaty that would only be understood by "diplomats or foreign offices or governments," he felt that if his treaty was accepted as it was, then it would be approved and enforced by the power of world opinion.[20]

The U.S. Navy's General Board, standing on the sidelines for most of the treaty, was aghast at Root's treaty. The Root treaty clearly aimed to emasculate the submarine and prepare it for abolition. Such an aim was at odds with the Navy's position, and soon the General Board of the Navy was forced to act on behalf of the beleaguered submarine.

ADMIRAL RODGERS, THE GENERAL BOARD, AND THE ROOT TREATY

At the center of the Navy's fight to save the submarine was the senior member of the General Board, Rear Admiral William Ledyard Rodgers. A former president of the U.S. Naval War College, Rodgers was known as an aggressive sailor and a scholar who eventually published two highly praised histories about oared warfare. Rodgers's views toward naval warfare were nuanced and reflected years of study and thought. Unlike Alfred Thayer Mahan, who believed that naval power alone could be decisive, Rodgers stressed that naval warfare ultimately served to support war on land: "Mankind lives on the land and draws its supplies from the land . . . the operations and consequences of war are primarily upon the land."[21] Rodgers fully understood the link between naval warfare and economic attrition: "All war upon the sea, therefore, has for its ultimate objective the control of sea-borne commerce . . . thus a navy's strategic role in major warfare is limited to the secondary one of facilitating supplies to one's own people and denying them to the enemy."[22]

Rodgers obviously did not believe in the Wilsonian paradigm of absolute freedom of the seas. In his view, deliberately targeting areas of production and routes of commerce was not only legitimate, but also vital. Hence, naval strategy needed to focus not on enemy battle fleets but upon controlling an enemy's trade.[23] Rodgers did not condone unrestricted warfare, but he also believed it was impossible to successfully ban new technologies like the submarine. Instead, the solution was to change international law to regulate submarine warfare against "public utilities" while outlawing unrestricted warfare against "consumer's goods" and noncombatants on passenger liners.[24]

Faced with Elihu Root's treaty, which attempted to ban commerce warfare by submarines, Admiral Rodgers responded with three considered reports that attempted to illustrate the fundamental flaws in Root's treaty as well as highlight the legitimate uses of the submarine.

The first report was released not by the Navy, but by a government advisory committee on submarines on which Rear Admiral Rodgers served. Rodgers's professional opinion heavily influenced the committee, and their report plainly reflected Rodgers's mindset. The committee agreed that the submarine was a valuable weapon of war and impractical to abolish. True to the Navy's viewpoint, the report declared that the real cause of unrestricted submarine warfare lay with armed merchant ships, which needed to be abolished instead of the submarine. The report also stressed the submarine's potential as a fleet scout and naval skirmisher.[25]

Elihu Root disregarded the committee's report. In deference to the aged statesman, the committee heard additional witnesses while following the ongoing negotiations of the Washington Naval Conference. After a month of deliberations, they reaffirmed their initial report.[26]

As the advisory committee submitted its final report, fundamentally disagreeing with the Root treaty, Rear Admiral Rodgers and the General Board submitted another report to the secretary of the Navy that directly attacked

Root's treaty. The General Board report pointed out that Root's attempt to ban "commerce destroyers" seemed ambiguous and open to various interpretations. The proposed ban also contradicted the cruiser warfare article of the treaty. As long as the two contradictory sections remained in the resolution, the General Board felt some fairly important questions were left open entirely to speculation, such as:

(a) May a submarine visit and search a merchant vessel, as provided in I (1)[?]
(b) May a submarine seize or capture a merchant vessel, as provided in I (1)[?]
(c) May a submarine escort a seized merchant vessel into port[?]
(d) May a submarine participate in a commercial blockade[?]
(e) Is a submarine denied the right to participate in a military and commercial blockade[?]
(f) What may a submarine do on sighting
   (1) An enemy merchant vessel[?]
   (2) A neutral merchant vessel[?]
(g) Does the article simply deny to the submarine any authorization to sink merchant vessels[?][27]

Rodgers and the General Board probably thought that between the advisory committee's report and the questions raised about the wording of the treaty by the General Board, Elihu Root's treaty suggestions would be revised or perhaps even dropped. Instead, the Root treaty was accepted as written. After being signed at the conclusion of the Washington Naval Conference on February 6, 1922, the Five-Power Supplemental Treaty was forwarded to the U.S. Senate for ratification.

The General Board then wrote one of its more remarkable documents, a long memorandum that asked rhetorical questions that might be asked by a civilian and to which the General Board offered caustic answers. The document, dated only a week after the treaty was signed, comprehensively debunked the Submarine Treaty by showing how the treaty was inherently contradictory, potentially open to abuse, and fundamentally opposed to existing international law. The memorandum also set forth how the U.S. Navy believed it could wage a legitimate war with submarines, as long as there were *no* armed merchant ships.

The document was probably written with a degree of anger on the part of Rear Admiral Rodgers and the General Board. They had been consistently ignored on this issue, as they noted:

QUESTION 34: When the Treaty was first proposed, were any objections raised to it?

ANSWER: Yes. On January 7, 1922, the General Board submitted certain adverse comments.

QUESTION 35: Were these comments accepted?

ANSWER: Apparently not.

QUESTION 36: Were any American technical naval advisors consulted when these articles were drafted?

ANSWER: No.[28]

The admirals clearly hoped that their long memorandum would not be similarly ignored.

Rodgers and the General Board began by noting that the Submarine Treaty was an ill-conceived attempt at absolute freedom of the seas that favored a powerful naval power over a weak one. In short, "[t]he commerce saving clause works only against that belligerent forced to use submarines. It is a trade restriction made in peace, which openly favors one belligerent in war."[29]

Rodgers and the General Board primarily focused on the main problem with the treaty: the contradiction of Article I, the cruiser warfare clause, by Article IV, which prohibited the use of submarines for commerce destruction. As a result, the treaty did not clear up the existing problems with international law, but rather exacerbated them.[30]

For instance, the General Board asked, what if a submarine sank a neutral merchant ship in accordance with Article I of the treaty, having taken off the crew and passengers in the same manner as a surface ship? Since the submarine had sunk the merchant ship, would it be guilty of violating Article IV of the treaty, which labeled commerce destruction an act of piracy? If so, would the submarine commander be liable to be hanged as a pirate under Article III of the treaty? The General Board hardly disguised their disgust with the treaty: "The Articles of the Treaty are ambiguous. According to Article I, a submarine may act in the same manner that any other surface war craft may act. Under Article IV, the use of submarines as commerce destroyers is prohibited. There is, therefore, the grave doubt as to what the rights of submarines are and as to what submarines may or may not do . . . Does the fact that a vessel has been built as a submarine preclude her from the rights which are vested in all war craft provided she acts in the same manner that other war craft act[?]"[31] From this point of departure, Rear Admiral Rodgers and the General Board ran through a litany of potential situations that would stress the treaty's ambiguity and contradictory nature. All the examples plainly demonstrated that as long as Articles I and IV remained as they were, the treaty was impossible to apply to the real world.[32]

Furthermore, Rodgers and the General Board alleged, the Root treaty missed the heart of the submarine problem: the armed merchant ship. Presuming that Article IV of the treaty did *not* mean that submarines were never to attack merchant ships, and assuming that submarines abided by Article I of the treaty, which forced submarines to act like surface ships, they would still be an easy target for a duplicitous merchant ship carrying even light or medium armament. The scholars on the General Board, probably Rear Admiral Rodgers, noted that merchant ships had once been armed for self-defense against pirates or to be placed into service as a naval auxiliary. However, privateers and piracy both had essentially vanished in the Atlantic and Mediterranean. In the First World War, ships had taken on armament for the sole purpose of fighting off submarines. In short, the purpose of the armament was inherently illegal.[33]

While Rodgers and the General Board might have sympathized with merchant ship sailors, unlike the idealistic diplomats at the Washington Naval Conference, they were unwilling to eliminate a form of naval warfare that had traditionally been legitimate:

> There are two recognized legitimate ways of waging war by sea against an enemy:
>
> (a) Against the armed forces;
>
> (b) Against the supply lines.
>
> Both methods are legitimate. The latter is the more effective. It was this pressure which finally brought Germany to terms. That nation which controls the sea surface can enforce surface blockade. That nation which does not control the sea surface can only hope to enforce economic pressure by its undersea forces. Both aims and practices are legitimate war aims and practices, provided humanitarian rules regulating war are not violated.[34]

Rodgers and the General Board then explained why the Submarine Treaty would also pose a definite danger to the United States, in a paragraph that spoke of the potential for war with an island empire like Great Britain or Japan:

Suppose that any other country with an equal or superior navy should also have a very superior merchant fleet. This second nation has really more sea power than the United States has. As an offset, and to secure fair play in sea transportation, the United States naturally turns to a policy of pressure through submarines, knowing that the threat of submarine operations against an island empire's lines of communications, where all lanes focus, will probably be sufficient to bring that nation to terms without resort to war in case of controversies. Without this asset through the limiting of submarines to operations against war craft solely, the tendency of that nation having superior sea control will be to continue on her way as she chooses. There is now no power back of any argument save that of understanding. If understanding fails, there must still be the resort to arms and in that case the United States is seriously handicapped in the effort to enforce her wishes because she has agreed not to use her most potent weapon, the submarine, against lanes of communication.[35]

Although Rodgers and the General Board were writing in generalities, they were probably writing about Great Britain, which would be equal with the United States under the terms of the treaty and which possessed the world's largest merchant marine. Should the interests of the two nations collide, the United States would have essentially hobbled itself by ratifying a treaty that eliminated a potential deterrent to war or, in the event of war, a decisive weapon.

The General Board was not suggesting unrestricted submarine warfare. For instance, the General Board did not believe that an escorted convoy gave a submarine the right to conduct unrestricted warfare. Instead, Rodgers and the General Board wrote, the submarine had to "attack without warning the belligerent convoying ship and to sink and destroy her if possible, and to search and to seize or to sink convoyed ships according to legitimate methods if it is possible for her to do so."[36] While this might have been more easily said than done, the General Board apparently believed it was possible.

Having discussed the problems of the treaty at length, the General Board concisely listed their objections with the articles of the Submarine Treaty:

(a) They are ambiguous.
(b) They probably give rise to more controversies than the older, simpler rulings.
(c) They prescribe drastic punishment, even though the legality of the

act may be clearly established from one point of view, or at least be open to argument.

(d) The rules drawn up consider only one side of the case. They are entirely one-sided. Their effect is to prohibit, not to solve the problems arising from the arming of merchantmen versus the submarine.

(e) From the reasons given in (a) and (d), and from the naval point of view, this Treaty is not practical and it is believed that it will not work.[37]

Furthermore, the limited number of nations signing it fundamentally flawed the treaty. Although the five nations signing the treaty were the world's principal naval powers, many other countries possessed submarines and could potentially use them. Unless every country in the world signed and genuinely honored the treaty, the General Board did not believe it could actually be enforced.[38] To illustrate this point, the General Board compared the treaty to an analogous U.S. domestic policy of the time: "Why is this Treaty like the Prohibition Law? ANSWER: It is forcing something on the majority of nations which they do not or will not want in war. It is made to be broken, and this in itself leads to a disregard for the law, which is a bad thing."[39]

Having dismissed the treaty, the General Board offered some solutions. They began by accepting Article I of the treaty, which reiterated accepted international law. All warships, whether surface ships or submarines, should obey the same laws of warfare regarding all merchant ships. In order to protect submarines and also maintain a clear-cut line between belligerent and noncombatant, no merchant ship that was not also a naval auxiliary should be armed. Only that sort of arrangement would be fair to all parties.[40] Furthermore, if a nation *did* order unrestricted submarine warfare, the General Board did not believe that subordinate submarine commanders should be hanged for the actions of their governments. Instead, the government leaders who ordered the illegal actions should bear the burden.[41] Until such a treaty could be worked out, the General Board recommended that the United States strike out Articles III and IV of the Submarine Treaty, which called for submarine commanders to be treated as pirates for unrestricted warfare and outlawed the use of submarines as commerce raiders. Having done so, the United States could then enact the suggestions of the General Board at another international conference.[42]

Whether or not the Senate actually saw the General Board's long memorandum is not clear. Whatever happened, however, the senators did not heed the General Board's advice. Instead, the Senate ratified both the naval treaty that scrapped dozens of warships as well as the Submarine Treaty. As events turned out, however, the Submarine Treaty never went into effect. Its enactment was contingent upon the ratification of all the signatories, and the French chose not to ratify it.[43]

Over a decade later, Lieutenant Hyman G. Rickover condemned the Washington Submarine Treaty as emotional, ineffective, and illogical. Rickover scornfully wrote:

> [I]t is difficult to escape the conviction that the delegates were still influenced by the "spirit of Versailles." No attempt was made to consider the submarine problem calmly and realistically. Everyone denounced the horror of the practices of the late enemy with becoming fervor; questions concerning the legality or practicality of the rules of the resolution were swept aside.
>   . . . An excellent critique of this treaty will be found in an article in this journal by Captain W. S. Anderson, U.S. Navy. He says:
>   "The most comprehensive rights of life and death over their naval personnel are conceded by the signatories to the officials of any country, in the heat of war, under the authority of a treaty containing inconsistent and ambiguous articles, and defying interpretation even by the eminent statesmen who signed it."[44]

Even Elihu Root's biographer, Philip C. Jessup, could not defend the Root treaty in his laudatory biography, published only a year after Root's death. Like the naval officers who had recognized the inseparable link between unrestricted submarine warfare and armed merchant ships, Jessup pointed out that Root's refusal to deal with this problem essentially doomed the treaty to irrelevance: "Merchant vessels have a right to arm, as Root insisted, but he failed to recognize that by so doing they lose their immunities as merchantmen. No final solution of the controversy over submarine warfare is possible without agreement upon the status of the armed merchantman."[45] Jessup concluded his description of Root and the Submarine Treaty by noting that Root's idea of imposing criminal sanctions on individual submarine commanders was dropped by subsequent naval conferences. Although he saw it as innovative, Jessup dismissed Root's treaty as "an evidence of war-time zeal rather than as a monument to his ability as a jurist or statesman."[46] However, the treaty did "serve to crystallize shortly after the war the sound proposition that submarines were bound by the rules of international law governing surface ships in their operations against merchant vessels."[47] Later treaties would reinforce this concept.

THE LONDON NAVAL CONFERENCE OF 1930

The first conference that could have addressed the submarine issue after the Washington Naval Conference was the Geneva Naval Conference of 1927. But because the Geneva Conference became mired in controversy over cruiser tonnage, it did not address the issue of submarines.[48] The issue arose a year later, at the Habana Convention on Maritime Neutrality of American States. The convention reiterated the traditional belligerent right of visit and search in international waters of any merchant ship at any time. As always, a merchant ship could not be sunk unless the crew and passengers were in a place of safety.[49] The convention specifically addressed submarines, stating: "Belligerent submarines are subject to the forgoing rules. If the submarine cannot capture the ship while observing these rules, it shall not have the right to continue to attack or to destroy the ship."[50] This article left no loopholes for unrestricted submarine warfare. If a submarine could not capture a merchant ship in accordance with cruiser warfare, it could not plead operational necessity and sink it anyway. Although a submarine could possibly shadow a merchant ship until a friendly surface ship intercepted it, this would hardly seem practical for a weaker naval power that could not contest control of the surface of the sea.

Two other, similar treaties followed the 1928 convention. The Pan-American Maritime Law Treaty of 1929 included similar language that bound a number of American nations, including the United States.[51] Even more important, in the London Naval Treaty of 1930, the world's major powers agreed on an article dealing specifically with submarine warfare. This became the most important resolution regarding unrestricted submarine warfare passed before the Second World War.

Like the 1921 American delegation in Washington, the U.S. delegation to the London Naval Conference was composed not of naval officers, but of diplomats and politicians, with the Navy limited to an advisory role. Admiral

William V. Pratt, the commander in chief of the U.S. Fleet, led the naval advisers. Pratt was a politically savvy admiral who had great faith in international treaties and was willing to carry out sweeping arms reductions.[52]

Once again, the British proposed abolishing the submarine. This time, however, the U.S. delegation completely agreed. The chairman of the U.S. delegation, Secretary of State Henry Stimson, stated before the conference:

> The essential objection to the submarine is that it is a weapon particularly susceptible of use against merchant ships in a way that violates alike the laws of war and the dictates of humanity. The use made of the submarine revolted the conscience of the world, and the threat of its unrestricted use against merchant ships was what finally determined the entry of my country into the conflict. In the light of our experience it seems clear that in any future war those who employ the submarine will be under strong temptation, perhaps irresistible temptation, to use it in the way that is most effective for immediate purposes, regardless of consequences. Those considerations convince us that technical arguments should be set aside in order that the submarine may henceforth be abolished.[53]

With both Great Britain and the United States in favor of abolition, it appeared that submarines would soon be eliminated, but France stepped in again. Traditionally opposed to abolishing the submarine and also leery of giving up a potential advantage against Great Britain, the French offered a counter-proposal to force submarines to obey the same rules of cruiser warfare as surface warships. Since this proposal reiterated what was becoming standard international law, the U.S. and British delegations eventually agreed to the compromise. One of the American delegates, Democratic senator Joseph T. Robinson, the Senate minority leader, soon reported that the proposed language of the submarine clause read something like: "[A]ll of the nations should agree hereafter submarines shall be forbidden to attack merchant ships, except after visitation and search, and provision made for the safety of passengers and crew in the same way that international law requires surface vessels to do."[54] The diplomats improved Robinson's language into what became Article 22 of the London Naval Treaty:

(1) In their action with regard to merchant ships, submarines must conform to the rules of International Law to which surface vessels are subject.

(2) In particular, except in case of persistent refusal to stop on being duly summoned, or of active resistance to visit or search, a warship, whether

surface vessel or submarine, may not sink or render incapable of navigation a merchant vessel without having first placed passengers, crew and ship's papers in a place of safety. For this purpose the ship's boats are not regarded as a place of safety unless the safety of the passengers and crew is assured, in the existing sea and weather conditions, by the proximity of land, or the presence of another vessel which is in a position to take them on board.

The High Contracting Parties invite all other Powers to express their assent to the above rules.[55]

In a sign of the importance assigned to this portion of the treaty, as well as the general agreement of all nations regarding this article, Article 22 of the London Naval Treaty was to "remain in force without limit of time."[56]

Afterward, Hyman G. Rickover felt the London Naval Conference evidenced "a marked difference in the spirit in which the submarine question was discussed," as opposed to the emotional discussions that had overwhelmed the Washington Naval Conference. He explained: "The new agreement is far less ambitious than the Washington treaty; the piracy clause is omitted, the tone of moral disapproval is wanting, and no attempt is made to lay down detailed rules of conduct." Rickover also approved of the recognition that lifeboats could be a place of safety, even if only in sight of land or with another vessel nearby. Finally, he particularly respected that Article 22 applied "both to submarines and surface vessels, thus expressing the sound principle that no particular type of warship should be singled out and subjected to special rules of warfare."[57]

In contrast to the Washington Submarine Treaty, Article 22 was generally unambiguous. Moreover, unlike the Habana Convention or the Pan-American Maritime Treaty, the London Naval Treaty was also signed by the major naval powers of Great Britain and Japan, which meant that it would almost certainly be binding upon the United States in a future maritime war. At last, the United States had legally bound itself to cruiser warfare, for better or for worse.[58]

Although Article 22 was to last indefinitely, the rest of the London Naval Treaty was set to expire on December 31, 1936, unless the five major powers that had signed it—Great Britain, the United States, Japan, France, and Italy— chose to renew its measures. In 1934 Japan announced that it would abrogate the London Naval Treaty, in order to build the fleet the Japanese Navy believed to be necessary. This set off a frantic attempt to entice the Japanese back into the fold at the Second London Naval Conference, held from December 1935 to March 1936. By January, however, the attempt had failed and the Japanese withdrew from the conference. Italy also refused to sign a new treaty. Nonetheless, the United States, Great Britain, and France still signed the Second London Naval Treaty in March 1936, with an escalation clause in case the Japanese or the Italians could not be persuaded to eventually sign the treaty.[59]

Even though the Japanese and the Italians chose not to renew the London Naval Treaty, they still reaffirmed their commitment to Article 22 of the original treaty.[60] On November 6, 1936, the United States, Great Britain, France, Italy, and Japan signed a *procès-verbal* reaffirming Article 22 and asked other nations to sign the document, which became known as the London Submarine Protocol. In response to this request, at least thirty-six additional nations signed the protocol, including Germany, the Soviet Union, and the Netherlands.[61]

The principles of the London Submarine Protocol of 1936 were actually put into practice in September 1937 when Great Britain, France, the Soviet Union, Bulgaria, Egypt, Greece, Romania, Turkey, and Yugoslavia signed the Nyon Agreement creating an International Naval Patrol and authorizing units of the patrol to sink submarines suspected of attacking merchant ships in the Mediterranean and Black Seas.[62] Although the United States did not sign the Nyon Agreement, its principles were entirely in agreement with U.S. foreign policy.

Despite the worldwide agreement with the London Submarine Protocol and the example of the Nyon Agreement, there was some question as to whether the protocol would actually be enforced in time of global conflict. As one legal professor, Edwin Borchard, noted, "It is well to remember that treaties which do not reflect the manners and customs of the people, such as the Kellogg Pact, are likely to become dead letters."[63]

A PREDICTION OF FAILURE

Borchard's point was more apt than he might have known. Article 22 of the London Naval Treaty and the London Submarine Protocol contained the seeds of their failure because they did not address the issue of armed merchant ships, an issue that the U.S. Navy had traditionally noted as inextricably entwined with that of the submarine. Even if the senior naval leadership had forgotten, Lieutenant Hyman G. Rickover had not. In September 1935 the U.S. Naval Institute *Proceedings* published his article "International Law and the Submarine." Not only was Rickover's article an excellent and concise overview of international law relating to submarines up until 1935, it also presciently noted the weakness of the London Naval Treaty and its potential for failure when put to the test.

By 1935 Rickover had been a commissioned officer in the U.S. Navy for thirteen years. He had graduated from the Naval Academy only months after the Washington Naval Treaty had been signed. Among other things, Rickover was a qualified submarine officer, and he served as both engineer and executive officer on board USS S-48. After his submarine duty, he went on to be the infamous assistant engineer on board USS *New Mexico* who resorted to extraordinary measures to win the Engineering Efficiency Award for three years in a row. After the Second World War, Rickover would leap to power and fame as the "father of the nuclear Navy." Rickover was also a versatile scholar. He earned a master's degree in electrical engineering from Columbia University, where he also studied international law in his spare time. Rickover's wife, Ruth Masters, earned her doctorate in international law from Columbia, and she probably helped Rickover write his 1935 essay.[64] Well-written and perceptive, Rickover's 1935 article on international law showed his grasp of legal and strategic concepts that should have been understood by his superior officers, if not his peers.

Like everyone else who seriously studied the topic, Rickover argued that submarines could not realistically conduct cruiser warfare: "The conclusion is inevitable that, except in rare circumstances, it is impossible for the submarine to carry on commerce warfare in accordance with international law as it stands today. Consequently, states must either renounce this weapon as a commerce destroyer or undertake a revision of the laws governing naval warfare, taking into account the changed conditions of modern war and the appearance of new weapons capable of operating under water and in the air."[65] As it was, the naval conferences since the First World War had not been able to solve the submarine problem because "they attempt[ed] a regulation of submarine warfare without at the same time considering the question of the armed merchantman; yet the two problems are intimately connected."[66] Although delegates from Italy and Japan had pointed out that armed merchant ships should probably be considered warships, the London Naval Treaty omitted any mention of armed merchant ships. As far as Rickover was concerned, this clearly set the treaty up for failure. Submarines could not be expected to conduct commerce warfare under conditions that were "suicidal."[67] In short, "it is doubtful whether any convention requiring submarines to comply with the existing rules of international law governing commerce warfare will receive general recognition unless it is also agreed that under the 'changed conditions of modern warfare' armed merchantmen are no longer entitled to the immunities of private vessels."[68]

Having established the underlying flaw with both the Washington Submarine Treaty and London Naval Treaty, Rickover ambitiously attempted to justify unrestricted submarine warfare as a legitimate form of warfare. He pointed out that there was virtually no difference between setting up a minefield and declaring it a war zone, and creating a war zone for unrestricted submarine warfare. The only difference was that the Allies had done the former and the Central Powers had done the latter—but the Allies had won.[69] Rickover saw no easy solution to what he viewed as an inevitable return to unrestricted submarine warfare. He recommended that neutrality legislation and international treaties stress a neutral's responsibility to prevent its ships from carrying contraband cargo to belligerent nations if it wished to remain at peace. If a neutral did so, no belligerent would have the right to stop, visit, search, or sink neutral shipping.[70]

Rickover's article clearly enunciated what astute U.S. naval officers had stated since the end of the First World War: submarines could not be held to cruiser warfare as long as merchant ships were armed. Although moments like the Nyon Agreement seemed to indicate the contrary, as long as armed merchant ships existed, unrestricted warfare remained the most effective and viable strategy available to a submarine force.

CHAPTER 4

Legislating Away Freedom of the Seas

In 1931, the tenuous world peace that had generally lasted since the Peace of Versailles was broken when Japanese troops invaded and occupied Manchuria. Within a matter of years, Fascist Italy and Nazi Germany began campaigns of overt and covert aggression and Spain dissolved into civil war. Faced with increasing world aggression, the American people had no desire to repeat what seemed to be the senseless slaughter of the First World War. Disillusioned with Woodrow Wilson's "war for democracy," the U.S. Congress enacted neutrality legislation that attempted to ensure that the United States would not be drawn into another world war.

THE NAVY AND NEUTRALITY LEGISLATION

The neutrality legislation focused on prohibiting the activities that had drawn the United States into war in 1917. Because outrage over unrestricted submarine warfare had been a pivotal factor in drawing the United States into the First World War, Congress tried to circumvent the issue by banning Americans from trading with belligerents and also from traveling on belligerent merchant ships, like the *Lusitania*. The desire to avoid war became so strong that the United States essentially abandoned its neutral rights with the Neutrality Acts of 1935 and 1939. By doing so, the U.S. Congress set the stage for unrestricted warfare by refusing to contest German activities in the North Atlantic.

The U.S. Navy consistently argued against the neutrality legislation for a number of reasons. The Navy wanted to protect U.S. munitions and arms industries, which would be unduly penalized by the act. The Navy also argued that the neutrality legislation would conceivably bind the United States to a certain course of action in time of war, and the precedent set by the legislation would allow other nations to deny aid to the United States in time of war. Finally, the acts implicitly surrendered Woodrow Wilson's conception of absolute freedom of the seas and inherently legitimized unrestricted warfare, because any ships trading with a belligerent were beyond the protection of the United States.

PROPOSED NEUTRALITY LEGISLATION, 1934–1935

On November 26, 1934, the Navy formally became involved with the proposed neutrality legislation when the secretary of state forwarded to the secretary of the Navy a memorandum of potential neutrality legislation written by the State Department's legal adviser, Green H. Hackworth. Hackworth proposed to ban all trade in munitions and other war matériel to belligerent countries, prevent armed merchant ships and submarines from entering U.S. territorial waters, and prohibit Americans from traveling on belligerent merchant ships, like the ill-fated *Lusitania*.[1]

Two days after receiving the secretary of state's request for the Navy's opinion, the secretary of the Navy, Claude Swanson, forwarded the proposed legislation to the chief of naval operations, the Navy's judge advocate general, the General Board, and the U.S. Naval War College. He requested their opinions on the legislation.[2]

A little over a week later, the Navy judge advocate general, Rear Admiral Claude C. Bloch, replied to Swanson. Bloch described the legal background behind neutrality and the specific portions of the proposed neutrality legislation that would affect the United States. Although Bloch did not go into the neutrality legislation's effect on unrestricted warfare, he concisely listed a number of legal, economic, and strategic reasons why the United States should not pass the legislation.

On the legal side, Bloch pointed out that the laws essentially abdicated U.S. neutral rights: "the proposed revised neutrality laws go far beyond the requirements of International Law."[3] Economically, Bloch argued against the legislation's potential restrictions upon arms and munitions industries, stating that a simple tax would be as effective and not quite as crippling.[4] Strategically, the proposed legislation could also feasibly set some important precedents, which would come back to haunt the United States later if it became a belligerent. For instance, if "the next war finds the United States as a belligerent and the proposed legislation has been enacted into law, then the United States could not well complain if her aviators, for example, who violated neutral territory were treated as criminals."[5] In Bloch's view, the proper way to ensure that the United States was not dragged into war, but still retained its national rights, would be with a practical "international agreement, and not by the enactment of the proposed legislation which surrenders some of our sovereign rights, in theory at least, and to which no other nation has agreed."[6]

Eight days later, the General Board issued their own opinion, discussing each paragraph of the proposed legislation. For the most part, the General Board fully supported Rear Admiral Bloch and the office of the judge advocate general (JAG). The General Board dismissed most of the legislation as superfluous, since it was already covered by existing U.S. laws and international law.[7] The idea of prohibiting Americans from traveling on whatever ship they pleased and to whatever destination they chose also seemed to be a drastic turnaround from the Wilsonian paradigm of absolute freedom of the seas.[8] Like Bloch, the General Board saw dangerous strategic precedents being set with the legislation. The General Board posed this hypothetical scenario: "If the United States were a belligerent, neutrals would have a strong position for denying requests for materials or munitions of war made by the United States, such as tin, manganese, and other strategic raw materials not produced by the United States."[9]

The next set of opinions, by the U.S. Naval War College, and signed by the college's president, Rear Admiral Edward C. Kalbfus, contained probably the most compelling arguments against the neutrality legislation. Unlike JAG and the General Board, which referred to the possibility for unrestricted submarine warfare by implication, Kalbfus explicitly connected the passage of neutrality legislation with a legitimization of unrestricted submarine warfare: "Such legislation might lead to the impression that this country would not seriously object to the sinking of its nationals traveling on foreign vessels by submarines and that such legislation might through inference appear to condone unrestricted warfare by this class of vessel."[10] Kalbfus's memorandum emphasized that the legislation represented an abandonment of absolute freedom of the seas. For instance, by establishing a "zone of naval hostilities" in which American ships and passengers were prohibited from traveling, the "proposed legislation might be interpreted by foreign nations as a form of implied approval of the establishment of such zones in any future war. That is certainly a radical departure from the historic stand of the United States concerning the freedom of the seas."[11] Kalbfus concluded with a strong plea against Section 8 of the proposed legislation, which prohibited the travel of American citizens on belligerent vessels: "It should not be assumed that belligerents will not abide by international law. To make such an assumption might well be considered by other nations as a form of approval of their failure to do so. If Section 8 were enacted with the above-quoted words included, it might be considered as a form of approval of unrestricted warfare against unarmed belligerent merchant vessels, by surface craft, submarines, or aircraft. The Naval War College recommends that this Section be not approved unless these words be deleted."[12] Secretary of the Navy Swanson forwarded the opinions of the judge advocate general and the General Board to the State Department on December 15, 1934, followed by the Naval War College's opinions on December 28.[13] Although the opinions brought up different points, they all stressed that the neutrality legislation was the wrong step strategically, economically, legally, and morally.

About nine months later, on August 31, 1935, Congress passed the neutrality legislation and President Roosevelt signed it. By that point, the legislation had gone through several different forms and revisions by numerous authors including Senators Key Pittman, Gerald Nye, and Bennett Champ Clark. However, the legislation ultimately retained most of Green Hackworth's suggestions, including the embargo on selling or carrying arms to belligerents and the prohibition against traveling on belligerent ships. Although the preamble asserted that the United States had not given up its sovereign rights, the entire point of the law was to ensure that the United States would not exercise its neutral rights as it had in the First World War.[14]

THE POPULARITY OF NEUTRALITY

Even though neutrality legislation made little sense to the U.S. Navy's leadership, it was extremely attractive to many Americans. In August 1935 the popular syndicated columnist Walter Lippmann expressed the isolationist viewpoint clearly and concisely. Lippmann had a great deal of expertise in foreign policy, and his friends in the government frequently contacted him for advice. For instance, the State Department had consulted him in 1934 regarding his views about the department's draft of the neutrality legislation.[15] Lippmann's popular column explained why the United States needed neutrality laws, what American objectives with neutrality legislation were, and how these objectives could be met.

Lippmann's column appeared as it became increasingly clear that Fascist Italy planned to invade Ethiopia. Although there was little chance that the United States could be pulled into the conflict, Lippmann felt that the Ethiopian crisis would be a litmus test for the Roosevelt administration in how it faced international crises. The precedent set by the neutrality legislation would play an important role in any coming major European wars.[16]

Lippmann listed several objectives that U.S. neutrality legislation would have to meet. He admitted that these objectives were often contradictory and would be difficult to achieve, but they reflected what most Americans wanted:

1. We desire not to be drawn into war to defend our trade or our honor.
2. But we would insist on not being insulted and outraged;
3. And we would not willingly let our normal export trade be destroyed.
4. We would like to be impartial as well as neutral;
5. But a policy of equal treatment for both belligerents would mean either that we became the tacit ally of the dominant sea power or came into conflict with it in defending our neutral right to trade with the blockaded power. If, for example, we prohibit shipments of munitions to both Italy and Ethiopia, the equal rule would prevent Italy from getting munitions she can get, whereas Ethiopia would only be prevented from getting munitions that she could not get anyway. If we insist on the right to ship to both, we have to deal with the Italian Navy, and we are, in effect, using our sea power to make up for Ethiopia's lack of sea power.[17]

In this list, Lippmann implicitly foresaw giving up the right of absolute freedom of the seas. He stated: "Historical experience shows plainly that in wars involving naval powers it is difficult, if not impossible, to defend trade and honor without entanglement and to be impartial in fact as well as neutral in law."[18] Lippmann believed that the first thing the United States needed to do was prohibit munitions shipments to either belligerent. He even proposed banning the shipment of any munitions on board American ships outside the Western Hemisphere. Furthermore, probably with the memory of the *Lusitania* in his head, Lippmann also proposed prohibiting U.S. citizens from traveling on board ships carrying munitions outside the Western Hemisphere. Most of these suggestions were already in the proposed neutrality legislation. However, Lippmann did not propose banning the shipment of munitions on ships other than American-flagged vessels. In a remark that presaged the modifications to the neutrality legislation, he wrote: "To sell arms to those who can come here and take them away is different from carrying munitions under the protection of the American flag to a nation at war."[19]

Lippmann concluded by summing up the potential effectiveness of the neutrality legislation and the legislation's consistency with the American people's will in the aftermath of the First World War: "Rules of this sort would not be a guaranty of immunity in a serious war. But they would reduce the danger of very serious embarrassments and, above all, of deliberate efforts to entangle this country. They would be consistent with the American feeling against profiting from war, and they would not be regarded as an ignominious surrender of national rights."[20] This was in accord with the feelings of most Americans, who generally applauded the passage of the 1935 neutrality legislation.

Over two and a half decades later, historian Robert A. Divine lambasted Lippmann and the isolationist philosophy, writing: "They accepted . . . glib historical doctrine . . . [and] they affirmed the arms embargo, the ban on loans, and the curb on passenger travel as a panacea that would prevent American involvement in world conflict."[21]

Although Congress asserted in the neutrality legislation that the United States gave up none of its sovereign rights, in hindsight, to historians like Divine, the neutrality legislation *did* surrender American sovereignty and rights. Even worse, the neutrality legislation of 1935 and the follow-on legislation of 1937 served to inform the powers of the Tripartite Axis that as long as they did not disturb American assets, the United States would not interfere with their rampages of conquest.

MORE PROPOSED LEGISLATION, 1939

In 1939, following the outbreak of war in Europe and President Roosevelt's call for a special legislative session, Congress revisited the neutrality legislation to ensure that the United States would not be pulled into the new European war. The new neutrality legislation reaffirmed the ban on American trade with belligerents and the prohibition of travel on belligerent merchant ships. At the same time it lifted the arms embargo against belligerents and facilitated the carrying of these munitions by including provisions for cash and carry, which would allow belligerent merchant ships to carry American goods and weapons.[22]

Although the Roosevelt administration saw the revised neutrality legislation as a belated victory, the Navy did not. On October 3, 1939, about a month after the war in Europe had begun, the chief of naval operations, Admiral Harold R. Stark, requested that various bureaus within the Navy study the proposed neutrality legislation.[23]

Like the 1935 act, the 1939 neutrality legislation sparked a strong reaction from the Navy. This time, however, the Navy attempted to win support by discussing the legislation's effect on vital war matériel. The Navy incorrectly assumed that no member of Congress would want to restrict the importation of matériel necessary for American defense.

The first naval personnel to attempt this argument was the War Plans Division within the Office of the Chief of Naval Operations. The War Plans Division was formally charged with creating war plans and strategic analyses. Because the division saw the neutrality legislation as a threat to the Navy's ability to effectively wage war, they felt it necessary to at least submit a memorandum. The War Plans Division concisely summed up their view, stating: "There are three provisions of this proposed Resolution, which, if enacted, may impose restrictions on United States commerce to an extent which will interfere with the importation, in sufficient quantities to meet the demands of the national defense, of strategic raw materials not native to the United States."[24] In particular, the War Plans Division saw the legislation as extremely harmful to the U.S. Merchant Marine, because it would strip American-flagged ships of the ability to transport goods to Europe and other "combat areas," while allowing foreign ships to take up the trading market without interference. Furthermore, the war planners did not trust foreign-flagged vessels to maintain the level of imports necessary for vital industries. They believed the United States might soon be seriously at risk because of a shortage of vital raw materials, such as manganese, tin, and tungsten. Although all of these materials existed in the Western Hemisphere, the United States traditionally relied on imports from countries that either were or soon would be at war. It would be difficult to make up the difference if trade with these countries was lost. Similarly, by prohibiting U.S. ships from traveling in combat zones, the neutrality legislation imposed lengthy delays or potential interruptions of trade with countries that were still neutral. Either way, the War Plans Division warned, the U.S. economy would be unduly harmed by the legislation.[25]

The Navy judge advocate general also weighed in with a memorandum that doubted the wisdom of the legislation. As in 1934, JAG pointed out that a number of sections of the legislation were already covered by existing U.S. law. JAG recommended against the law for economic, practical, and legal reasons.[26]

Rear Admiral Edward Kalbfus had recently been reassigned to the U.S. Naval War College, and he suddenly found himself having to discuss the legislation again. As in 1934 Kalbfus and his staff recommended against the legislation. This time, however, Kalbfus relied upon economic arguments. Like the War Plans Division, he argued that the legislation would unduly harm U.S. trade. Unlike the impassioned 1934 discourse about surrendering freedom of the seas, there was nothing about unrestricted warfare in Kalbfus's 1939 letter.[27] This emphasis on the economic effects of the proposed legislation was supported by the Naval War College's official statement, which focused almost entirely on economic effects with no mention of freedom of the seas.[28]

This left the Navy's General Board to defend the right of freedom of the seas. The Navy's senior admirals issued a shrill denunciation of the neutrality legislation, claiming it violated the traditional American right of freedom of the seas, damaged American trade grievously, and left the United States extremely vulnerable by shifting weapons production away from American shores and allowing American opponents to arm as U.S. industries stagnated. Like the War Plans Division and the Naval War College, the General Board focused on the economic dangers of the legislation, but they also made a strong principled argument on the basis of the sovereign right of freedom of the seas.

The General Board began by justifying their right to question congressional legislation. Although the Navy was constitutionally bound to follow the laws of Congress, the General Board believed that because maritime law could potentially affect the Navy's ability to wage war and because the Navy did enforce the law, it should at least have the right to offer an opinion regarding proposed legislation. If anything, not only did the Navy have the right to offer an opinion, it was obligated to do so as part of its duty to the nation.[29]

Like the War Plans Division and the Naval War College, the General Board pointed out the potential effect of the neutrality legislation on American munitions and arms industries, as well as trade. The board believed that by prohibiting munitions and arms plants from doing business with belligerents, American industry would be woefully unprepared should the United States be thrust into war. The General Board also predicted that the neutrality legislation would be copied by other powers, especially in the Western Hemisphere; "[if] then we ourselves become involved in war, we may find ourselves so isolated as to make it impossible to obtain certain essential raw materials and unduly difficult to prosecute even a defensive war."[30]

Although the 1935 act had been restrictive, it at least had only embargoed one type of cargo to a certain destination. The proposed legislation, on the other hand, while permitting weapons trading for cash and carry, would simultaneously cut off *all* American trade with a belligerent power. By doing so, the General Board stated ominously, the United States would, "in effect, surrender the doctrine of the freedom of the seas."[31]

The General Board defined freedom of the seas as a nation's "right to continue its international trade during war," and an emphasis on "neutral commercial rights as opposed to the restrictions upon those rights imposed by belligerents."[32] The General Board drew directly from Woodrow Wilson's second of the 14 Points, relating to absolute freedom of the seas. The General Board admitted that this was an extreme view, and the experience of the Paris Peace Conference showed that this view was hardly embraced by all nations. The General Board set the Wilsonian view of absolute freedom of the seas as "an ideal objective toward the attainment of which our neutrality legislation should be shaped."[33] No matter what, however, no form of freedom of the seas should be given up. The board admonished its potential congressional readers: "History teaches that no country has escaped war or consequences worse than war by a surrender of its national rights."[34]

The General Board directly tied the concept of freedom of the seas to economic strength. As long as the United States maintained its sovereign right to trade freely with all powers at all times, then its economy would not be endangered. The General Board, however, thought it was dangerous to assume that the economy would continue to run well with the restrictions of neutrality legislation, particularly in the era of the Great Depression:

> We cannot afford to surrender our traditional doctrine of the freedom of
> the seas for a set of self-imposed restrictions which initiate precedents that
> may well work to our disadvantage in the future. Moreover, if it becomes
> unlawful for the American merchant marine to operate freely during

foreign wars, then, in wars of wide extent, as the present war threatens to be, our merchant marine becomes unprofitable to operate; we are left to the mercy of foreign competitors; and our merchant marine, currently being greatly augmented by public moneys, largely because of its potential value to our own national defense, necessarily languishes. There is also set up a distinct invitation to transfer registry to some nation less restrictive.[35]

By tying the concept of freedom of the seas to the economic dangers of the neutrality legislation, the General Board thus made the issue both moral *and* economic. The topic of freedom of the seas would at least resonate with those who remembered Woodrow Wilson's call to arms of 1917, while the economic dangers of the legislation would have relevance for those who prized the economic recovery of the United States.

The General Board stridently declared that giving up national rights amounted to surrendering to a belligerent without even going to war. If the United States yielded its rights to the belligerents in Europe, then the General Board thought the neutrality legislation would not eliminate European interference with American affairs, but rather serve as an invitation for greater interference by Europeans with all sorts of American trade. Instead, the General Board recommended: "A strong assertion of national rights has the effect of reducing the natural hazards inherent in war. Such hazards do not disappear by our withdrawal from them, but rather tend to increase to the degree that neutrals yield their rights to the prerogatives (not rights) exercised by hard-pressed or arbitrary belligerents. Our national well-being consequently is jeopardized to the degree that we accede to the impositions of belligerent powers, let alone the extent to which we hamper ourselves by self-imposed restrictions."[36] In particular, the General Board pointed to the embargo on trade with belligerent powers and the declaration of "combat areas." To the General Board, "combat areas" were precisely the same as "war zones." If the United States, as a neutral, declared "combat areas," then it would be countenancing the establishment of war zones by powers like Great Britain and Germany. The General Board strenuously warned against this action, since "[h]istory indicates clearly that many of the accepted tenets of international law have been established in this manner."[37] In short, just as the Naval War College had warned in 1934, the legislation would essentially legitimize unrestricted warfare.

The General Board concluded its memorandum by calling for Congress to scrap the current legislation and replace it with legislation that would protect

American rights. The board summed up its view of the problems with the legislation with the following points:

(a) By self-imposed restrictions, it impairs the exercise of neutral rights recognized by international law and never seriously challenged in principle.

(b) It surrenders, in large measure, the traditional American doctrine of the freedom of the seas.

(c) It allows foreign powers free access to our basic sources of munition supply, without setting up appropriate safeguards to conserve such supply.

(d) It makes it unprofitable for us to operate our merchant marine, thus tending to reduce or destroy its value as a war asset.[38]

The General Board concluded by recommending that the legislation be rewritten to correspond with international law regarding neutral rights and that Congress take steps to ensure that the munitions and arms industry would not be endangered or, worse, moved overseas. Most important, however, the General Board recommended eliminating the provision for the trade embargo and the combat zones, and called for changing the legislation so "that the law be implemented to assert, rather than to yield, such rights."[39]

Such a stout stand for American rights would hardly have impressed isolationists like Senators Gerald Nye and Bennett Champ Clark, both of whom favored giving up neutral rights for peace at any price. Ignoring the General Board's assertion that giving up neutral rights would only lead to more infringements on American national rights, isolationists asserted that the only way to prevent a repeat of the First World War was to remove as many potential stumbling blocks as possible.[40] Faced with such opposition, the Navy and its defense of the freedom of the seas had no chance. The neutrality legislation passed.

Shortly thereafter, President Franklin Roosevelt established the first combat area, prohibiting all American ships from going to any belligerent ports in Europe or Africa north of the Canary Islands. The president defined a combat area as an "area in which the actual operations of the war appear to make navigation of American ships dangerous."[41] Five months later he extended the combat area up to the Arctic waters around the Soviet Union, and in June 1940 he added the Mediterranean and the Gulf of Aden. Although he eventually removed the Gulf of Aden from the combat area, the combat area was still impressively large as of August 1941: "In substance, therefore, American ships may not now legally proceed to any ports in France, Great Britain, Ireland, Norway, European Russia, or other Baltic ports, or Germany, Sweden, Denmark, Netherlands, or Belgium. All neutral ports, belligerent or neutral, in the Pacific and Indian Oceans and dependent waters, and all ports in Africa south of the latitude 33°-10' N., are still open."[42] By establishing the precedent of "combat areas," the United States essentially freed Germany to conduct unrestricted warfare within a portion of the North Atlantic. Although the Germans initially trod lightly for fear of upsetting the United States, they slowly intensified unrestricted warfare as it became clear that the United States would not make any effort to prevent it.[43]

THE IMPORTANCE OF THE U.S. NEUTRALITY LEGISLATION

Because the United States was eventually drawn into the Second World War, many historians have implicitly dismissed the U.S. neutrality legislation as an abject failure that actually helped lead to world war.[44] Samuel Flagg Bemis especially scorned the legislation, on the grounds that it "repudiated the policy of Woodrow Wilson of 1914–1917 for the defense of neutral rights, and was thus intended to keep the U.S. out of the next war by applying the lessons of the last war."[45] To a certain degree, however, the neutrality legislation fulfilled its intended function: the laws prevented the United States from being drawn into the war over sunken U.S. merchant ships.

To a surprising extent, Nazi Germany respected the boundaries of the U.S. combat area in the Atlantic. When the German Navy eventually proclaimed its war zone, its borders generally matched those of the U.S. combat area. Furthermore, both Adolf Hitler and Admiral Karl Dönitz issued explicit orders to their U-boats to avoid harassing or sinking U.S. merchant ships and even to avoid shooting at destroyers that might be American.[46] Notably, before Germany declared war on the United States, only four American merchant ships were sunk: *Robin Moor* on May 21, 1941; *Lehigh* on October 19, 1941; *Astral* on December 2, 1941; and *Sagadahoc* on December 3, 1941. Of those, *Robin Moor* and *Sagadahoc* were actually sunk in conformity with the cruiser rules of warfare: their masters showed their papers to the U-boat commanders in question, who decided to sink their ships on the basis of contraband, but who also attempted to provision and tow lifeboats to an area of perceived safety. Both *Lehigh* and *Astral* were sunk under conditions of mistaken identity.[47] Furthermore, despite the decidedly nonneutral actions of the United States by escorting British convoys up to the mid-ocean transfer point, where the German war zone began, German U-boats sank only one U.S. Navy ship: destroyer USS *Reuben James* on October 31, 1941, with the loss of 115 American sailors. Destroyers USS *Kearny* and USS *Greer* were also attacked by U-boats, but without success.[48]

That there were not more American maritime and naval losses was owing to both the restrictions of the neutrality legislation and to Hitler and Dönitz's desire to avoid making the same mistake that Germany had made in 1917. Although U.S.–built ships were lost in the combat area, they had almost all been flagged as British merchant ships. Although American travelers were still killed by U-boat attacks, unlike the situation in the First World War, the onus was on the American for traveling into danger, not the German who sank his ship.[49] Consequently, despite the increasing involvement of the United States in the Battle of the Atlantic, the U.S. neutrality legislation succeeded in its goal: the United States was not drawn into the European war over German unrestricted warfare.

The success of the U.S. neutrality legislation, however, came at a great cost. Unrestricted warfare, which had once been denounced by President Wilson as warfare against humanity, was inherently legitimized by the U.S. neutrality legislation. Within the American combat area, the German U-boats, aircraft, and surface raiders could sink any ship at any time without warning and without any fear of adverse consequences. Although the Germans initially attempted to abide by cruiser warfare, they steadily escalated up to de facto unrestricted warfare when it became clear that the United States would not stand in the way. The implicit message of the neutrality legislation could not have been clearer: the United States would no longer stand up for absolute freedom of the seas.

No group understood this better than the senior leadership of the U.S. Navy. In both the Navy Department and at the Naval War College, naval officers had fought against the neutrality legislation for economic and strategic reasons and, more important, for moral reasons: they had once fought a great naval war over this issue. Their protests ignored, they could only watch as the U.S. Congress, by fiat, ceded the sovereign right of freedom of the seas that had been won and legitimized by U.S. involvement in the First World War.

Bound by the neutrality legislation, the United States stood by as Germany steadily escalated to full unrestricted warfare in the North Atlantic. In 1940 the British War Cabinet "belatedly" realized that cruiser warfare in enemy-controlled waters was almost impossible, and Great Britain unleashed unrestricted submarine warfare in the Skagerrak, the Kattegat, and certain portions of the Mediterranean.[50] In the United States, many naval officers seemed to agree that unrestricted submarine warfare was inevitable. This sense of inevitability was encapsulated in an August 1941 U.S. Naval War College staff presentation that discussed the latest trends in submarine warfare and international law. The United States was clearly teetering on the brink of war, and the presentation implied that the Navy expected that the rules governing commerce warfare would soon change.

The presentation began with a fact that must have been painfully clear to all by this point in the war: the submarine was here to stay because it possessed the advantage of stealth and it was extremely cost effective.[51] Furthermore, unlike the situation in the First World War, American naval officers were unwilling to regard German unrestricted submarine warfare as abhorrent. Rather, they saw it as a natural reaction to British armed merchant ships and convoys. Consistent with two decades of naval thought, the naval officers implicitly placed the onus for unrestricted submarine warfare on the British, who had insisted on arming their merchant ships. The Naval War College instructors concluded, in a sentence reminiscent of Hyman G. Rickover's *Proceedings* article: "It cannot easily be presumed that armed merchant vessels could be tolerated while submarines should be required to conform to Article 22."[52]

By recognizing the impossibility of waging cruiser warfare against armed merchant ships, the Naval War College staff implied that unrestricted submarine warfare might be permissible instead: "Submarines can be used in commerce warfare for attack with torpedoes and guns, for laying mines, and in the service of information. Also, under favorable circumstances they may be able to exercise the right of visit and search on unarmed merchant ships."[53] By recognizing that the ability of submarines to conduct visit and search was limited to only "unarmed merchant ships," the Naval War College staff implied that they expected that U.S. submarines would be free to attack armed merchant ships in the event of war.

Given the realities of modern warfare, submarines were the natural choice to fill in for blockade duty. Because "the advent of torpedoes, mines, and aerial bombs has made the positions of surface vessels in a close blockade untenable ... [t]he submarine is the only weapon which is capable of operating and maintaining its position in areas near the enemy coast."[54] Like Admiral Hermann Bauer, who had commanded German U-boats in the First World War, the Naval War College staff believed that any ship that chose to brave an announced blockade and attempted to enter enemy ports should be prepared to suffer the consequences if she were sighted. This was a major change from the American attitude in the First World War, but it was perfectly in keeping with an attitude that favored belligerent rights. Having said that, the War College Staff still quoted from *Neutrality for the United States* (1937) by Edwin Borchard and William Potter Lage, which stated that the legality of war zones or of submarine blockades was highly questionable.[55]

Whether or not the German submarine campaign was legal, the reality of the Battle of the Atlantic indicated that the London Submarine Protocol was virtually a dead letter. Although the Naval War College did not discuss what American submarine warfare might be like in a war with Japan, the implications of their presentation were clear: cruiser warfare apparently belonged in the past.

Although officers at the Naval War College seemed to realize that cruiser warfare was almost impossible, there was no sign that the U.S. naval leadership agreed. If anything, a memorandum of October 27, 1941, from the Bureau of Navigation implied that the U.S. Navy's leadership intended to conduct cruiser warfare. The memorandum discussed possible plans for supplying prize crews and armed guards to captured prizes in the event of war. Astonishingly, even at this late date, some officers in the U.S. Navy foresaw an ocean war that would be more like the War of 1812 than the First World War.[56]

As 1941 drew to a close and war with Japan became increasingly likely, the U.S. Navy still clung to the London Submarine Protocol, even as the world around it realized the realities of modern warfare and waged unrestricted air and submarine warfare. Furthermore, as far as the Navy's submarine force could tell, there was little reason to expect that that policy would change, except under the reality of war.[57]

CHAPTER 5

The Accidental Commerce Raider

U.S. SUBMARINE DEVELOPMENT, STRATEGY, AND TACTICS

As the Washington and London Naval Treaties toyed with the fate of the submarine, the U.S. Navy forged ahead with a submarine design that met its strategic vision. It was not a vision that accepted unrestricted submarine warfare. Instead, the U.S. Navy's leadership believed the submarine could play an important role in supporting the battle fleet. By the 1930s the U.S. Navy had formulated a strategy and concurrent technical specifications for its submarine force that focused almost entirely on the concept of the "fleet submarine."

ESTABLISHING ROLES FOR THE SUBMARINE

Even though the specified role of the fleet submarine did not coalesce for some time, in the years immediately following the First World War the Navy was already justifying the continued existence of the submarine by pointing out its potential as an integral part of the battleship fleet paradigm. Submarines could serve as fleet scouts and naval skirmishers, detecting the enemy fleet and even softening up the enemy before a major engagement.

In late 1921 and early 1922, the Advisory Committee on Submarines, set up to advise the U.S. government during the Washington Naval Conference, highlighted these possible roles. The committee's report stressed three potential uses for submarines: scouting, combatant, and minelayer.

Because of their stealth, submarines were perfectly suited to serve as scouts, advancing deep into enemy waters to report enemy ship movements. During the First World War, both the Allies and the Germans used submarines as a principal source of information on activities of the opposing fleets in the North Sea.[1]

The submarine's success as a commerce raider had also overshadowed its success as a naval combatant. During the First World War, German submarines sank 5 out of the 13 British battleships lost in the war. In a naval war in which battleships were supposed to sink each other, it is significant that submarines sank over a third of the British battleships lost in the war.[2]

Submarines also had proven their worth as minelayers, leaving vast fields of mines for enemy surface ships to sail into. According to the Advisory Committee, another 5 British battleships of the 13 that were sunk had been lost to mines. It was only logical to assume that at least two or three of those losses to mines were due to submarine-laid mines. Furthermore, the "only material damage to the United States Navy on the Atlantic Seaboard during the World War was caused by mines laid by German submarines. The *San Diego,* a large armored cruiser, was sunk off New York, and the *Minnesota,* a battleship, was badly damaged off the Delaware capes by these mines."[3]

Although the report highlighted the submarines' potential, the Advisory Committee did not undermine the paradigm that set up the rest of the Navy. Instead, the report supported the notion of a three-dimensional naval force that could strike in the air, on the sea, and beneath the waves. Because a proper Navy "must consist of capital ships and auxiliaries . . . the submarine, lawfully used, is a legitimate and effective part of a well balanced Navy."[4] In short, the report did not endorse the belief that submarines could be the dominant type of vessel in any navy. While submarines could deny control of the seas, they were not capable of simultaneously controlling the sea or keeping lines of communication secure. Consequently, aircraft and surface ships remained necessary.[5]

The roles noted by the Advisory Committee would lay the foundation for interwar U.S. submarine design. These missions focused on the submarine's role as a naval combatant, not as a potential commerce raider. Although the commerce-raiding role of the submarine would be repeatedly recognized, U.S. submariners ultimately chose design characteristics to support the mission of fleet combat.

THE CONTEXT: WAR PLAN ORANGE

The roles of U.S. submarines as fleet scouts, naval skirmishers, and minelayers fit neatly into the context of the dominant American naval war plan: War Plan ORANGE. War plans were all assigned a rainbow color for a potential enemy, with RED for Great Britain and BLACK for Germany. There were even random rainbow colors for unlikely conflicts, such as GARNET for New Zealand or EMERALD for Eire. As a standard color, ORANGE denoted a more likely conflict. Many naval officers believed that a war based on ORANGE was inevitable. Their belief turned out to be correct, for ORANGE stood for Japan.[6]

Since 1906 the Navy had worked on ORANGE, exploring and rejecting numerous scenarios, such as a forward-deployed naval base like Gibraltar or Singapore, and the idea of a quick trans-Atlantic dash to reach the Pacific in the event of war. Eventually the Navy settled on a war plan that stressed a methodical trans-Pacific offensive, taking islands in the Japanese Mandate as stepping-stones to Japan. By the late 1930s naval planners expected the war to last for approximately three years before the U.S. Navy finally reached Japan and enforced a crippling blockade that would presumably force the Japanese to sue for peace.[7]

Historian Michael Vlahos credited the broad strokes of War Plan ORANGE to Rear Admiral Raymond P. Rodgers, whose March 15, 1911, war plan basically set the objectives that the Navy would adopt and follow, with some exceptions, for the next thirty years:

- The Fleet would sortie from Hawaii and anchor at the end of the line: Okinawa.
- The axis of advance would cut the Central Pacific, and incur the island-hopping seizure of the Marshalls and the Carolines.
- Manila would be re-captured.
- The Fleet would hike out with its own mobile, advanced base.
- Japan would be brought to its knees through blockade: economic strangulation.

There would be no short war, there was no certainty even of a climactic, setpiece sea battle: a Trafalgar-like decision. Drawn on a canvas of early dreadnought technology, *sans* radar, *sans* Zero, *sans* B-29; it was a remarkable picture of "the shape of things to come."[8]

Edward S. Miller's authoritative history of ORANGE explains that the war plan went through many iterations over the years; the one thing that never changed was the objective—total victory over Japan.[9]

War Plan ORANGE's projected blockade against Japan preyed upon Japan's greatest strategic vulnerability: its reliance upon the importation of war matériel by sea. Except for a few natural resources, Japan required its merchant marine to import oil, steel, aluminum, and even foodstuffs. Indeed, despite Japan's natural supply of coal, it still required significant imports of coal to meet domestic demand, as well as the higher grade coal necessary for industrial use. Japan also needed a strong merchant fleet to supply its many island possessions with the military necessities they needed to survive. If the supply lines could be cut off, not only would Japan be unable to supply its war machine, but even the Japanese home islands would be choked with inexorable economic pressure.[10]

However, the blockade envisioned by War Plan ORANGE was not like the German war zones of the First World War. War Plan ORANGE presumed that sufficient naval forces would be available to destroy the Japanese fleet and gain control of the sea in order to enforce such a blockade. Consequently, such a naval blockade could be maintained by surface ships and with cruiser rules of warfare.

Under the ORANGE war plan, the submarine force's primary mission was that of a naval combatant. Since the Japanese would hold several advantages in the event of war, including the ability to decide the field of battle, submarines would play an important role in softening up the Japanese fleet before the two battle lines engaged. Until the Japanese fleet had been destroyed and control of the seas won, commerce warfare was hardly considered.[11] With this role in mind, American naval planners went about designing a fleet submarine.

DESIGNING THE CAPABILITIES OF FLEET SUBMARINES

Initially, the General Board of the Navy issued the specifications for prospective American submarines. However, the General Board's orders for the first large American submarines in the early 1920s flew in the face of the logic of the submarine officer community, who did not concur with the specifications.[12]

As a result of the General Board's mistakes, in 1926 the secretary of the Navy and the chief of naval operations charged the Submarine Officers Conference (SOC) with advising the General Board. The SOC had been established by officers, including then-Captain Thomas C. Hart, as an informal advisory group after the First World War, but it did not gain formal status until 1926.[13] The SOC's responsibilities included design specifications, submarine doctrine, and strategy, as well as determining submarine names.[14] Many of the SOC's members would go on to lead the U.S. submarine force in the Second World War, including Robert H. English, Charles A. Lockwood, Ralph W. Christie, and Charles W. Styer.[15]

At the start of 1930, the SOC and the General Board had concluded the Navy needed a "fleet submarine" that could keep up with the Battle Fleet, scout ahead, and attack the enemy battle fleet as it prepared to engage the American battle line. In keeping with War Plan ORANGE, American submarines needed to have the ability to advance across the Pacific, staying ahead of the Battle Fleet. To do this, submarines required long range, reliable engines, and sufficient weaponry.[16]

To build submarines with the necessary range required a large displacement to carry the fuel and supplies needed for extended operations. The smaller submarines favored by some naval officers could only be used for coastal operations, such as defending the Panama Canal and Hawaii. Rear Admiral Harry E. Yarnell, chief of the Bureau of Engineering, pointed out that making these small submarines did not meet U.S. strategic goals since the Battle Fleet was "going to advance across the Pacific when the war comes out there and . . . the Panama Canal and Honolulu would be protected by the advance of the Fleet across the Pacific apart from raids."[17]

In terms of speed, submarines had to be able to keep ahead of the U.S. Fleet under normal conditions. In 1930 the commander-in-chief of the U.S. Fleet, Admiral William V. Pratt, identified the optimum speed as 15 knots. Pratt felt that it was unrealistic to expect a submarine to make 21 knots, a speed that other officers called for, based on the diesel engine capabilities of the 1920s. Instead, Pratt wanted a submarine that could consistently achieve 15 knots, the cruising speed of the battleships. As long as the submarines left before the Fleet, they could stay far ahead of the Battle Fleet.[18]

A report released in March 1931 discussed the necessary characteristics for submarines as determined by a Control Force Conference, made up of many of the Navy's most experienced submariners and chaired by Rear Admiral Thomas C. Hart. The officers discussed subjects such as the history and future of submarine warfare, the proper size and purposes for submarines, and submarine specifications that would be capable of meeting the challenges inherent in "Blue-Orange, Blue-Red, and Blue-Red-Orange Campaigns," the color codes denoting an American-Japanese, American-British, or American-British-Japanese conflict, respectively.[19]

To their credit, the submarine officers examined the submarine doctrine and history of a variety of other nations, particularly Germany, France, and Great Britain. As a result of their thorough study of the history of submarine warfare, the American submarine officers pointed out that the desired use of submarines in coordinated fleet actions was largely not supported by history, which normally "dealt with individual submarine action against merchant shipping and protective vessels rather than with Fleet action."[20] Despite this, however, the conference concluded:

(a) That although the use of submarines was restricted almost entirely to trade warfare, submarines nevertheless demonstrated their effectiveness against combatant vessels.

(b) That the failure of submarines to play an important part in Fleet action was due to the failure of the higher command to use them to the best advantage rather than to any inherent defect in submarines.

(c) That the major effort in submarine design during the World War was to develop a type for commerce destruction rather than for Fleet use.

(d) That a feature of this development was the large, long radius type with heavy caliber guns.

(d) [sic] That even occasional raids on communications by submarines imposes on the enemy extensive measures for defense. These defense measures involve the use of large numbers of small craft, divert manpower from other war activities, and cause a general slowing down or stoppage of traffic in the sea lanes threatened.

(f) The importance of silent operation, long submerged radius and freedom from oil and air leaks—particularly when operating in enemy waters.

(g) The importance of recognition signals, underwater sound devices and radio.[21]

Clearly, the conference was not about to reject the concept of the fleet submarine. Although the submariners recognized that the submarine was a natural commerce raider, their armament choices emphasized the submarine's role as a naval combatant, not a commerce raider. By intellectually connecting large deck guns to commerce warfare, the Control Force Conference implicitly explained their subsequent decision not to include a deck gun in their recommended submarine. This conclusion would remain with the report's senior author, Admiral Hart, for the next ten years, and he would consistently oppose the placement of large guns on submarines.

Based on their conclusions that submarines *could* operate in conjunction with the Fleet and could serve as a valuable naval combatant, particularly in a conflict against Japan or Great Britain, the Control Force wrote out a long list of recommendations for future submarines. Although not all submariners agreed on the characteristics, the recommendations reflected the majority opinion of the submariners who attended the conference. The desired U.S. fleet submarine would be no longer than 250 feet, displace about a thousand tons, and carry enough fuel and provisions for a ninety-day patrol. The Control Force called for six bow tubes, two stern tubes, and enough space for sixteen torpedoes. There would be two 50-caliber machine guns, but no deck guns. The submarine would require at least three diesel engines, for a minimum surfaced speed of 18 knots, and sufficient battery capacity to go at 10 knots submerged, or maintain 4 knots for fifteen hours. In terms of surface cruising radius, presuming the submarine maintained only 10 knots, the fleet submarine could go as far as 12,000 nautical miles with a full load of fuel. The amount of personnel projected for such a submarine was small: only five officers, three chief petty officers, and thirty-eight enlisted men, for a total of forty-six officers and men.[22]

The recommendations reflected both the experience of the First World War and the poor characteristics exhibited by the Navy's S- and V-type submarines. In reaction, the recommendations of the Control Force Conference called for submarines like the German U-boats, which were small and packed with gear and weapons. Moreover, by recommending against any type of major deck gun, the Control Force Conference seemed to be implicitly ensuring that "commerce destruction" would not even be a temptation.

Five years later, in 1935, the SOC reiterated these design characteristics, with some new wrinkles from operational experience. Submarines still needed to be small in order to be maneuverable, but at the same time they required more space to make long ocean voyages and carry enough weapons to be effective. Additionally, the SOC left open the option of adding more berthing space to make submarines habitable for extended patrols.[23] As far as speed was required, the submarine was still a fleet submarine: "Sufficient sustained speed in the normal condition to maintain the fleet cruising speed. The highest practicable speed is desirable but of secondary importance as compared with other characteristics. Battle line speed not required."[24] In short, the submarine needed to be able to stay ahead of the Fleet in order to be an effective scout and naval skirmisher. However, there was no need to force submarines to match the speed of the battleships in battle. Neither submariners nor surface admirals had any intention of maneuvering submarines *with* the battle line once a surface battle was joined.

Having decided upon the fleet submarine's mission and requisite characteristics, the submarine force resisted limited missions that were seen as a step backward. In 1938, in response to the General Board's decision to construct two coastal defense submarines, both the Commander-in-Chief of the U.S. Fleet, Admiral Claude C. Bloch, and the Commander Submarine Force, Rear Admiral C. S. Freeman, repeated the strategic vision that had been developed for almost twenty years. Admiral Bloch explicitly declared that he had no use for coastal-type submarines, and that constructing the submarines contradicted the nature of War Plan ORANGE as he understood it.[25] Rear Admiral Freeman agreed, declaring that American submarines were meant to "operate offensively in distant waters generally controlled by the enemy and consequently denied to all other types of naval vessels or aircraft . . . [and also] to operate strategically or tactically with our own fleet, either in distant scouting areas or disposed to cover areas through which an enemy fleet may be expected or drawn."[26] To meet these goals, American submarines required "surface ability, sea endurance, large radius of action, and as much speed as can be reliably installed in the designed hull."[27]

With the exception of the two coastal submarines authorized in 1938, the strategic mission of the submarine remained that of a long-range fleet submarine. With the desired characteristics of a practical fleet submarine in mind, the Navy set about building and refining fleet submarines throughout the 1930s. After various refinements, the Navy finally produced a submarine with all the necessary design characteristics by 1941, just in time for the Pacific War.

BUILDING FLEET SUBMARINES

Just as the Navy finally settled on the characteristics it wanted in its submarines, the submariners found their ability to experiment limited by treaty restrictions. In 1930 the United States signed the London Naval Treaty, limiting

the tonnage it could place into submarines at 52,700 t
the Navy could not put too much displacement into i
submarines.

Unfortunately, the Navy had already devoted a signifi
nage to submarines. In 1916 Congress had authorized th
"fleet submarines" to investigate the characteristics nece
marines.[29] These submarines were known as the V-subn   ...., ...y
were all different from each other in design. By 1930 only six of them had
been laid down, with V-5 and V-6 both entering service in 1930.[30] The six
V-submarines had become progressively larger, with V-5 and V-6 displacing as
much as 3,158 tons when fully loaded.[31] The massive displacement had been
considered necessary to install large diesel engines for the V-submarines to
achieve surface speeds up to 17 knots. However, starting in 1927, submarine
officers began to argue against these bulky and sluggish submarines.[32]

Submariners began looking for smaller submarines that could still operate
with the necessary speed and deliver a significant load of torpedoes. The first
of these smaller and experimental submarines was V-7, later renamed Dolphin.
Dolphin displaced only 1,550 tons and her layout foreshadowed the future fleet
submarines of the war. In a continuing trend to decrease the size of submarines
in order to make as many as possible, the next two submarines, V-8 and V-9,
soon to be renamed Cachalot and Cuttlefish, displaced only 1,110 tons.[33] The
small size of the sister submarines, however, severely limited speed and endurance. Furthermore, their diesel engines hardly measured up to the design
characteristics for fleet submarines.

After World War I, the Bureau of Engineering had copied the successful
wartime German diesel engines and steadily developed the engine during the
decade after the war. By 1930, however, it was clear that U.S. submarines required more efficient diesel engines. Unfortunately, no American company
had progressed far enough in diesel technology to be considered suitable for
developing a next-generation submarine diesel engine. Instead, for Cachalot
and Cuttlefish, the Bureau of Engineering purchased the rights to the improved M.A.N. engine, designed in Germany and made in Switzerland.[34] Between the lightweight M.A.N. engines and the Bureau of Engineering's choice
to install only two engines, the Navy succeeded in launching Cachalot and
Cuttlefish with very small displacements.[35] Unfortunately, the M.A.N. engines
performed poorly, and submarine commanders were uncomfortable with the

of being in enemy waters with only two main engines. Consequently, Cachalot and Cuttlefish served through most of the Second World War as training submarines.[36]

With the Depression's sudden influx of federal money into industry and engineering, American companies began to leap ahead in diesel technology. In 1933, with new technology available from the General Motors Winton diesel division, the Bureau of Engineering installed four engines and an all-electric drive into the new Porpoise-class submarines. The all-electric drive transferred energy directly from the diesels to the electric motors, which turned the propeller shafts. The all-electric drive enabled Porpoise to reach 19 knots on the surface, a speed that American submarines had never reached before.[37]

With the 1936 Salmon-class, the Bureau of Engineering shifted to a composite power plant, with two diesels feeding into the electric motors and the other two diesels directly coupled to the shafts, an engine design continued with the 1937 Sargo-class submarines.[38] Due to torsional vibration problems connected with the direct diesel drive, the Bureau of Engineering shifted back to all-electric drive with the 1938 Seadragon-class. Although Admiral Hart, assigned to the General Board at the time, felt that flooding could disable an all-electric drive, the Bureau of Engineering argued that there was no existing hydraulic clutch to buffer the shafts from engine vibration and transmit the horsepower a submarine required.[39] The all-electric drive would power the mainstay U.S. submarines of the Second World War, the Gato-, Balao-, and Tench-classes. By 1943, new slow-speed electric motors permitted the designers of the Tench-class to directly couple the electric motors to the shafts instead of to easily damaged reduction gear. In addition, by the end of the war, American submarines had far surpassed the modest 15-knot speed requirement Admiral Pratt had called for in 1930. Starting with the 1940 Tambor-class, American submarines regularly and reliably made up to 20.25 knots on the surface.[40]

As U.S. submarines increased in speed and displacement, the Submarine Officers Conference pressed the General Board for greater armament. As early as 1930, submariners requested six bow torpedo tubes from the General Board and four torpedo tubes in the stern for over twenty torpedoes and mines. Submariners pointed out that if they made contact with an enemy capital ship, they wanted to be sure they would sink it. With only four torpedoes in a standard spread, the odds were that only two would hit and two would miss. With six torpedoes, submariners could reserve torpedoes for a second attack, or ensure more hits on a target. Some critics felt that submarine commanders would "shotgun" their shots, wasting six torpedoes at once instead of using "rifle" tactics to carefully use one torpedo at a time, making each hit count. Experienced submariners countered these critics by pointing out that during the First World War, making any surface contact at all was rare. These experienced officers wanted to be able to use as many torpedoes as possible during the one opportunity they might have.[41]

For early fleet submarines like *Dolphin* and *Cuttlefish,* the General Board chose not to modify the weapons load-out of the boats. The submarines were already under construction, and the board did not want to increase the displacement any more than necessary due to the constraints of the London Naval Treaty.[42] As the submarines began to increase in size, however, the board was continually assailed to increase the number of torpedoes and tubes in submarines. With the *Salmon*-class in 1936, the General Board agreed to add two torpedo tubes aft, giving the submarines four torpedo tubes fore and aft.[43] The *Salmon*s also carried twenty torpedoes, with four torpedoes stored externally. However, the externally carried torpedoes were removed during the war after *Nautilus* developed a hot run with an externally stowed torpedo during a depth charging and other submarines found it impossible to conduct any maintenance on the external torpedoes.[44] In 1939 the *Tambor*-class was launched with six torpedo tubes forward and four torpedo tubes aft. With the extra space, the submarines were capable of carrying twenty-four torpedoes. This interior layout for torpedoes and tubes would be repeated with the wartime submarines of the *Gato-, Balao-,* and *Tench*-class.[45]

Despite the advice of the Control Force Conference of 1930, all submarines, starting with *Cachalot* and *Cuttlefish,* were also fitted with a 3-inch/50-caliber deck gun aft of the conning tower.[46] Such a step was quite a concession from the naval leadership, which was typified by men like Admiral W. R. Furlong, chief of the Bureau of Ordnance in 1939, who said, "I can't imagine a submarine wanting to fire in a battle on the surface. She should dive and avoid action."[47] However, many submarine officers, particularly Commander Charles A. Lockwood, felt the deck gun was not a weapon for self-defense, but rather a multipurpose weapon for offense.[48] At Lockwood's insistence, the General Board agreed to provide the foundation for a 5-inch/50-caliber deck gun starting with the *Tambor*-class. Halfway through the war, the 5-inch deck guns were added fore and aft, providing U.S. submarines with formidable firepower on the surface. The deck guns would be used in desperate surface battles and against lightly armed, small merchantmen that were not worth a torpedo.[49]

Equipment aboard the late interwar submarines developed greatly as well. In 1930 submariners were using rudimentary "is-was" circular slide rules to aim torpedo salvoes. The system was woefully inaccurate.[50] Starting in 1932, the Bureau of Ordnance coordinated with Arma and Ford Instruments to develop a small but advanced analog fire control computer. The first torpedo data computer, or TDC, was completed in 1938. The Arma Mk 1 TDC turned out to be very complicated, and further competition between Arma and Ford Instruments produced the Arma Mk 3 TDC. The Mk 1 TDC was back-fitted onto submarines from *Dolphin* to *Seawolf,* while the *Tambor*s were designed with a specified location for the Mk 3 TDC inside the conning tower in order to concentrate the fire control party in the attack center of the submarine.[51] The Mk 3 TDC turned out to be extremely successful during the Second World War. No other navy, including the vaunted *Kriegsmarine,* fielded a submarine fire control system that matched its performance during the war.[52]

Another system that helped solve torpedo-shooting problems was the "bubble eliminator." Every time a submarine launched a torpedo using a slug of air, massive bubbles would gurgle to the surface, upsetting the delicate trim necessary to accurately launch torpedoes and giving away the submarine's position. Developed by Lieutenant Marshall M. Dana at Portsmouth Navy Yard, the bubble eliminator was actually a poppet valve that vented air and water from the torpedo tube into a tank in the torpedo room bilges. The bubble eliminator was introduced with the *Porpoise*-class and almost instantly solved the trim problems associated with launching torpedoes.[53]

Perhaps the most important technological advance that allowed for operations in the tropics of the Pacific Ocean was the inclusion of air conditioning aboard submarines. After a hellish shakedown cruise for *Narwhal* in 1930, the General Board realized that submarines required air conditioning to operate in the heat of the tropics. During her cruise, temperatures inside *Narwhal* rose to over one hundred degrees, and within a few days the accumulated moisture in the air reached a humidity of 100 percent. The resulting moisture caused electrical short-circuits, metal corrosion, and mildew in mattresses and clothing. Personnel could not be expected to work for extended periods in these conditions.[54] Starting with experiments aboard *Cuttlefish,* the Navy began designing all submarines with air conditioning. In addition to making the submarines capable of seventy-five-day patrols in the mid-Pacific, air conditioning genuinely improved their habitability.[55]

As the Second World War was about to begin, submarine officers had generally fine-tuned the fleet submarine design that had evolved over the past decade, starting with *Dolphin*. In response to the General Board's decision to build two coastal submarines in 1938, Rear Admiral C. S. Freeman, Commander Submarine Force, highlighted the vastly superior capabilities of the new, medium-sized fleet submarines: "The type found most effective is an intermediate size of about 1500 surface tons displacement, as included in our current building program. This submarine has a turning circle approximately the same as our smaller S-Class, it is not restricted to any special field of operations, it meets all the defensive requirements, and is immeasurably superior in its primary offensive role. Furthermore, it fulfills all the functions of a submarine as called for by our war plans, and is more reliable because of its power unit consisting of four main engines as compared with two main engines for the small type."[56] Freeman's letter was correct. The small, 800-ton *Marlin* and *Mackerel* proved to be utterly unsatisfactory for operations, and ended up as training submarines during the Second World War.[57] Only the large fleet submarines would prove capable of meeting the Navy's needs in the Pacific War.

PREWAR SUBMARINE DOCTRINE

Even though the General Board and the SOC created the characteristics for the highly successful American submarine of the Second World War, the missions envisioned for these submarines turned out to be greatly different from the actual experience of war. Throughout the interwar period, naval officers expected to use submarines as scouts and as the first line of attack against an enemy battle fleet. The submarines' "most important employment [was] in operations against enemy capital ships, and until that type of operation [was] reduced in its importance to the general employment of naval forces [the United States] would not contemplate using submarines against commerce."[58]

The submariners' priorities meshed with the strategic vision of the naval leadership. For instance, at the beginning of 1936 the commander-in-chief of the U.S. Fleet, Admiral Joseph M. Reeves, stressed the use of submarines against ORANGE warships. An innovative leader, Reeves acknowledged that he eventually expected to use submarines against merchant ships at a future stage of a BLUE-ORANGE war, but definitely not at the beginning.[59] However, there was no doubt about the main objectives of the submarine force: "The primary employment of submarines will be in offensive operations against enemy larger combatant vessels, although it will be necessary initially to divert small detachments to: (1) training purposes; (2) local defense at the Canal Zone; and, (3) to local defense forces at Hawaii . . . No submarines will be assigned in the early stages of the war to operate against enemy trade routes."[60] In Reeves's vision of the Pacific war, his submarines would scout out and engage the enemy fleet about one month into the war. Although Reeves did not expect his submarines to win the war, he did expect them to find and damage the enemy battle line: "The objectives of these submarines would be the enemy main body. Before attacks could be made on the Main Body, it would have to be located *at sea*."[61]

The U.S. submarine strategy was codified in April 1939, when the submarine force released its tactical doctrine. This was a detailed set of guidelines by the Commander Submarine Force, Rear Admiral C. S. Freeman, who had labeled two missions for the submarine force in 1938: the first was to operate independently in enemy waters in place of aircraft and surface ships; the second was to operate as a scout ahead of the fleet or a naval skirmisher to soften up the enemy fleet before the U.S. surface fleet engaged.[62] In keeping with these missions, the submarine force doctrine dictated that the submariner's primary target was to be capital ships. As long as it was possible to attack capital ships, submarines were not permitted to attack any other targets.[63]

The doctrine explicitly separated attacking fleet units from secondary missions like "patrol."[64] It explained that submarine patrols differed from "attack" because their purpose was to attack lines of communication, not fleet units.[65] The doctrine discussed commerce destruction as part of attacking lines of communication, limiting commerce raiding to armed merchant ships and convoys:

> Patrol against enemy lines of communication may include the destruction of commerce. It may be expected that the convoy system will be used, especially at focal and terminal points. On the high seas circuitous routing will be employed. Due to the limitations of submarines in exercising the right of visit and search, and the difficulty of distinguishing between enemy and neutral shipping because of the disguise of enemy shipping as neutral, submarine operations against enemy commerce is limited to attacks on convoys, or attacks on positively identified armed enemy shipping, *unless*

unrestricted commerce destruction is directed as a last resort. The torpedo is the major weapon in these operations, as the submarine is not equipped with gun power to equal that which may be expected on modern merchantmen. The submarine gun may be employed against vessels known to be unarmed or small vessels of minor resistant qualities.

... The principles of the submarine attack against commerce does not differ from that against other types of vessels.[66]

Although documents from the General Board during the Washington Naval Conference and other writings from directly after the First World War indicated that attacking armed merchant ships or even escorted convoys was considered tantamount to unrestricted submarine warfare, Rear Admiral Freeman's doctrine concluded that armed merchant ships or convoyed merchant ships were *not* protected by the London Naval Treaty. The doctrine also identified troop transports as enemy combatant vessels and even recommended attempting to sink the transports during troop disembarkation, when the transports were most vulnerable.[67] Traditional cruiser warfare was impossible, however, because of the danger of armed merchant ships: "Under the limitations imposed by the laws of war and as interpreted in the Treaty of London, submarines cannot be used effectively against merchant ships without running undue risk of destruction."[68]

Although the doctrine indicated the possibility that unrestricted submarine warfare would occur only "as a last resort," it was the most explicit formal consideration given to unrestricted warfare by the submarine force until the war began. Within the submarine force, individual submariners clearly recognized the efficacy and probability of unrestricted submarine warfare. Commander Edward E. Hazlett remarked in front of the General Board in 1937, "I realize we are committed not to use the submarine for economic warfare but ... we might some day be forced into that by our adversary."[69] Among others, Hazlett, Lieutenant Joseph C. Hubbard, and then-Lieutenant Hyman G. Rickover echoed this view in the pages of the U.S. Naval Institute *Proceedings.*[70] However, doctrine and training ignored their pragmatic opinion.

For instance, the submarine force doctrine rated the hierarchy of targets in no uncertain terms: "Normally the primary objectives of submarine attack are capital ships or aircraft carriers. For special reasons heavy cruisers or lighter combatant or auxiliary ships may be designated as targets. Attack on other than capital ships or aircraft carriers *will not be made* unless such other vessels are designated as primary objectives or attack on capital ships is definitely impracticable or will not be jeopardized thereby."[71]

TRAINING TO BE CAUTIOUS

With its emphasis on attacking enemy fleet units, particularly capital ships, the published doctrine established what the U.S. Navy expected from its submarines. But even though the published doctrine stressed aggressiveness, the submarine force deliberately hobbled itself by inculcating a culture of caution and a fear of detection, based on an undue belief in the excellence of antisubmarine warfare. Naval officers and submariners believed that if a submarine was detected, it would be easily destroyed: "Once a super-sonic-equipped destroyer made sound contact with an attacking submarine the odds went down. It was estimated that depth-charge attacks which would surely follow such a contact would result in a submarine kill in one attack out of four."[72] In hindsight, the Navy clearly misjudged the capabilities of antisubmarine warfare. Submariners improperly assumed that aircraft could easily spot submarines at depths shallower than 125 feet because most naval exercises were held in unusually clear waters around the Hawaiian Islands or in the Caribbean. Sonar conditions in those waters were also unusually excellent. Consequently, submariners believed airpower and sonar to be omnipotent over submarines.[73]

The exaggerated belief in the dominance of antisubmarine warfare would come back to haunt the submarine force during the war. One submarine commanding officer actually broke down upon the realization that his Japanese attacker had sonar, and another refused to make attacks on targets with sonar-equipped escorts.[74] After the war, Captain Wilfred Jay Holmes, a prewar submariner and wartime intelligence officer, explained that "the caution that was essential to [attacking screened warships] was unnecessarily restrictive in [commerce raiding], and when U.S. submarines were diverted to war against commerce it took time to develop effective tactics for the new task."[75]

Based on their erroneous belief in the superiority of antisubmarine warfare, the submarine force staged training exercises that required submarines to attack almost entirely by sound. Periscope observations were generally prohibited, despite the published doctrine. According to W. J. Holmes, submarine commanders in the Asiatic Fleet were threatened with relief from command if their periscope was sighted in an exercise.[76] Even when it was not sighted, submarine commanders were criticized for using their periscope. Captain

Slade D. Cutter recalled a prewar exercise in which his submarine, USS *Pompano*, and other submarines in the Pacific Fleet had attempted to infiltrate a screened force of battleships, using only sonar. Cutter's commanding officer, Lewis Parks, eventually grew impatient with attempting to find a target in the clutter of noise generated by the destroyers and the battleships. He briefly used his periscope to make an observation, and shot an exercise torpedo. It was the only torpedo hit of the entire exercise, but afterward Parks was accused of "losing his nerve" by risking a periscope observation.[77]

After the war, W. J. Holmes scathingly criticized the prewar doctrine of sound approaches as a recipe for failure: "Of the 4873 U.S. submarine attacks that it was possible to analyze after the war, only thirty-one could be described as sound attacks and none of these was successful."[78]

Virtually all submarine exercises were unrealistic. Submarines practiced in scenarios in which potential targets zigzagged, while under heavy protection by extremely alert aircraft and surface vessels. To avoid detection, submarines remained below 125 feet and relied upon passive sonar for an attack.[79] Although the scenarios reflected attacks against a well-escorted enemy battle fleet, they hardly reflected the conditions of potential commerce warfare. One of the few times that submarines actually attempted to attack an exercise convoy, in January 1940, turned out to be just another exercise in attacking an incredibly well-screened, high-speed force: "[T]he attackers operated submerged, and the merchant ships had a destroyer and aircraft escort imposing a high degree of caution on the submariners' part. Worse still, the convoy sailed at either 12 or 17 knots, at the high end of most merchant vessels' capabilities, making them harder to "torpedo." In such a hostile environment, this exercise provided an illustration of the requirements of attacking a group of well-defended enemy troopships, and not a strike at [a] more lightly defended merchant convoy."[80] Furthermore, this unrealistic exercise was the *only* exercise that trained submarines against commerce in the two years before the war. The other thirty-five exercises of 1940 to 1941 were submarine attacks against naval units.[81]

Night surface attacks turned out to be another neglected phase of training. Published doctrine *did* allow such attacks, even recommending that a submarine commander maintain his submarine's stealth by using the quieter electric motors instead of diesel engines.[82] The reality, however, was much different. Unwilling to risk collisions between submarines and surface ships running without lights, most of which were not equipped with radar, the Navy rarely, if ever, formally practiced night surface approaches. Furthermore, even if the submariners attempted night surface attacks, they actually had no way of observing a target from the bridge and then easily transmitting the information to the fire control computers. Only shortly before the war did Mare Island Naval Shipyard begin fielding the Target Bearing Transmitter (TBT), which accomplished this purpose. Even so, most submarines were not equipped with a TBT at the beginning of the war.[83] Consequently, night surface attacks were next to impossible.

The tempered aggressiveness of the submarine force was personified in the last prewar commander of the Pacific submarine force, Rear Admiral Thomas Withers. Withers took command of the Pacific Fleet's submarine force shortly before the Pacific war began. To prepare his force for war, Withers suspended exercise regulations that he felt were unnecessarily restrictive, allowing submarine commanders greater freedom to shoot exercise torpedoes. However, most of Withers's exercises were worst-case scenarios: the submarines practiced against targets that were highly screened by surface ships and aircraft.[84] Following the published doctrine, submarines practiced evading destroyer screens, while also attempting to penetrate a screened force of capital ships, preferably battleships when possible.[85] Withers did not record any practices involving slow and poorly escorted merchant ships.

Withers also ordered submarine commanders to start regularly diving below 100 feet, which had been the typical submarine operating depth. Withers directed submarines to make regular dives to test depth, forcing submarine officers to become proficient at operating at deeper depths and using temperature gradients to elude sonar screens. This experience at deeper depths would prove vital during the war.[86] Unfortunately, Withers's deep-diving approach also stressed a doctrine that discouraged periscope attacks. Withers directly fostered this by overestimating the ability of aircraft to see submarines. As noted previously, the unusually clear waters around the Hawaiian Islands fooled submariners like Withers. He gave several effective demonstrations that convinced submarine commanders of their vulnerability to aircraft, even dropping firecrackers from an aircraft that exploded over the deck of a submerged submarine.[87] Consequently, the doctrine of remaining deep and attacking by sound became entrenched in the psyches of most prewar submarine commanders.

When the war began, Withers continually tempered his orders for boldness with simultaneous orders not to be foolhardy. In personal interviews before a submarine went on patrol, Withers "preached aggressiveness but warned against rashness," particularly warning against surface gun actions.[88] For most early submarine commanders, these contradictory orders compelled them to err on the side of caution.

Some prewar submarine commanders, however, instinctively prepared for unrestricted submarine warfare and bolder doctrine. One such was Lewis Parks of USS *Pompano*, who typified aggressiveness. Parks instilled battle-mindedness into his junior officers, who included the famous submarine ace, Slade Cutter. Unlike many of his peers, Parks remained sublimely self-confident in the face of criticism by superior officers. Before the war, *Pompano* patrolled between Pearl Harbor and Wake Island to practice approaches on unsuspecting Japanese merchant ships, as well as making night surface attacks, including one on battleship USS *California*.[89] Even in port, Parks remained aggressive. He often sent Cutter to study Japanese merchant ships moored in Pearl Harbor in order to develop mental tricks to help determine the angle-on-the-bow for a certain ship.[90]

Unfortunately, Parks was the exception to the rule. For the most part, submarine commanders and even the submarine force commanders, like Admiral Withers, were unprepared for unrestricted commerce warfare. For instance, the operations orders of the Asiatic Fleet's submarine force, issued on December 2, 1941, emphasized that submarines would attack ships in the following "priority of objectives[:] (a) capital ships (b) loaded transports (c) light forces, and transports and supply ships in ballast."[91] Although the operations orders implicitly recognized the possibility of unrestricted submarine warfare by noting that the rules governing naval warfare could be changed, the emphasis remained on attacking the Japanese naval units that would be attacking the Philippines. Less than a week before Pearl Harbor, the submarine force continued to focus on the mission they had created for themselves over the last twenty years: to scout out and sink enemy warships in support of the U.S surface fleet.[92]

THE ACCIDENTAL COMMERCE RAIDER

Although the submarine force doctrine acknowledged the remote possibility of unrestricted submarine warfare, "at the lower levels, in its operational and tactical preparations, the service held a consistent view: the U.S. Navy would not allow its submarine captains to attack merchant shipping without warning."[93] Submarine commanders like Dick Voge, who commanded USS *Sealion* at the outbreak of hostilities, even believed that to conduct unrestricted submarine warfare would make them liable for the punishment that American statesman Elihu Root had pushed for at the Washington Naval Conference in 1922: "submarines who violated [Article 22] were subject to being 'hunted down and captured or sunk as pirates.'"[94]

U.S. submarines would eventually prove to be natural commerce raiders, but not because they had trained for the role. When war came, the submariners quickly had to adjust to a wartime environment that did not match their prewar expectations. Dick Voge flatly stated that the war submariners found themselves fighting was not the war they were prepared to fight: "a campaign of torpedo attacks against enemy combatant ships; occasionally a gun attack if the odds were favorable and the expected results were commensurate with the risks; some tactical scouting; possibly a few mine laying missions to harass the enemy. *Neither by training nor indoctrination were the submarines prepared to wage unrestricted warfare.*"[95]

In one of many signs of the submarine force's unreadiness for unrestricted warfare, Voge noted that submariners had to develop tactics such as the "end-around" and high-speed night surface attacks, neither of which had been developed before the war.[96] In a brief study on the readiness of the U.S. submarine force for unrestricted warfare, naval historian Randy Papadopoulos cited a story of a communications officer who, upon the receipt of the orders to conduct unrestricted warfare, asked his commanding officer what "unrestricted" meant. The commanding officer replied, "I don't know."[97] While the story may be apocryphal, it certainly reflected the submariners' prewar training.

For two decades, following the strategic goals they had chosen, the submarine force had focused on naval combat to the exclusion of all else. Consequently, their new mission caught them almost completely off balance. The reaction of many could be typified by submariners like Dick Voge, who later wrote that he found the order to conduct unrestricted submarine warfare to be "as startling as the Japanese attack on Pearl Harbor."[98]

The U.S. submarine force eventually proved capable of carrying out unrestricted warfare not because the fleet submarine had been designed for that purpose, but because the submarines had been designed for the difficult mission of naval combat in the Pacific Ocean. For such a mission, the submarines required characteristics that enabled them to carry out a variety of different tasks that naval planners had not envisioned. The U.S. fleet submarine's high speed allowed it to proceed far ahead of American surface forces and maintain contact with enemy battle fleets, but it also allowed submarines to outflank slower merchant convoys. Submarines had the range to shadow Japanese fleet movements all the way from the Sea of Japan, but they could also stay on station for almost two months, allowing them to sink virtually anything crossing their patrol area. The large number of torpedoes and torpedo tubes on U.S. submarines allowed a submarine to shoot a mortal salvo of torpedoes into heavily protected battleships and aircraft carriers, but it also allowed American submarine commanders to persistently and tenaciously continue convoy battles when other, less-well-armed submarine commanders might have broken contact.[99]

The orders to conduct unrestricted warfare came as a surprise to the submarine force, but the orders had been in the process of formulation for a year. Starting in November 1940, with a global war increasingly likely, the U.S. Navy's senior leadership had to squarely confront some strategic choices. One of these would be the matter of commerce warfare in the Pacific, and it would force the leaders of the U.S. Navy to weigh the principles of international law against the imperatives of military strategy.

CHAPTER 6

Laying the Strategic Groundwork

Ever since the First World War, unrestricted submarine warfare had been considered immoral and illegal. But as the Second World War progressed, new strategic realities facing the United States made American unrestricted submarine warfare increasingly necessary. These strategic realities were encapsulated in a document that would lay the foundation for the U.S. national military strategy in the Second World War—Plan Dog.

PLAN DOG

Unlike many U.S. war plans, Plan Dog was the brainchild of one man, the U.S. chief of naval operations, Admiral Harold R. Stark. Stark assumed the post on August 1, 1939, and he quickly found himself bringing the Navy up to wartime readiness when the Germans invaded Poland only a month later. Stark worked hard to enlarge the Navy, while also devising an appropriate strategic vision for employing the forces he had. Shortly after the unprecedented reelection of President Roosevelt to a third term, Stark committed his thoughts to paper. His memorandum, which became known as "Plan Dog," became the national military strategy of the United States for the Second World War and the basis for cooperation between Great Britain and the United States even before the war began.[1]

Plan Dog was actually part of a long memorandum that assessed the strategic situation facing the United States in December 1940. Initially written by Admiral Stark in November 1940, the memorandum was studied and revised by both then-Captain Richmond Kelly Turner and his Army counterpart, Colonel Joseph T. McNarney.[2] The memorandum was then studied and approved by a Joint Board consisting of General George C. Marshall, Army chief of staff;

Admiral Stark; Major General William Bryden; Rear Admiral Royal Ingersoll, Brigadier General Leonard H. Gerow; and Captain Turner.[3] From there, the memorandum then went to the secretaries of state, war, and the Navy, who then forwarded it to the president of the United States.[4] Although he never formally approved the plan, President Roosevelt agreed with its general principles.[5]

Admiral Stark, Captain Turner, and Colonel McNarney identified three primary goals for the United States. In keeping with the popular isolationist sentiment of the time, the United States would first focus upon hemispheric defense. From there, the national goals became far more global in scope. The United States would prevent the dissolution of the British empire and also stop all further Japanese territorial aggression.[6] This not only ran counter to the isolationist sentiment in the United States, but also was hardly the action of an unqualified neutral. Admiral Stark and his subordinates clearly felt that an Axis victory was intolerable.

Although the planners mentioned Japan as one of the threats to U.S. national security, it was a lower priority than hemispheric defense and aid to Great Britain. Despite the clear threat posed by Japan, the memorandum continued to circle back to preserving Great Britain. At one point, the authors wrote: "Our interests in the Far East are very important. It would, however, be incorrect to consider that they are as important to us as is the integrity of the Western Hemisphere, or as important as is preventing the defeat of the British Commonwealth."[7]

The assessment offered several possible scenarios for war involving the United States, and several concurrent plans to go with those scenarios. The authors listed the advantages and disadvantages of each plan, before settling upon the fourth—Plan D—as the most advantageous to the United States no matter how war came, whether from Nazi Germany or imperial Japan. The planners hoped not to fight a two-ocean war, but they called for immediate aid to Great Britain upon the commencement of hostilities, regardless of how war began. As a result, even though the planners recommended the United States do everything in its power to avoid war with Japan, should the United States be forced into a war in the Pacific, it "should, at the same time, enter the war in the Atlantic, and should restrict operations in the Mid-Pacific and the Far East in such a manner as to permit the prompt movement to the Atlantic of forces fully adequate to conduct a major offensive in that ocean."[8] Almost a full year before Pearl Harbor, the United States had already adopted a plan that called for first winning the war in the European theater, while fighting a delaying action against the Japanese.

Plan Dog's influence on the decision to conduct unrestricted submarine warfare came in its call for an economic war of attrition against Japan. Because the bulk of U.S. forces were to be sent to Europe and the Atlantic in the event of war, the American war planners believed the United States would have to "settle upon a war having a more limited objective than the complete defeat of Japan. The objective in such a limited war against Japan would be the reduction of Japanese offensive power chiefly through economic blockade."[9] The United States and its allies would cut off all supplies to Japan from Malaysia, the Western Hemisphere, Indochina, China, the Philippines, and the rest of the Pacific. While Japan might still be able to shuttle some supplies through the Sea of Japan from Russia (assuming Russia remained neutral), the supplies would only be enough for the Japanese to subsist on, but certainly not enough to wage any offensive actions. While the Japanese were thus bottled up, the United States would be winning the war in the Atlantic and Europe.[10]

In a sense, this economic blockade was no different from what the Navy's war plan for Japan, War Plan ORANGE, had always projected. Even from the first ORANGE war plans in 1906, naval war planners proposed to defeat Japan by imposing a blockade that would economically strangle the Japanese.[11] War Plan ORANGE, however, presumed that sufficient naval forces would be available to destroy the Japanese fleet and gain control of the sea in order to enforce such a blockade. Consequently, such a naval blockade could be maintained by surface ships and with cruiser rules of warfare. Unfortunately, by late 1940 the United States simply did not have the overwhelming naval forces necessary to conduct the blockade envisioned by War Plan ORANGE.

The U.S. Navy was therefore in a tough position. It had to cut off Japan's maritime trade, but lacked the surface fleet necessary to control the Western Pacific. Without U.S. control of the Western Pacific, there was only one force that could still deny control of the sea to the Japanese, despite the preponderance of Japanese warships in the area—the U.S. submarine force.

Hiding beneath the waves, submarines could cruise into Japanese waters and strike undetected. To maintain their stealth and chances of survivability, however, meant abandoning cruiser warfare. Consequently, the campaign of economic strangulation, to be waged before the United States could gain control of the sea, implicitly required unrestricted submarine warfare. As Samuel Flagg Bemis noted in 1961: "The motives which impelled the United States in the Second World War to resort to unrestricted submarine and air warfare against Japan . . . were coolly, studiously strategic: to cut off the enemy's vital overseas trade and thereby weaken his capacity to fight and win a long war. Submarines were the only American naval instrument which could reach across the Pacific at the beginning of the conflict, and they were put promptly to this prearranged task!"[12] Unrestricted submarine warfare carried a great deal of moral and legal baggage, but for naval war planners, the strategic necessity for unrestricted submarine warfare dovetailed with over thirty years of U.S. naval war planning. As Edward S. Miller concluded: "The old concept of blockade by surface vessels could not have been made effective until late in the war. The decision for undersea predation magnified the success of one of the Orange Plan's most basic prescriptions."[13]

Thus, it was probably no coincidence that even as Admiral Stark and Captain Turner were writing and revising Plan Dog, they were also revising the Navy's war plans, including, for the first time, the authorization to fleet commanders to create war zones.

RAINBOW 3 AND "STRATEGICAL AREAS"

Stark's Plan Dog was remarkable, but he did not have time to convert his strategic vision into a viable naval war plan. To do that, he needed an efficient and driven war planner, administrator, and naval leader. Stark settled upon the fiery and dynamic Captain Richmond Kelly Turner, commanding officer of the heavy cruiser USS *Astoria*.[14]

Few U.S. naval officers have excited the sort of controversy that Admiral Richmond Kelly Turner has. Even Turner's most ardent supporters admitted that "'good nature' and 'good fellow' were probably the furthest deviation from the truth."[15] Yet Turner's abilities impressed many superiors, and he was often sought after as a war planner. Although Turner would take up many responsibilities when he became director of War Plans Division, his most important duty was to convert Stark's vision into an effective RAINBOW war plan.

The RAINBOW war plans were joint service plans meant to fight against a broad spectrum of multinational enemies, almost all of which were part of the Axis. Drawn up by officers from both the Army and the Navy, the RAINBOW war plans set out detailed and achievable goals for both services, while leaving specific details and planning up to unit commanders. The Navy, of course, drew up its own, Navy-specific RAINBOW war plan, and then fused it with the concurrent Army RAINBOW war plan to create a Joint RAINBOW war plan. Like most joint service projects, this process was far from painless.[16]

When Turner arrived at the War Plans Division, only RAINBOW 1 and RAINBOW 4 had been drawn up in any detail. Turner quickly decided that both war plans, which were meant only to defend the Western Hemisphere, were unrealistic. Instead, he focused on creating war plans that addressed a more likely scenario: war in both the Atlantic and Pacific.[17]

Given the threat emanating from Germany, both Rear Admiral Turner and Admiral Stark believed that the massive trans-Pacific offensive envisioned in War Plan ORANGE was unfeasible. Instead, the two planned to conduct the war just as Stark believed it needed to be fought: with the emphasis first upon defeating Germany, and then on tackling Japan. Both the RAINBOW 3 and RAINBOW 5 war plans reflected this emphasis, although in reality, only RAINBOW 5 was meant to be the embodiment of Plan Dog. As the Navy's RAINBOW 3 entered print, Stark and Turner retired the ORANGE war plan on December 17, 1940, after thirty-four years of guidance to the U.S. Navy.[18]

Even if War Plan ORANGE was dead, RAINBOW still reflected its influence, as well as that of Stark's Plan Dog. The specific tasks and orders issued to the two Pacific fleets in RAINBOW 3 made it clear that the overarching goal of the RAINBOW 3 war plan was to defeat Japan by cutting off its economic sources: "[The] Naval Establishment, in cooperation with the Army and the forces of our Allies, will . . . [s]ever Japanese sea communications in the Pacific Ocean and the Bering Sea to the eastward of the 180th meridian, and through the Malay Barrier; and raid Japanese sea communications in other areas in the Western Pacific, and South China Sea and contiguous waters, in order eventually to destroy the economic power of Japan to conduct offensive warfare."[19]

The tasks were split between the U.S. Fleet, soon to become the Pacific Fleet, and the Asiatic Fleet. The U.S. Fleet would cut off the trade to the east of the 180th meridian, while the Asiatic Fleet was assigned responsibility for the Western Pacific and the Malay Barrier.[20]

In keeping with the focus on economic warfare, RAINBOW 3 also adjusted the rules of war governing naval officers. The only prior naval RAINBOW war plan to be officially approved, RAINBOW 1 from July 1940, was strikingly different from RAINBOW 3 regarding the conduct of war at sea. The specific change lay in a section entitled "Rules of Warfare." RAINBOW 1's "Rules of Warfare" section included only a very terse passage enjoining all Navy units to follow the 1917 *Instructions for the Navy of the United States Governing Maritime Warfare.*[21] RAINBOW 3, in contrast, provided for "strategical areas":

> The Commander-in-Chief, U.S. FLEET, the Commander-in-Chief, U.S. ASIATIC FLEET, and the Commander, ATLANTIC FORCE, are authorized to declare such "Strategical Areas" as in their opinion are *vital.* They must give wide publicity to the exact boundaries of the areas involved and, at the earliest opportunity, notify the Chief of Naval Operations of these actions. A "Strategical Area," as here used, means an area from which it is necessary to exclude merchant ships and merchant aircraft to prevent damage to such ships or aircraft, or to prevent such ships or aircraft from obtaining information, which, if transmitted to the enemy, would be detrimental to our own forces.[22]

Although there was no mention of unrestricted submarine warfare within these strategical areas, naval officers could hardly have mistaken their resemblance to the sort of areas that the Germans called "war zones," the British termed "zones dangerous to navigation," and the United States neutrality legislation phrased as "combat areas." In all these cases, these were areas that strictly prohibited noncombatant commercial vessels.

At the same time, Stark and Turner were not yet willing to explicitly condone unrestricted warfare, despite their focus on economically defeating Japan. RAINBOW 3 not only ordered all U.S. naval units to continue to obey the 1917 *Instructions,* but also specifically called for the enforcement of the *Instructions* in regard to "[m]erchant vessels and merchant aircraft [and] Bombardment and bombing of shore positions and establishments."[23] The "Rules of Warfare" also included a section on what to do with prizes, recalling the days of sailing warships. In short, the rules indicated that sinking merchant shipping was still generally unacceptable.[24]

Furthermore, the specific instructions to the fleet commanders indicated that unrestricted warfare was not yet being explicitly considered. In its orders to the commander-in-chief of the U.S. Fleet, RAINBOW 3 specifically ordered the U.S. Fleet not to destroy commercial shipping, but to "CAPTURE

ENEMY NAVAL AND MERCHANT SHIPPING, AND NEUTRAL MERCHANT SHIP-
PING BOUND FOR ULTIMATE ENEMY DESTINATIONS, WHICH MAY BE FOUND IN
THE PACIFIC THEATER."[25]

Even though RAINBOW 3 explicitly prohibited the use of unrestricted warfare, Admiral Stark seemed to believe that it was implicitly condoned by the
circumstances regarding Japanese merchant shipping. As soon as RAINBOW
3 was complete, he sent advance copies to the commander-in-chief of the U.S.
Fleet, Admiral James O. Richardson, and his relief, Rear Admiral Husband
Kimmel, and the commander-in-chief of the Asiatic Fleet, Stark's Naval War
College classmate and friend, Admiral Thomas C. Hart.

Of all the senior officers in the U.S. Navy when the Second World War
began, Admiral Thomas C. Hart arguably had the greatest experience in submarines. He had commanded submarine flotillas and divisions during their
nascent years, helped establish the submarine base at Pearl Harbor and helped
draft the specifications for the fleet submarine. His biographer, James Leutze,
properly credited Hart with an influential role in the creation and survival
of the interwar submarine force: "He pioneered in the administration of the
[submarine] service; he helped organize the influential Submarine Officers
Conference; he lobbied against the abolition of undersea weapons, unless
coupled with a more sweeping disarmament measure; and he fought hard,
and ultimately effectively to get German design features incorporated into U.S.
submarines . . . Tommy Hart was in the forefront of the submariner's battle all
along and could surely take considerable pride for these developments. He
was not always right, but he was always in the center of the fray."[26] Now, as
commander-in-chief of the Asiatic Fleet, Hart commanded a puny force that
consisted of a few cruisers, a handful of destroyers, and a number of submarines. In the event of war, Hart planned on his submarine force to take the
leading role in disrupting enemy landings in the Philippines, while most of his
surface ships would join up with the British and the Dutch to the south.[27]

Given his emphasis on submarine operations, Admiral Hart immediately
noticed the ambiguous phrasing regarding strategical areas and raiding of
Japanese sea communications in the RAINBOW 3 war plan, and in a letter of January 18, 1941, he queried Stark about how much freedom he had
regarding merchant shipping: "The possibilities in raids on Japanese sea
communications,—meaning shipping other than naval forces,—would be
great if our submarines were free to wage 'unrestricted' war." However, Hart

quickly added, "Unless we are otherwise ordered, our submarines will not be directed to depart from the War Instructions now in force."[28]

Admiral Stark replied on February 7, 1941:

'Sever sea communications' indicates that you should make the fullest possible defense of the three straits mentioned, in order to prevent Japanese naval forces from approaching the final vital positions, and in order to prevent enemy raids on the associated communications in the Indian Ocean. It is believed that further careful study of these tasks will reveal all their implications. The term 'sea communications' includes all naval as well as merchant shipping. Raids on military and naval supply ships should prove very profitable. The question of inability to sink merchant shipping by submarines, without warning, is unlikely to arise, since it is probable that all shipping within your reach will be under Japanese naval operation or control . . .

. . . The employment of submarines as proposed is considered suitable and highly desirable.[29]

Admiral Stark's reply did not highlight the portions of the RAINBOW war plan that called for cruiser warfare or adherence to the 1917 *Instructions*. Instead, he essentially told Admiral Hart to assume that virtually all Japanese shipping would be under the control of the Japanese Navy or military. His comments seem to leave little doubt that Stark's vision of cutting off Japanese trade entailed unrestricted warfare. However, in February 1941, the only rationale Stark could give for conducting unrestricted warfare was to claim that virtually all Japanese shipping would be under military control. Fortunately for Stark, his views were about to receive critical legal and ideological support from an unexpected source.

In his letter to Admiral Hart, Admiral Stark had informed Hart that "a revised 'Instructions for the Navy of the United States Governing Maritime Warfare' will soon go to press."[30] Although Stark could not have known it in February 1941, the prospective *Instructions for the Navy of the United States Governing Maritime and Aerial Warfare* would soon initiate another series of letters directly related to the subject of unrestricted warfare.

THE NEED FOR NEW *INSTRUCTIONS*

When Admiral Stark sent RAINBOW 3 to Admiral Richardson, Rear Admiral Kimmel, and Admiral Hart, all three of the fleet commanders pointed to the antiquated nature of the *Instructions for the Navy of the United States Govern-*

ing Maritime Warfare. Admiral Richardson and Rear Admiral Kimmel, in a joint letter to Admiral Stark in January 1941, pointedly wrote of the need for new *Instructions:* "The only 'Instructions for the Navy of the United States Governing Maritime Warfare' now available are those prepared in 1917–1918. There is no copy of this publication in the files of the Commander-in-Chief, Pacific Fleet, and it is known that many ships are likewise without copies. It is considered imperative that they be brought up to date, taking into account modern weapons and methods of warfare. *The distribution of the revised instructions should be expedited.*"[31]

The Navy keenly felt the absence of any revision to the *Instructions for the Navy of the United States Governing Maritime Warfare, June, 1917.* As the title indicated, the *Instructions* had not been updated since the First World War, and it was clearly a product of its era. It hardly addressed the new technologies that had reshaped naval warfare, like the submarine and the airplane. The coming of the Second World War made clear that it was time to update, revise, and reissue the *Instructions for the Navy of the United States,* something that Admiral Stark had realized shortly after entering office in August 1939.

Numerous naval officers had tried to revise the *Instructions* during the interwar period. In July 1922 Rear Admiral William L. Rodgers and Marine Corps Lieutenant Colonel L. C. Lucas had actually submitted a proposed code of naval warfare to the General Board based upon Rodgers's views about the need to change maritime law, but nothing came of it.[32] Perhaps in response to the Rodgers and Lucas code, the secretary of the Navy in October 1922 ordered the General Board of the Navy to revise the *Instructions,* but no revised edition was ever published.[33] The General Board of the Navy had called for new *Instructions* numerous times, and they repeatedly consulted Naval War College professor George Grafton Wilson for his opinion on the necessary revisions. However, the only revisions the Navy actually made to the *Instructions* were in two pamphlets issued in 1935 concerning the new neutrality legislation.[34]

Part of the problem was deciding who was responsible for preparing the new *Instructions.* Naval Regulations vested the sole authority for matters of naval law within the Office of the Judge Advocate General, so only JAG had the authority to write the *Instructions,* unless otherwise directed. However, the Naval War College had traditionally taken an important role in preparing the regulations guiding U.S. naval forces in relation to international law. Professor George Grafton Wilson, after all, had been one of the principal authors of the 1917 *Instructions*.[35] At the same time, the War Plans Division also claimed responsibility for the *Instructions*, since the *Instructions* would directly govern the actions of the Navy at war.[36] Last, but not least, the State Department held the final veto over any *Instructions* the Navy produced. Although the Navy was a separate department, and JAG held authority regarding international law and the Navy, the State Department held overarching authority regarding all matters of international law. After all, State Department lawyers had drafted most of the treaties that made up the *Instructions,* and they were supposed to best understand the views of other nations regarding certain acts of war. Although the Navy judge advocate general had actually written two revised *Instructions* during the interwar period, the State Department had rejected both of them.[37]

As war became imminent, the same pressures that had driven Admiral Stark to draw up Plan Dog and replace the ORANGE war plans with RAINBOW led him to call for new *Instructions*. Initially, Stark turned to the General Board of the Navy, but the War Plans Division argued in a memorandum that it was the proper office to write the new *Instructions*.[38] Consequently, Stark ordered the War Plans Division to draw up new *Instructions,* assisted by the Navy judge advocate general. By April 1940 the first draft of the new *Instructions* was ready. After receiving approval from the General Board, the prospective *Instructions* was sent to the State Department and the Office of the Navy Judge Advocate General for review and critique.[39]

THE NEW *INSTRUCTIONS* AND THE SUBMARINE

If naval officers were hoping for a major change in the regulations regarding submarines, they must have been keenly disappointed. From the initial version of April 1940 to the tentative copy that was sent to the Fleet in February 1941, the regulations regarding submarine warfare quoted verbatim Article 22 of the London Naval Treaty of 1930, which forbade unrestricted submarine warfare in no uncertain terms.[40]

The introduction of the new *Instructions* made it clear that the regulations were to be enforced uniformly against all enemies of the United States, even if those enemies had chosen to violate international law themselves or had not even signed or ratified the treaties in question. However, the naval leadership reserved the right to change the *Instructions* under certain circumstances: "It is the responsibility of higher authority, as occasions arise, to determine and instruct forces afloat as to which, if any, of the instructions herein are not legally binding as between the United States and the other powers immediately concerned and as to which, if any, for that reason are not for the time being to be observed or enforced."[41] Still, the *Instructions* was implicitly clear: under ordinary circumstances, unrestricted submarine warfare would not be considered.

The reactions of JAG and the State Department did nothing to change the *Instructions* regarding submarines. If anything, they both reinforced the emphasis against unrestricted submarine warfare and in support of the cruiser warfare.

Although a representative from the Navy JAG had worked with the War Plans Division to draft the new *Instructions,* JAG took almost four months to respond with a comprehensive memorandum. While JAG may have recognized the difficulties inherent in traditional blockades under current conditions of warfare, it was clearly unwilling to consider unrestricted submarine warfare.

The judge advocate general first rejected any legal connection between a blockade and a war zone. Blockades, announced JAG, only affected neutrals that were attempting to trade with a particular enemy port or coastal area. Blockades did *not,* however, stop neutrals from trading with a belligerent nation through neutral neighboring countries or even through non-blockaded enemy ports. In short, the only legitimate way to stop neutral trade with an enemy nation was with a blockade that prevented the flow of supplies to a clearly designated location, as opposed to a war zone, which unfairly assumed that any ships traveling in a certain area *had* to be trading with the enemy, even if they were not.[42]

As far as the rules of naval warfare were concerned, JAG did not seem to believe that naval warfare had changed from the classic era of blockades. JAG believed there were only four basic types of blockade, which had hardly changed since the eighteenth century. *Strategic blockades* assisted with a campaign against a particular port or location. *Short-range* or *close commercial blockades* were the traditional type of blockade, where warships stayed close offshore to interdict shipping that was visibly trying to enter or leave a blockaded port. These blockades, however, were no longer practicable with the advent of land-based aviation and submarines, which could easily sink the blockading vessels. The solution, as the British had discovered in the First World War, was the *long-range commercial blockade.* Instead of stopping ships based on their port of origin or destination, a long-range blockade looked for contraband cargoes. The unspoken problem with long-range blockades, however, was that they also penalized innocent neutral countries that might lose a vast amount of supplies that had been confiscated as contraband. Unlike President Wilson, JAG apparently accepted that long-range blockades were legal. The final type of blockade was the *stone blockade,* which used stones or block-ships to block a vulnerable channel and bottle up trade until the channel could be recleared and dredged. Once again, under the conditions of modern warfare, such a blockade was easier to describe than to carry out. Although JAG must have known of these problems, it presented all four types of blockade as equally valid and possible.[43]

In the end, instead of challenging the practicality of any type of blockade, JAG merely insisted that the *Instructions* include an explanatory note that differentiated the four types of blockade and explained how each was to be carried out. Once again, JAG implicitly lashed out at unrestricted warfare: "In the case of the 'close' commercial blockade and the strategic blockade, the operation is against enemy and neutral vessels seeking to enter the blockaded territory regardless of whether they are carrying supplies to the enemy. The long range commercial blockade is aimed at the supplies destined for the enemy and only incidentally against the vessels in which they are being carried."[44] By calling for long-range blockades that required an exhaustive search of cargo to determine a vessel's neutrality, JAG clearly endorsed cruiser warfare and implicitly rejected unrestricted warfare. After reviewing the JAG memorandum, the General Board essentially adopted virtually all of JAG's recommendations.[45]

Like JAG, the State Department refused to acknowledge there was a submarine problem, by utterly ignoring it. In January 1941 the Department of State finally replied to the General Board with a lengthy memorandum from the legal office containing problematical sections and requested changes. Happily, most of the changes were acceptable to the General Board, which rapidly began work on revising the *Instructions* for a final draft. However, despite the ongoing German unrestricted submarine campaign in the Atlantic, the State Department's memorandum did not discuss submarine warfare at all. As far as the State Department was concerned, apparently, Article 22 of the 1930 London Naval Treaty was enough guidance in such confusing times. Furthermore, based on its pleas to safeguard noncombatant lives during shore bombardments, the State Department would hardly have entertained the notion of unrestricted warfare, in which civilian casualties were unavoidable.[46]

By February 1941, having collated and included the comments of the Navy judge advocate general and the State Department, the General Board released yet another draft of the *Instructions,* labeled *Tentative Instructions for the Navy of the United States Governing Maritime and Aerial Warfare, February 1941.* The Office of the Chief of Naval Operations then distributed a copy of the *Tentative Instructions* to all ships and stations in preparation for superseding the old *Instructions* of 1917. However, they noted, the *Tentative Instructions* was not to go into effect until so ordered by the secretary of the Navy via an All-Navy message. The memorandum included a note that the *Tentative Instructions* was subject to updates and revisions.[47]

The *Tentative Instructions* was issued on the last day of February 1941, and arrived at the U.S. Naval War College in Newport, Rhode Island, just as the War College was completing its Winter 1941 International Law Situation. Since the International Law problem touched directly upon the issue of unrestricted submarine warfare and war zones, the Naval War College faculty and students examined the new *Tentative Instructions* to see if the Navy's official position had changed. Since the *Tentative Instructions* merely continued the policy of cruiser warfare, the Naval War College felt the need to take action. For the Naval War College, by sheer coincidence, had just concluded that the U.S. Navy needed to conduct unrestricted warfare in a designated war zone in order to achieve victory in a prospective Pacific war.

FIG. 1. USS *Covington* sinks after being torpedoed by a German U-boat, her American colors still flying. Indiscriminate attacks by German U-boats against shipping, regardless of nationality, defenses, and passengers, proved to be the pivotal factor that drew the United States into the First World War.

Naval Historical Center Photo #NH 61488

FIG. 2. The senior naval leadership of the United States, including some members of the General Board of the Navy, assembled for a group photo in December 1920. The senior member of the General Board, Rear Admiral William Ledyard Rodgers, stands on the far right of the back row, with a light pole directly behind him. Rodgers would lead the General Board's vigorous protest against Elihu Root's attempted emasculation of the submarine as a warship in 1922.

Naval Historical Center Photo #NH 50445

FIGS. 3, 4. Above, USS *S-44* off Cuba in 1929.

Naval Historical Center Photo #NH 42264

Designed at the end of the First World War, the small S-boats were the mainstay of the U.S. submarine force in the 1920s and early 1930s, but they did not possess the range, weaponry, or habitability necessary for extended patrols across the Pacific Ocean. After a decade of experimentation, the U.S. Navy entered the Second World War with the "fleet submarine," exemplified by one of the most famous fleet submarines, USS *Barb*, pictured below. Although designed for naval warfare, these fleet submarines turned out to be perfect commerce raiders.

Naval Historical Center Photo #19-N-83952

FIGS. 5, 6. Above, Admiral Harold R. Stark on his first day as chief of naval operations.

Naval Historical Center Photo #NH 49928

Stark authored Plan Dog, which eventually became the national military strategy for the United States in the Second World War and the strategic foundation for unrestricted submarine warfare. Stark's trusted war planner, Rear Admiral Richmond Kelly Turner, below, turned Plan Dog from a broad set of strategic goals into a viable strategy with the RAINBOW war plans.

Naval Historical Center Photo #38-MCN-537-1

FIG. 7. Admiral Edward Kalbfus during the Second World War, presiding as a member of the Naval Court of Inquiry into the Pearl Harbor attack. Before the war, Kalbfus became the second naval officer to serve twice as president of the U.S. Naval War College. Under his leadership in 1941, Professor Payson S. Wild and his class of naval officers called for the use of unrestricted submarine warfare in the event of hostilities with Japan.

Naval Historical Center Photo #80-G-46137

JAMES FIFE
Captain U S N
McCLELLAND BARCLAY
U S N R

FIGS. 8, 9. Above, James Fife as a captain in the Second World War.

Portrait by McClelland Barclay, Naval Historical Center Navy Art Collection #85-236-W

Just before the war, Fife carried Admiral Stark and Admiral Turner's intent to carry out unrestricted submarine warfare "immediately upon the outbreak of war" to Admiral Thomas C. Hart (below), commander-in-chief of the U.S. Asiatic Fleet and one of the oldest and most respected submariners in the U.S. Navy.

Naval Historical Center Photo #NH 81734

FIG. 10. Sailors assigned to the submarine base at Pearl Harbor stare at the carnage caused by the Japanese sneak attack on December 7, 1941. In the foreground is the submarine USS *Narwhal*, whose crew claimed partial credit for destroying a Japanese aircraft during the attack. Before the smoke had even begun to clear, both Admiral Hart and Admiral Stark issued orders to conduct unrestricted air and submarine warfare.

Naval Historical Center Photo #80-G-32704

FIGS. 11, 12. Above, Admiral Harold Stark is decorated by President Franklin D. Roosevelt.

Naval Historical Center Photo #NH 93290

There is no documentary evidence that Stark discussed the decision to conduct unrestricted warfare with either President Roosevelt or his direct superior, Secretary of the Navy Frank Knox (below) until December 7, 1941.

Naval Historical Center Photo #80-G-399009

FIG. 13, 14. The victors and vanquished. Above, USS *Wahoo* (SS 238) enters Pearl Harbor in February 1943 after the most successful war patrol in the war up until that point. Note the broomstick signifying a "clean sweep" next to the periscopes, as well as the pennant reading "SHOOT THE SUNZABITCHES."

Naval Historical Center Photo #80-G-35726

Below, one of *Wahoo*'s confirmed victims, *Nittsu Maru,* on her way to the bottom in March 1943.

Naval Historical Center Photo #80-G-60948

CHAPTER 7

Debating Law, Ethics, and Strategy

When the *Tentative Instructions* was issued in February 1941, the U.S. Naval War College was under the leadership of Rear Admiral Edward C. Kalbfus. At the time, Kalbfus was one of only two admirals to hold the post of president of the Naval War College twice (the other being William S. Sims). Under his leadership from 1934 to 1936, the Naval War College added an Advanced Class, composed almost exclusively of Naval War College graduates who studied international law, naval policy, and naval warfare under the personal guidance of the president of the War College. In addition, there were normally two other classes, a Senior Class and a Junior Class. The Senior Class focused on Battle Fleet tactics and major strategy, particularly the strategy of the ORANGE war plan, while the Junior Class focused upon tactics and minor strategy. All three classes studied international law and international relations. Although the Naval War College was one of the few institutions of higher learning that devoted itself to matters of national strategy and security, Admiral Kalbfus found that the Navy, Congress, and the public were generally uninterested in the work the Naval War College was carrying out. As a sign of the times, Kalbfus even had to cope with an attempt to remove the word *war* from the institution's name.[1]

NAVAL WAR COLLEGE INTERNATIONAL LAW "MAJOR SOLUTION"

Admiral Kalbfus credited his reassignment to the Naval War College to his work on a book called *Sound Military Decision*. During his first tour at the Naval War College, Kalbfus had grown extremely dissatisfied with the "Estimate of the Situation," the college's traditional method for solving strategic and tactical problems. As far as Kalbfus could tell, the value of the "Estimate" had entirely dissipated because instead of focusing on strategic and tactical problems, officers became more concerned about meeting the required format of the "Estimate," and graders accordingly evaluated "Estimates" based more on form than on content. Furthermore, Kalbfus put little stock in "manuals," and he derided attempts to learn "principles of war," which he felt were constantly in a state of flux. As a result, he began work on *Sound Military Decision* during his first tour. Recognizing the work's value, the Navy reassigned him to Newport in 1939.[2] Consequently, Kalbfus focused the Naval War College upon the task of making difficult strategic decisions in war, such as a decision regarding unrestricted warfare.

Three days into 1941, the Senior and Junior Classes of 1941 were given their assignments for the international law course. The purpose of the course was to provide the naval officers with a basic understanding of international law sufficient to make difficult decisions in complex maritime situations with other nations. The students were required to do introductory readings, as well as any supplementary readings that would help them with their written assignments; attend all lectures; and turn in written answers to minor situations and one long essay regarding a "major situation." The course would conclude with a critique of the students' "major situation" solutions.[3]

Advising the Naval War College and guiding the international law course was a thirty-five-year-old Harvard professor named Payson S. Wild Jr. Wild graduated with a degree in political science from the University of Wisconsin in 1926, received a master's degree in government from Harvard in 1927, and earned a Ph.D. from Harvard in 1931, where he had already started teaching in 1929, while still a graduate student. As a professor at Harvard, Wild became known as one of the top scholars in international affairs, and he taught both Joseph and John F. Kennedy.[4]

Wild was probably recommended for the position of associate professor at the Naval War College by his Harvard colleague, Professor George Grafton Wilson. Professor Wilson had been an associate for international law at the Naval War College since 1900, and his views and teaching influenced several generations of U.S. naval officers. After thirty-eight years of service to the War College, Wilson stepped aside and allowed Wild to take over.[5] Wilson had been instrumental in shaping the Navy's regulations regarding naval warfare just before the First World War, and he had also shown a progressive, if slightly unsettling, bent toward the acceptance of new weaponry, even recommending in 1925 that the Navy should reevaluate its policy toward poison gas.[6] If Wilson expected Wild to follow in his footsteps, the younger Harvard professor did not disappoint his mentor.

At the beginning of 1941 Wild issued an international law directive to his Naval War College students. The directive consisted of five parts, or annexes. The first part contained the students' schedule, followed by an introductory reading. The next two parts, Annexes C and D, were the meat of the international law course, because they contained the minor situations and the major situation, respectively, that the students needed to solve. Annex E listed possible sources to which the students could refer.[7]

The minor situations, while difficult, did not call upon the students to think about matters of statecraft or national policy. For example:

> Japan has declared a pacific [sic] blockade of the port of Canton, China. A Japanese gunboat meets the PRESIDENT HOOVER, an American merchant vessel, 6 miles off the port, and announces that, as the HOOVER is known to be carrying a number of airplanes to the Chinese Government, she will visit and search the HOOVER. You are commanding the U.S.S. AUGUSTA, nearby, and the master requests your protection.
> What should you do?[8]

The students were expected to use the various treaties signed by the United States, the *Instructions* of 1917, and their experience as naval officers to guide them in reaching a solution. However, the students were told that the international law course was meant to be a realistic guide to future events, not a wishing game. The directive piously intoned: "It may be remarked here that, in spite of events of the past few months, the military profession of the United States is still bound by certain international rules. The course will stress what legally *is,* rather than what *ought to be.*"[9]

The injunction to the Naval War College students to look only upon actual legal codes and not upon potential and favorable change did not stop Professor Wild and his fellow instructors from including a major situation that asked students to judge whether or not the current laws and regulations restricting U.S. naval officers might also prohibit victory. The major situation specifically addressed the question of unrestricted warfare, with the following hypothetical scenario:

> War has existed between Japan and the United States allied with Great Britain for six months. All other states are neutral.

The allied fleet is now in a position to exert economic pressure on Japan. The principal theatre of war is the Western Pacific, and the Commander in Chief, U.S. Fleet, is in command of all allied naval forces in that theatre.

The following despatch has been received by the Commander in Chief, U.S. Fleet, from the Navy Department:

"EFFECTIVE JANUARY THIRTY FIRST STOP ALL CONTRABAND TRAFFIC WITH JAPAN. IT IS THE POLICY OF THE ALLIED GOVERNMENTS TO ACT IN ACCORDANCE WITH THE LAW OF NATIONS."

The Commander in Chief believes that a strict interpretation of conventions to which the United States is a party might seriously restrict his freedom of action. He therefore decides to act in this matter in accordance with practice of democratic states. Because certain modern practice is legally controversial he expects to inform the Navy Department of his views, which will thus indicate his actions in certain cases.

The Commander in Chief is aware of the elementary legal considerations involved. He desires to go deep into this problem, in a realistic way, getting away from mere text book considerations. He desires to give full scope to *practical* naval experience and thought in the matter. With this in mind, he issues the following to his staff:

Assuming that a blockade (in the historic legal sense) of Japan is impossible, draft a memorandum in regard to other means available to Allied naval forces for stopping all Japanese commerce. Taking into account, as far as necessary, the geographical situation, and the probable Japanese needs and resources, the draft should present opinions on the following points:

(a) *The nature of a contraband list.* Should it be itemized or general? Should there be a distinction between absolute and conditional? Should there be any contraband statement at all by the Allied authorities? In other words, give an estimate of the possibility of the concept of contraband in naval warfare with Japan.

(b) *Visit and search.* Should there be search upon the high seas? If not, should the Allies establish 'control stations'?

(c) *The Declaration of Paris of 1856.* Should the Allies continue to adhere to its principles? What would be the effect of their application, e.g., "free ships, free goods" in a war with Japan? The statement in regard to (c) obviously depends greatly upon what has been said in (a)

(d) *Control of air traffic.*[10]

Despite the major situation's attempt to call for a legal method of constraining Japanese trade, the wording of the question made it quite clear that it expected students to look "outside the box." The scenario indicated that visit and search would probably be impractical by first mentioning that the hypothetical commander-in-chief U.S. Fleet expected that strictly following international law would inhibit his "freedom of action," and then pointedly asking, "Should there be search upon the high seas?" The scenario then set up the potential for stepping outside of accepted U.S. national policy by advocating following the policy of "democratic states." With France invaded and most of Europe under some form of dictatorship, the only democratic state capable of waging long-range naval warfare was Great Britain, and Great Britain had established its own war zones for unrestricted submarine warfare in the Skagerrak, the Kattegat, and portions of the Mediterranean. So, by looking at the example of Great Britain and using their own "*practical* naval experience," the students were probably expected not to advocate some sort of pre-1914 close blockade.

Every student had to turn in a thirty-page essay that responded to the hypothetical scenario, drawing mostly upon legal and historical precedents, but also upon their own personal experiences at sea. Professor Wild and the staff would read the papers and prepare a universal critique for the students. The individual papers would not receive a written grade, in keeping with the current practice of the Naval War College. Instead, on February 12, Professor Wild would address the Senior and Junior Classes of 1941 with his critique of their work, and the officers could determine for themselves how well they had done in the context of Wild's comments. Professor Wild and the Naval War College staff also noted that the students were expected to use Admiral Kalbfus's *Sound Military Decision* to help them make a judgment in the situation.[11]

Although the students' essays and any record of Professor Wild's critique were not preserved in the Naval War College archives, Wild and the naval officers seemed to have agreed that the current state of affairs regarding submarine warfare and war zones was clearly inadequate. Wild, the staff of the War College, and the students all helped draft a short "Solution to the Major Situation" that listed their concerns and their conclusion: wage unrestricted warfare in a declared war zone.[12]

Wild's solution began by declaring that the needless and wanton destruction of noncombatant personnel and property was abhorrent. However, with the advent of the submarine, the old practice of visit and search had been superseded by the needs of submarine warfare. Wild pointedly shrugged off the attempts to legislate the actions of submarines, pointing out that new weapons were bound to be used in the most efficient way possible in order to maximize the damage to the enemy as well as safeguard the lives of one's own personnel. In short, the current rules were bound to be broken, just as they were being broken in the North Atlantic by the German U-boats. Wild called for changing the rules to reflect the realities of modern day warfare: "The job of lawyers and the military profession is to adapt old principles to new situations. Clinging to obsolete legal formulae does not make for respect for law. On the contrary, it may hasten the end of the effectiveness of law."[13]

Having laid the legal groundwork for revising the regulations regarding submarine warfare, Wild and the other authors of the composite solution turned to the practical aspects of condoning unrestricted warfare. Using the hypothetical scenario as their backdrop, Wild and the naval officers claimed that with a declaration of war, the United States would immediately halve Japan's outgoing commerce and reduce incoming tonnage by at least 20 percent. The problem facing the U.S. Navy, therefore, was to cut off the rest of Japan's trade.[14]

The Naval War College emphatically recommended against a formal blockade. They listed a number of reasons, first pointing out that most formal blockades were set up to intercept neutral shipping. Since Japan dominated the Western Pacific, the Naval War College students, like Admiral Stark in Washington, did not expect there to be many, if any, neutral vessels. Second, a formal blockade was not necessary to capture enemy merchant ships, which could be seized at all times. Third, the War College did not seem to agree with JAG's judgment regarding the numerous types of blockades, insisting that a formal blockade *had* to be a close blockade. Unlike JAG, which had not recognized the problems with a close blockade, the Naval War College fully recognized the impossibility of a close blockade against a modern military power that could launch submarine and air attacks against the vulnerable blockading vessels and sink them. In support of this view, the Naval War College pointed out that Great Britain had not formally blockaded Germany in either world war. Instead, the Naval War College recommended adopting the British system from the First World War, which JAG and most observers had termed a "long-range blockade," and which the Naval War College called a "long range patrol." The college posited that such a patrol, using the traditional methods of visit and search, would effectively cut off any trade with Japan, without exposing U.S. forces to the dangers of a close blockade.[15]

Unfortunately, a long-range blockade only worked at a certain distance from an enemy country. Closer in, any U.S. naval unit, whether surface, submarine, or aircraft, would be vulnerable to land-based aircraft or coastal submarines if it attempted to conduct visit and search according to the traditional rules of warfare. Instead, the Naval War College called for establishing war zones around the islands of Japan and other areas that were under the nominal control of the Japanese Navy, where few neutral ships were expected to be anyway. In such war zones, any merchant ship could be sunk without warning by mere virtue of its presence in the war zone. Professor Wild attempted to justify war zones on legal grounds by noting that declaration of war zones had become common practice during both the First World War and the current war, and that the United States had accepted an already established war zone when it entered the First World War in 1917. Furthermore, the Harvard Draft Code on Rights and Duties of Neutral States in Naval and Aerial War, published in the *American Journal of International Law* in July 1939, allowed a belligerent to create war zones in which to lay mines. In short, war zones were not only eminently practical, they also had a legal precedent for their establishment, even if the only previously accepted war zones had been solely for mines. The Naval War College planners called for creating war zones in "strategic areas, e.g. in the seas between the Philippines and Japan, the Sea of Japan, and in certain waters in and around the Netherlands East Indies."[16] Professor Wild and his colleagues finished their call for war zones by asserting: "Neutral or non-combatant persons and property have always been subject to danger and loss without warning. The war zone is merely a development of that long standing rule. Of course war zones may be extended unreasonably, but the fact that a right may be abused does not signify that the right should not exist. The war zones envisaged in this paper would be limited in such a manner that they would not bring any undue hardship upon neutrals."[17] Not content to merely reverse American doctrine regarding unrestricted warfare and war zones, Professor Wild and the Naval War College also called for a clear-cut definition regarding neutrals whose actions favored one belligerent over another. Wild called these "non-belligerents" instead of "neutrals." Since Wild and the Naval War College were essentially proposing to create the same sort of war zones that Germany had created in the First World War, they had no desire to repeat history. By refusing to recognize a nation aiding an enemy as a "neutral" but instead calling it a "non-belligerent," they felt they could get away with different rules of warfare that would allow them to treat "non-belligerent" shipping like enemy shipping. Since numerous nations, including the United States, were "non-belligerents" in reality, if not by admission, Professor Wild and the Naval War College felt that taking this new stance would not undermine international law.[18]

Professor Wild's brief solution did not address in detail all the criteria of war zones, unrestricted warfare, and non-belligerency. Wild's legal rationale for war zones was particularly weak, since it relied principally upon war zones that were established solely for mine fields. Had Wild and the Naval War College instead focused on implicit war zones like the U.S. "combat area" around Great Britain, perhaps their argument might have been stronger. In addition, the Naval War College apparently had not been able to review the RAINBOW 3 war plan, which permitted "strategical areas." Had Wild and the Naval War College been able to tie their solution to RAINBOW 3, their recommendations might have carried greater weight.

As it was, Professor Wild and the Naval War College called for actions that would change the way the U.S. Navy waged war as well as reject the Wilsonian paradigm of absolute freedom of the seas. If the Naval War College's suggestions were accepted, then the United States would not closely blockade Japan, but instead economically strangle it with a long-range blockade throughout the Pacific Ocean and a war zone in the Western Pacific. Even outside a war zone, submarines would have permission to attack any armed vessel, whether warship or merchant ship.[19]

The officers at the Naval War College fully recognized the importance of their conclusions. One of the assistant professors in the Department of Intelligence, Commander James M. Steele, enclosed Wild's solution in a memorandum to Admiral Kalbfus, prefacing it with a brief explanation of the origin of the memorandum and his own personal belief "that rigid adherence to the 1917 Instructions would seriously restrict the freedom of action of the Commander in the Western Pacific. Indeed, under those instructions, trade warfare in that area might be ineffective and make the accomplishment of certain tasks impossible."[20]

Steele noted that the Naval War College had recently received the revised *Tentative Instructions,* but the *Tentative Instructions* had the same problems as the old 1917 *Instructions.* Consequently, the Naval War College solution needed to be immediately sent to the Navy Department to help change the *Instructions*. In particular, Steele worked from Professor Wild's solution, calling for changes to the *Instructions* that would recognize and provide instructions for non-belligerency, war zones in which the United States could wage unrestricted warfare, and legal permission to attack, at any time or place, "all armed craft, whether planes, surface vessels, or submarines."[21] Steele concluded by recommending that the *Instructions* be revised with the help of Professor Wild, since Professor Wilson had been so instrumental in writing the 1917 *Instructions*.[22] Although this was a sensible solution, both Navy JAG and the War Plans Division might have interpreted such an action as an attempt by the Naval War College to seize control of the *Instructions*, a move that neither bureaucracy seemed willing to contemplate.

Admiral Kalbfus acted quickly. He wrote a letter to the chief of the Bureau of Navigation, Rear Admiral Chester W. Nimitz, inquiring whether the Naval War College could offer comments regarding the new *Instructions*. Nimitz forwarded the letter to Admiral Stark, who asked Kalbfus to send him the Naval War College's recommendations.[23] Kalbfus enclosed Professor Wild's solution with a cover letter, most of which Kalbfus directly lifted from Commander Steele's memorandum, recommending a number of changes to the *Instructions*. Kalbfus, unlike Steele, apparently understood the turf wars of naval bureaucracy, and wisely did not include the recommendations that would have transferred authority for writing the *Instructions* from JAG and the War Plans Division to the Naval War College. Instead, he contented himself with strongly endorsing the need to change the rules governing U.S. naval warfare as well as to abandon the policy of absolute freedom of the seas for a policy of war zones and unrestricted attack against armed merchant ships.[24]

THE INITIAL REACTIONS

Admiral Kalbfus's letter must have come as a fairly rude surprise to Admiral Stark and the War Plans Division, after all the time they had put into producing the new *Tentative Instructions*. In a sign of how much weight the Naval War College's opinion merited, however, the college's ideas were not immediately rejected.

But just because Admiral Kalbfus's letter was not immediately rejected did not mean it was well received. On a copy of the letter archived in the confidential correspondence of the chief of naval operations and the secretary of the Navy is a series of notations indicating that someone at the higher levels of the chain of command did not favor the recommendations of the Naval War College.

Next to Kalbfus's recommendations to provide for non-belligerency and to establish a certification program to regulate neutral goods was handwritten "No," while next to the recommendation to create war zones was jotted down "covered in WPL," a note that was clarified on another copy of this letter, which had a handwritten "WPL-44" next to this recommendation. Whoever marked Kalbfus's letter clearly knew about the provisions for "strategical areas" in RAINBOW 3, which was also known as Navy Basic War Plan (WPL) 44.[25] Since these letters were sent to the chief of naval operations, via the Bureau of Navigation, Admiral Stark himself might have written these notations, though copies of the letter apparently reached other personnel.

One of the recipients of Admiral Kalbfus's letter was the War Plans Division, which was not pleased with the interference of the Naval War College. Two of Admiral Turner's top officers, Captain F. L. Lowe and Commander L. S. Fiske, both looked at the Naval War College's recommendations, and neither one was willing to support the college. In a memorandum to Commander Fiske, Captain Lowe confessed that "[t]here are a lot of other ideas in this study which I can't quite fathom," before taking the Naval War College to task for simplifying the rules regarding war zones and also casually waiving the accepted and traditional U.S. view of unrestricted warfare and freedom of the seas.[26]

Lowe immediately criticized Wild's solution for its definition of war zones, pointing out that the war zone Wild was talking about was one in which submarines and aircraft could attack any merchant ship, while the only war zone that the United States had participated in had been for mine fields only.[27] He then noted that RAINBOW 3 essentially authorized the sort of war zone that Wild and the Naval War College were referring to, though perhaps "not to the extent that the War College would go, but . . . to adopt the rules suggested by the War College, we might as well say that the whole of both oceans is a war zone and nobody permitted to enter them without our expressed approval."[28]

Similarly, Lowe was not impressed by the Naval War College's recommendation to sink all armed vessels, since that had been the exact issue over which the United States had gone to war in 1917. Whether or not armed merchant ships made any sense, Lowe could not imagine the United States being so willing to turn its back on the legacy of Woodrow Wilson and the First World War in the blink of an eye.[29]

Lowe regarded the Naval War College's recommendations regarding non-belligerency more generously, noting that it would be a simple matter to merely insert a definition of non-belligerency in the *Tentative Instructions*. However, he noted it would be fairly difficult to set down rules regarding non-belligerents, since every nation was its own judge of the extent of its non-belligerency and hence its risk of attack by belligerent forces. For instance, although the United States and Spain were both non-belligerents, they each accepted different risks regarding their merchant ships and citizens. As far as Lowe was concerned, it was not the province of the U.S. Navy to make rules regarding this.[30]

Finally, Lowe took exception to Admiral Kalbfus's recommendation that the United States set up special treaty exemptions regarding certain contraband materials. However, his comments about treaty exemptions could be seen as applicable to virtually all of the Naval War College's suggestions, which essentially called for the United States to turn its back on the London Submarine Protocol as well as its traditional view of freedom of the seas: "What is recommended is that we break all treaties we don't like for the time being. *If we wish to do that we ought to do it without publishing it ahead of time.*"[31]

Having mulled it over, the Office of the Chief of Naval Operations did what it normally did when it came up against a particularly difficult or controversial problem. On April 1, 1941, Rear Admiral Royal E. Ingersoll forwarded the Naval War College's recommendations to the secretary of the Navy and suggested that the recommendations then be sent to the General Board of the Navy for a comprehensive review. Three days later Secretary of the Navy Frank Knox approved Ingersoll's suggestion and forwarded the whole package to the General Board.[32]

When the package was received at the General Board, the admirals who made up the board picked one of their members, Admiral A. P. Fairfield, to look it over and draft a tentative opinion. Fairfield's initial letter still exists and shows that he was swayed by the Naval War College's arguments. His tentative opinion endorsed the Naval War College's recommendations regarding non-belligerency, war zones, no formal blockade, and sinking armed merchant ships without warning.[33]

Fairfield's letter did not merely agree with the Naval War College's recommendations, it also proposed various articles that could be added to the *Tentative Instructions*. Regarding non-belligerency, Fairfield called for a paragraph that explained the concept of non-belligerency, declared the fact that the United States was currently a non-belligerent, and also conceded that non-belligerent states like the United States could not expect to be treated with the same sort of respect as a wholly neutral power.[34]

Fairfield's letter acknowledged that war zones in which unrestricted warfare took place were now common practice. Furthermore, given the advances in technology, modern warfare made it virtually impossible to conduct a blockade, so Fairfield saw no alternative but to establish a war zone. Although Fairfield acknowledged that the only war zone the United States had ever been involved with dealt entirely with mine fields and not unrestricted warfare, it would be foolish not to recognize the current trends in naval warfare and act accordingly. As a result, the draft letter from the General Board wholeheartedly endorsed the concept of war zones and the belief that war zones should be established in lieu of a traditional close blockade.[35]

Although the Naval War College had only mentioned in one sentence the sinking of armed merchant vessels, Admiral Fairfield's letter directed a great deal of attention to the matter. Fairfield recommended adding passages to the section on visit and search in the *Tentative Instructions* that would allow "All armed enemy merchant ships [to] be sunk at sight, without warning, even though encountered outside a war zone." Fairfield then explained that even though the United States had traditionally opposed the unannounced sinking of any vessel, armed or unarmed, it was obviously impractical for submarines or aircraft to attempt visit and search on armed merchant ships.[36]

Like most military bureaucracies, however, the Navy would not overturn the traditional rules of warfare on the suggestion of one of its subordinate branches. As a result, having reviewed the findings of the Naval War College and Admiral Fairfield's letter, the General Board decided to hold a hearing on the subject on April 30, 1941. The board did not request the presence of any staff members from the Naval War College. Evidently, even Admiral Fairfield felt that the Naval War College had played enough of a role in the *Tentative Instructions*. Although Fairfield wrote to the Naval War College for clarification, there is no evidence that he or anyone else on the General Board requested any testimony from Professor Wild, Admiral Kalbfus, or Commander Steele.[37]

Instead, the General Board asked only the War Plans Division and the Office of the Judge Advocate General to send representatives.[38]

The result of the General Board hearing was certainly not assured. The issues the Naval War College brought up were not new. Naval officers and submariners had been pointing out the problem with cruiser warfare and armed merchant ships since the First World War. Similarly, the Naval War College's suggestions were entirely in keeping with the Navy war planners' conception of victory through economic warfare. Finally, the War Plans Division had already sanctioned the creation of strategical areas in which merchant shipping was prohibited.

The decision to invite only the War Plans Division and the Navy JAG had significant ramifications. To begin with, it is likely that neither the War Plans Division nor JAG appreciated the Naval War College's intrusion on what they saw as their turf. Next, although the War Plans Division had already made allocations for strategical areas, their viewpoint had already been summarized by Captain Lowe: the war planners of the U.S. Navy were not prepared to violate international law, and if they were, they certainly were not going to tell anyone. Finally, the General Board, JAG, and the War Plans Division had already spent a significant amount of time earning the Department of State's approval for the *Tentative Instructions,* something that the Navy had failed to achieve for over twenty years. Probably no one imagined that the State Department would suddenly waive the traditional rules of naval warfare solely on the basis of a letter from the Naval War College, no matter how compelling the logic might be.

Consequently, while the Naval War College's suggestions smacked of practical sense and reflected two decades of grievances by naval officers, the naval officers reviewing the Naval War College's recommendations were bound to view the suggestions with a certain amount of skepticism, if not outright hostility.

THE GENERAL BOARD HEARING OF APRIL 30, 1941

Like many General Board hearings, that of April 30, 1941, was transcribed in its entirety. This is fortunate because the hearing fully explains what historian Samuel Flagg Bemis only guessed at: why did the General Board, after initially favoring the Naval War College's recommendations, choose not only to reject them in scathing terms but also to propose a letter of information that would have clearly solidified the U.S. Navy's adherence to cruiser warfare and opposition to war zones?[39]

The short answer is that while the General Board, the War Plans Division, and JAG may have sympathized with the viewpoints of the Naval War College, they felt that the college's ideas were not applicable to the *Tentative Instructions,* which was meant to be a guide to current international law, not a textbook regarding all possible contingencies. Furthermore, the Navy had to be careful, in order to maintain the U.S. neutral advantage over Germany by keeping all consideration of this topic extremely quiet. Finally, the naval officers were so relieved that the Department of State had approved the *Tentative Instructions* that they were unwilling to lose what they had gained.

When the General Board convened on the morning of Wednesday, April 30, 1941, it had only four men in front of it for testimony. Captain Lowe and Commander Fiske represented the War Plans Division, while Captain Thomas Gatch and Mr. Leslie C. McNemar, a civilian lawyer, represented the Office of the Navy Judge Advocate General.[40]

It quickly became clear that one of the points of contention between the Naval War College and virtually everyone else was the nature of the *Tentative Instructions.* While the Naval War College viewed the *Tentative Instructions* as a set of guidelines in the event of war, most of the General Board viewed the *Tentative Instructions* merely as a listing of the current international laws governing the Navy. One of the General Board's admirals, Rear Admiral Frederick J. Horne, directly pointed this out: "Aren't you getting away from the character of this book? It is not to tell what may or may not happen but to give them the rules of international law that this government is bound by."[41] At another point the admirals of the General Board ignored the representatives sitting before them to argue among themselves about the nature of the *Instructions.* Admiral Snyder noted that expanding the *Instructions* into "a textbook . . . is not advisable," to which Admiral Horne agreed that the *Instructions* was "not a textbook." Admiral Rowcliff, however, pointed out that the *Instructions* should at least mention the existence of the forms of warfare currently in existence, even if those forms of warfare were not legitimate under international law. However, Admiral Horne argued against adding definitions, saying that they would only confuse a naval officer.[42] In the end, the *Instructions* would remain a compilation of the laws affecting naval warfare to which the United States was a signatory, not a comprehensive primer about current forms of naval warfare and their legality.

Furthermore, and perhaps most important, the naval officers knew that whatever they proposed had a very slim chance of being accepted by the State Department. In a revealing moment, Captain Lowe noted that the State Department had been extremely reluctant even to approve the *Tentative Instructions*. Admiral Rowcliff complained, "The State Department will never recognize any precedent before it happens. That is their natural attitude." Admiral Horne agreed that "[i]t is the attitude of the State Department not to have anything new published."[43] At another point, Admiral Horne flatly stated that he sincerely doubted that "the State Department . . . will ever . . . approve the question of war zones or navicerts or quasi-neutrality."[44]

With the contested nature of the *Tentative Instructions* and the obstinacy of the State Department as a context, the General Board addressed the specific recommendations of the Naval War College.

The first point they addressed was the question of non-belligerency. Leslie McNemar, representing JAG, argued against publishing any official Navy doctrine on non-belligerency, since the United States was currently the world's "principal non-belligerent, [so] anything printed on this subject will be held against us and we want to be very careful about letting them be able to hurl back at us what we may say on the subject."[45] In particular, McNemar noted, the term *non-belligerency* did not exactly mean what the Naval War College and Professor Wild said it did. It was a very broad term covering a wide range of possible options. McNemar credited the current definition of the term to Italian dictator Benito Mussolini, who had used it instead of the more accepted phrase *qualified neutrality*, which meant favoring one belligerent over another. Furthermore, McNemar noted, it was really up to a belligerent to decide whether the actions of a neutral power were not entirely neutral. If a neutral power actually declared itself to be a "non-belligerent" with the definition that the Naval War College wanted, the end result was that "[w]hatever we say is certainly going to be held against us . . . It just depends on the belligerent."[46]

The clause regarding war zones evoked considerable discussion among the board members and from Captain Lowe and Mr. McNemar. Captain Lowe spoke first for the War Plans Division, with a concise argument that laid out the crux of the problem: "We entered the last war on this question and our government has never yet officially said we would not enter the war under similar circumstances again. I can't help but think we place the stamp of approval on it when we put it in this book. I don't think we would want either Mexico or Brazil establishing a war zone in the Caribbean."[47] Lowe's answer pointed out two of the primary problems with considering war zones. For one thing, the United States had gone to war only twenty-four years earlier over the issue of war zones, something that most senior naval officers, who had been on active duty in 1917, could hardly forget. Furthermore, the United States, despite its neutrality legislation, did not yet fully recognize the legitimacy of Germany's war zones, which helped constrain the German war zones to a portion of the Atlantic Ocean away from American shores. As Admiral Walton R. Sexton, the senior admiral on the General Board, noted, "Even though there is this Neutrality Act which makes it an offense for our ships to go into a zone which we establish ourselves, yet if the ship did go there and was sunk by a German submarine without warning we would make an awful fuss about it."[48]

However, if the United States suddenly announced publicly in its *Instructions* that it recognized the legality of war zones and unrestricted warfare, Nazi Germany could extend its war zone to the shores of the United States and the United States would have limited legal ground to argue against them. Significantly, Lowe did *not* mention RAINBOW 3's provisions for strategical areas. Obviously, Lowe felt that if war zones were going to be established, then he wanted the United States to do it first, and the only way to accomplish this was to ensure that no one else knew the United States was planning to do so.

Leslie McNemar added to the argument against the Naval War College's recommendations by describing three different types of war zones—something it seems the naval officers of the Naval War College were not fully aware of, nor even most of the naval officers attending the General Board hearing.

The first type of war zone was a defensive zone contiguous to a nation's territorial waters. The zone could extend as far as necessary to cover a nation's coastline and was governed only by the needs of a nation and common practice of international law. Inside such a war zone, a nation could mine the waters so that maritime traffic would have to travel down certain designated lanes, ensuring that no belligerent warships could launch a surprise attack. Such a war zone, noted McNemar, was fully recognized and accepted under international law. The Naval War College had attempted to use this type of war zone as a precedent for its own proposed war zone. In a sign of how contentious war zones were, however, and despite the legality and practicality of such a war zone, McNemar still expected difficulties from the State Department and the Department of Justice over the establishment of such a defensive war zone.[49]

The second type was a "strategic war zone which may be established by the Commander-in-Chief for purposes of protection of the Fleet."[50] The rationale behind a strategic war zone held that if a sizeable portion of the Navy was in a vulnerable position, such as the Philippines, the fleet commander could declare the area off limits and mine it for the protection of his forces. In short, a strategic war zone was essentially a defensive war zone that had been forward-deployed to wherever the U.S. Fleet was operating from. While it denied the passage of the sea to neutral shipping, its intention was self-protection, not the destruction of commerce. However, McNemar admitted, the strategic war zone had "less recognition than the first in international law, but it can be done."[51] This was the type of war zone that the RAINBOW 3 planners overtly envisioned as a "strategical area," Admiral Stark's confidential comments to the contrary. In a sign that McNemar had probably seen the RAINBOW 3 war plan, he mentioned that the "Commander-in-Chief has the authority to issue proclamations for establishing strategic war zones for the defense of the Fleet."[52]

The third type of war zone, however, was the type the Naval War College was proposing. Such a war zone directly attempted "to prohibit neutral commerce" by establishing a zone for unrestricted warfare against all shipping. McNemar explained the implications of such a decision to the General Board, using the example of a belligerent cutting off New York City. He then tied such an action to the current actions of Nazi Germany, saying: "That is what Germany has done. International law has not recognized such a war zone. We would not stand for such a war zone being established off the Port of New York . . . Winston Churchill in his speech on Sunday denied the right of the Germans to establish the type of war zone that is indicated in here. It is a type of blockade which is not recognized in international law."[53]

Admiral Fairfield, who had written the initial and favorable response to the Naval War College's recommendations, asked McNemar about the Naval War College's point about the impracticality of blockades. After all, Fairfield noted, if blockades were impossible under modern law and if the German Navy was going to conduct unrestricted warfare against the United States if the United States entered the war, should not the United States realistically plan for war by planning to establish a war zone of unrestricted warfare instead of a blockade?[54]

McNemar's response was unequivocal and remarkably similar to the view expressed by Captain Lowe: "*We certainly shouldn't admit it at the present time.*"[55]

The General Board clearly was faced with a dilemma. Obviously, the *Tentative Instructions* was out of touch with the reality of modern warfare. At the same time, however, if the General Board attempted to update the document, then they would not only risk the disagreement of the State Department but also possibly give Nazi Germany the ammunition it needed to wage unrestricted submarine warfare against the United States without a declaration of war. Admiral Horne, with what must have been a sense of frustration, said, "There are no specific instructions we can issue to a commanding officer."[56] McNemar certainly thought so, and he recommended that this was not a matter for the *Instructions* but for war plans.

However, the admirals were unable to back away as easily. After all, what use was the *Tentative Instructions* if the first thing the United States did during a war was issue new orders countermanding the document? Unfortunately, none of the admirals could agree on what they could say that would not raise the ire of the State Department or jeopardize the publicized policy of the United States. In the end, the admirals were forced to agree with Admiral Horne: "We ought not to fill this up with anything but bona fide instructions."[57]

The General Board then turned to the problem of armed merchant ships. Admiral Fairfield took the side of the Naval War College, explaining the impracticality of visit and search by aircraft or submarines against armed merchant ships that were not bound to a code of naval warfare. The admirals debated whether they could add a section that would implicitly allow a submarine or aircraft to attack an armed merchant ship, such as a qualifying section permitting attack on a ship that was not heaving to for visit and search. Captain Lowe pointed out that the language of Article 22 of the London Naval Treaty already permitted this. The Navy, however, was not willing to allow a submarine commander to merely plead that he felt danger and thus sink any armed merchant ship he wanted when he wanted.[58]

In one case, however, a submarine could attack without much warning—the case of escorted convoys. In 1922 the General Board had confidently believed that a submarine could conduct cruiser warfare by sinking a convoy's escorts and then searching the convoy's ships one by one. By 1941, however, according to Captain Lowe, "the resistance of the escorting vessel is the resistance of the others."[59] In this case, law was finally conforming to reality.

The admirals agreed that armed merchant ships would be an unacceptable threat to submarines in the event of war. Admiral Sexton sagely predicted, "Our governmental attitude is one thing. What we ought to do in time of war is something else . . . Our people should receive instructions at the proper time as to what they should do. In order [sic] words, there is another instruction that should be drawn up, ready for distribution prior to our going into war."[60]

Admiral Rowcliff disagreed with Sexton, asking why the instructions could not be added to the *Tentative Instructions* immediately and save the Navy the trouble of doing so later. Sexton's reply reflected Lowe and McNemar's view that the United States should not make any public commitments before hostilities began: "I don't believe the United States would want to do that ahead of an actual entry into war. I think they would stand out for visit and search but the moment that some other nation sank one of our vessels without going through the regular proceeding, as a matter of retaliation we would then take the matter up and do the same to him."[61] Once again, while the officers of the General Board recognized the practicality of the Naval War College's recommendations, the recommendations plainly were not politically acceptable before the beginning of hostilities.

In the end, the General Board decided to make no changes to the *Tentative Instructions*. Admiral Fairfield concluded, perhaps glumly, since he had written the initial and now-dismissed letter: "We haven't agreed to anything in this paper," to which Admiral Snyder replied, "Very little; we can recommend no changes."[62]

With that, the hearing ended. For various reasons, Captain Lowe and Leslie McNemar had succeeded on behalf of their offices in forestalling the suggestions of the Naval War College until the outbreak of hostilities.

THE GENERAL BOARD'S NEW LETTER

About two weeks after the hearing, the General Board significantly revised Admiral Fairfield's letter into a rejection of virtually every suggestion of the Naval War College. The suggestions the General Board did accept entailed no change to the Navy's *Tentative Instructions*. However, based on the minutes of the General Board's hearing, it seems that the General Board did sympathize with the Naval War College. If the language of the revised General Board letter seemed unduly harsh, it was undoubtedly because the General Board did not want to leave any doubts that the United States was abiding by its treaty obligations, a situation that the board members had already said they expected to change in the event of war. The chairman of the General Board, Admiral Sexton, signed the letter, even though he had stated during the hearings that "[o]ur governmental attitude is one thing. What we ought to do in time of war is something else."[63]

At the same time, however, the General Board letter reflected the Wilsonian paradigm of absolute freedom of the seas, staunchly defending a nation's right to arm its merchant ships as well as refusing to possibly countenance the legality of war zones and unrestricted warfare. The language of the letter when discussing points related to Wilsonian freedom of the seas was markedly more emotional and illustrated the passions that the issues of the First World War still evoked for some of the senior naval leadership.

The revised General Board Serial No. 154, regarding the proposed changes to the *Tentative Instructions,* was an absolute reversal from Admiral Fairfield's letter. The General Board reversed its stance regarding non-belligerency, war zones, and sinking of armed merchant vessels. To make sure that naval officers were clear regarding the current state of naval warfare, the General Board also enclosed a proposed letter of information to supplement the *Tentative Instructions.*

The General Board first negated the Naval War College's call for a definition of non-belligerency, since only a few nations actually had declared themselves to be non-belligerents. Furthermore, since non-belligerency was not yet well defined under international law, official discussion of it seemed premature. Finally, the General Board preferred the term *qualified neutrality,* which had been used previously during the First World War, and adequately and accurately described the attitude of the United States during the current war. However, while the General Board preferred *qualified neutrality,* they believed "that any definition of such a status is not appropriate in a publication of this nature."[64]

The General Board's rebuttal of the Naval War College's call for war zones was far sharper. After criticizing the Naval War College for recommending a type of war zone that was *not* the sort of war zone the United States had conducted during the First World War, the General Board made it clear that not only was the type of war zone recommended by the Naval War College utterly opposed to Wilsonian freedom of the seas, it was also absolutely impossible for the Navy to suddenly announce its acceptance of war zones before the beginning of hostilities: "These zones have no justification in International Law, and the United States and other nations have vigorously protested the establishment of such zones. To announce beforehand in written instructions to Naval Officers that the United States countenances such 'zones' *would constitute a surrender of the position which this country has long maintained.* The Board firmly believes that the United States should maintain its traditional position under International Law until circumstances render modification thereof advisable."[65] While the General Board's language was strong, the last sentence, which left open the possibility of establishing war zones under certain "circumstances," was not an afterthought. Rather, it reflected the philosophy of the General Board, the War Plans Division, and particularly the Office of the Navy JAG, all of whom had strongly recommended holding off on any public pronouncements regarding war zones or unrestricted warfare until war had broken out. Until then, the United States had too much to lose by ceding its neutral advantage.

As for the Naval War College's recommendation not to blockade Japan, the General Board nimbly sidestepped the entire issue. Instead of making a decision, the General Board merely concurred with the Naval War College's recommendation to retain the section in the *Tentative Instructions* regarding blockades, but made no statements regarding the practicality or impracticality of blockading Japan.[66]

Like its answer concerning war zones, the General Board's rebuttal of the Naval War College's suggestion regarding armed merchant vessels directly harkened back to the First World War and the Wilsonian paradigm of absolute freedom of the seas. Although the General Board recognized that armament on merchant ships was mostly used to fight off submarines attempting visit and search, they stated that the rationale for armament was to provide a means of defense against threats such as piracy. As a result, the General Board refused to countenance the idea that "the United States [should] abandon its former stand against sinking without warning. *Such action would constitute a surrender to the German viewpoint.*"[67]

The General Board concluded its letter by recommending that "none of the changes suggested by the Naval War College in its Serial 6838 of March 20, 1941, be incorporated" in the *Tentative Instructions*. Instead, the General Board attached a "Letter of Information Concerning Maritime Warfare," which enumerated the various practices of modern warfare, including non-belligerency, war zones, and unrestricted warfare, "which practices may or may not be within the purview of International Law as generally accepted by the majority of nations and concerning which, definite instructions cannot now be issued."[68]

The General Board had found a solution to their dilemma by attaching the proposed letter of information. By doing so, the board avoided having to go to the State Department for approval or making a public pronouncement regarding the U.S. Navy's current or planned position regarding non-belligerency, war zones, or unrestricted warfare. The letter of information defined the status of non-belligerency and war zones for 1941. The General Board intended to issue the letter of information with every copy of *Tentative Instructions*.[69]

However, the letter of information did not merely define terms. It also reiterated, in the strongest possible language, the Navy's overt hostility to war zones and unrestricted warfare, while repeating the Navy's endorsement of cruiser warfare in the event of war. When discussing the third type of war zone, the war zone proposed by the Naval War College and currently used by Nazi Germany, the General Board insisted that this was a "war zone which has no standing in law . . . In such zones merchant ships have been sunk without warning."[70]

Although the General Board's letter of information was technically correct and reiterated the stated position of the U.S. Navy, the chief of naval operations and the secretary of the Navy did not act upon it. Admiral Stark and Rear Admiral Ingersoll, who had acted swiftly when queried by the Naval War College in March, now sat on the General Board's recommendations. Since there were no changes to the *Tentative Instructions,* this is partly understandable, but they also chose to ignore the General Board's proposed letter of information. When asked whether the matter regarding the Naval War College would be dealt with in the *Tentative Instructions,* Stark's direct subordinate, Rear Admiral Turner, responded: "The matters referred to are being handled in another manner."[71]

In fact, Admiral Stark did not endorse the General Board's judgment for almost seven months. When he finally did so—significantly, on *December 10, 1941*—he had already issued orders to conduct unrestricted warfare three days previously. Having already "surrendered" to the morally indefensible position of the Germans, the chief of naval operations dismissed the General Board's proposed letter of information as no longer relevant: "In view of the fact that the 'Letter of Information Concerning Maritime Warfare' was intended to cover the period when the United States was a non-belligerent, and the fact that the 'Instructions for Maritime Warfare' will be altered from time to time as may be found necessary, it is recommended that the proposed letter of information not be issued."[72]

Stark's inaction regarding the General Board's letter of information appears to have stemmed from the personal effect the Naval War College's arguments made upon him and his vision of the future. Admittedly, the importance of the Naval War College's bold challenge to the status quo is hard to evaluate. But although the Naval War College, Professor Wild, and Admiral Kalbfus had ostensibly been defeated, they seem to have made an indelible impression upon Admiral Stark and Rear Admiral Turner. Stark had clearly favored unrestricted warfare in his previous confidential correspondence with Admiral Hart, but before Admiral Kalbfus's letter, whenever Stark and Turner had discussed strategical areas, they had been describing "strategic war zones" for the defense of the Fleet. Stark had been forced to resort to a subterfuge about Japanese military control of shipping in order to justify unrestricted warfare in his confidential letter to Admiral Hart. From this point on, however, "strategical areas" would come to mean war zones for unrestricted air and submarine warfare. As future events would illustrate, the Naval War College's arguments *had* influenced the key decision makers in the U.S. Navy's leadership.

CHAPTER 8

"Immediately upon the Outbreak of War"

The first sign that Admiral Stark and Admiral Turner's vision of strategical areas had changed came in May, when the War Plans Division released the working copy of RAINBOW 5 or Navy Basic War Plan 46 (WPL-46). RAINBOW 5 built directly off RAINBOW 3, but there were important differences.

RAINBOW 5, THE TWO-OCEAN NAVY, AND THE ROYAL NAVY

Just like RAINBOW 3, RAINBOW 5 included a section regarding the conduct of war at sea. Like its predecessor, the new war plan stressed compliance with the *Tentative Instructions,* except when the *Instructions* were modified by the naval leadership.[1] Unlike RAINBOW 3, however, that was all RAINBOW 5 enjoined naval officers to follow. The little note to pay special attention to sections of the *Instructions* regarding merchant shipping had been excised.

Similarly, the war planners deleted the rules for taking prizes. This implicitly indicated that the war planners expected there to be no such prizes in the upcoming Pacific war. Unlike the War of 1812, modern warfare had no time for gentlemanly courtesy or profit. With the excision of the rules for prizes, the war planners implicitly acknowledged that the prospective Pacific war would be a destructive and brutal affair.[2]

Finally, the war planners continued to make provisions for strategical areas. The wording from RAINBOW 3 to RAINBOW 5 remained virtually unchanged, except for updating the names of the various fleets. The U.S. Fleet had been renamed the U.S. Pacific Fleet, and the Atlantic Force had become the U.S. Atlantic Fleet. Other than that, however, the explicit language of RAINBOW 5 continued the impression that strategical areas would work just like "strategic war zones," existing solely for the defense of a fleet.[3]

In a July 3, 1941, letter to Admiral Hart, Admiral Stark concisely reiterated the broad authority granted to his fleet commanders regarding strategical areas: "You have all the authority from us about a strategic area as per War Plans so I will not touch further on it."[4]

Stark, Turner, and Hart were not the only senior naval officers to realize the value of the submarine against Japanese commerce in the event of a Pacific war. Even as Stark and Turner's beliefs regarding unrestricted warfare crystallized, the commander-in-chief of the U.S. Atlantic Fleet, Admiral Ernest J. King, wrote of the potential boons of unrestricted submarine warfare in a memorandum regarding the U.S. Navy's building program for the "two-ocean Navy."

King's memorandum demonstrated that the realization of the submarine's worth as a commerce raider extended across the senior leadership of the Navy. King rated submarines as the Navy's top building priority, ahead of destroyers, carriers, cruisers, and battleships.[5] He explained his decision by pointing out that "submarine attacks on Japanese communications would prove very effective."[6]

Even though it is unclear whether King had seen the Naval War College's memorandum or heard of the General Board's subsequent hearing and rebuttal, he clearly sided with the Naval War College in advocating a commerce-raiding role for the submarine force. As war with Japan became more likely, it was becoming increasingly clear that the senior leadership of the U.S. Navy was determined to use its submarine force effectively.

It would be the Royal Navy, however, that forced Admiral Stark and Rear Admiral Turner to commit to unrestricted warfare. Since 1940 the U.S. Armed Forces had been informally and formally negotiating with the British Army and Royal Navy regarding the role of the U.S. Navy in protecting merchant traffic in the Western Hemisphere and the prospective role of the United States in the Far East in the event of war with Japan.[7] In the Far East, the two chief representatives for the United States and Great Britain were Admiral Hart, commander-in-chief of the U.S. Asiatic Fleet, and his Royal Navy counterpart, Vice Admiral Sir Geoffrey Layton, the commander-in-chief of the Royal Navy's China Station. In the summer of 1941 Hart's and Layton's staffs drew up plans for an Allied defense against Japan in the Far East, which included a provision for a "combat zone": "any enemy or neutral ship entering this zone will do so at her peril, and no responsibility will be taken should she be damaged or sunk."[8] The wording was similar to RAINBOW 5's defensive strategic war zone, but Hart implicitly considered this area to be a zone for unrestricted warfare, and he mentioned his intentions to Vice Admiral Layton.

Layton found what Hart told him to be so remarkable that he wrote to London, informing his superiors that the United States was contemplating a major change in policy regarding unrestricted warfare. In response, the British Joint Staff's mission to Washington, D.C., wrote a letter to their U.S. Navy liaison, Commander McDowell. In the letter, the British Joint Staff's secretaries, Commander R. D. Coleridge and Major R. F. G. Jayne, informed McDowell that Admiral Hart had discussed the "subject of submarine attack on merchant ships in the Far East" with Admiral Layton, and that the British government was now very interested in the U.S. government's official position regarding unrestricted warfare and war zones.[9]

The British officers started their letter by reiterating the British government's official position, which was strong aversion to the practice of war zones and unrestricted warfare. In retaliation for German depredations, however, the Royal Navy had established war zones in the Skagerrak and other areas that were primarily traveled only by enemy shipping. The British called these areas "zones dangerous to navigation," but in intent and practice they were precisely the same as "war zones," "strategical areas," or "combat areas." The British officers then revealed that the British wanted "to follow a similar policy vis-à-vis Japan, but consider that danger zones should not be declared until they are satisfied that Japan is not abiding by the rules of submarine or air warfare."[10] In short, the British wanted to prepare for unrestricted warfare in designated war zones, but would only establish such a war zone as a retaliatory measure.

This, of course, brought the British to the question of what the United States was planning to do. After all, the United States had traditionally been opposed to war zones and unrestricted warfare; the British could hardly forget what had brought their old allies into the last world war. However, based on Admiral Hart's discussions with Admiral Layton, the British were now under the impression that "it is the intention of the U.S. Authorities to make a declaration of 'combat zones.'" If so, the British naturally wondered if the American "combat zones" were "equivalent to 'danger zones' in which submarines will be given authority to sink merchant ships at sight." If the United States did intend to conduct unrestricted warfare in a war zone, the British then asked if the United States would agree to the British position that such a war zone could only be established as a retaliatory measure.[11]

Assuming the United States agreed, the British wanted to negotiate the boundaries of the Western Pacific war zone in advance. Currently, the proposed war zone that Admiral Hart and Vice Admiral Layton had tentatively agreed upon "comprise[d] that part of the Far Eastern Area as defined in ABC-1, to the south and west of a line joining positions latitude 30°N longitude 122°E and latitude 7°N longitude 140°E."[12] The British joint chiefs of staff, however, wanted a far larger war zone that would include the Japanese home islands. Furthermore, the British wanted to reach an understanding with the United States whereby the United States could conduct unrestricted warfare in other areas of the Pacific, while the British would carry out unrestricted warfare in portions of the Indian Ocean and the area around Australia and New Zealand.[13]

The British letter was deceptively enticing. After all, like most military officers, U.S. naval officers preferred to enter a conflict with a prepared plan and not improvise every step of the way. The general adherence to the ORANGE war plan, from the early twentieth century to its revised form as RAINBOW 5, could plainly show that U.S. naval officers wanted a plan of action. As a result, the British invitation to map out war zones ahead of the conflict must have been tempting.

However, therein lay the danger of accepting the British proposal. For if the United States did so, then it was formally committing itself to unrestricted warfare before the initiation of hostilities, something that the General Board, Admiral Stark, and Admiral Turner had done everything to prevent. After all, secret diplomatic agreements had a nasty habit of becoming public knowledge. The naval leaders of the United States must have known that they could not make a formal or binding promise to the British.

Instead, in a sign of the U.S. Navy's willingness to consider the prospect of unrestricted submarine warfare, the War Plans Division actually drafted a letter to request the formal support of the U.S. Department of State regarding the prospect of U.S. unrestricted submarine warfare in a designated Pacific war zone in the event of war.

THE UNSENT LETTER

The Americans delayed responding to the British letter for almost two months. During that time Rear Admiral Turner's War Plans Division used it to draft a proposed letter for the secretary of the Navy to the secretary of state.

The draft letter began by discussing the British proposal to create a joint war zone in the Western Pacific, as well as the possibility of other war zones in the Pacific, the Indian Ocean, and around Australia and New Zealand. However, Turner and the War Plans Division went one step further than the British proposal. Instead of waiting to retaliate for planned Japanese actions, the War Plans Division proposed actually conducting unrestricted warfare in a designated war zone from the start of hostilities. The naval war planners cited a number of possible justifications for the proposed American decision, including Japanese atrocities in China and Japan's shared guilt, as a member of the Axis, for the German unrestricted warfare. The proposed letter offered a direct insight into the desires of Rear Admiral Turner and his War Plans Division regarding war zones and unrestricted warfare, showing that by September 1941, the U.S. Navy's senior leadership was fully ready to commit itself to conducting unrestricted air and submarine warfare.

The proposed letter began by summarizing the background of the letter from the British Joint Staff. Unlike the British, who focused on the concept of war zones, the War Plans Division focused on unrestricted warfare, explicitly stating that "the question has arisen as to whether or not the naval forces of the three Powers [the United States, Great Britain, and the Netherlands East Indies] might properly, and without violation of national policy applicable to that area, engage in unrestricted submarine warfare."[14] The war planners then cited the portion of the British letter that stated Great Britain's aversion to unrestricted warfare, and its decision to conduct unrestricted warfare in clearly defined war zones as retaliation for German war zones. The letter's introduction then concluded by having the secretary of the Navy state that he "construe[d] United States naval policy as substantially the same in this regard as that of the United Kingdom."[15]

Having said that, however, the war planners then launched into a litany of reasons why naval warfare in the Western Pacific would be vastly different from naval warfare in other parts of the world. To begin with, "there would probably be no neutral shipping in the Far East Area, and almost certainly there would be none engaged in trade with Japan or with areas which Japan controls. All seagoing shipping except Chinese junks would, therefore, be belligerent shipping."[16] The war planners then stated that north of the Malay Barrier, the string of islands from Singapore to Australia, virtually all shipping would be Japanese and would be employed in the military service of the

Japanese empire. So, as far as the United States and its allies would be concerned, "the mission of any vessel, public or private, traversing the sea within the area described, except the vessels of the three Powers mentioned, must be presumed hostile."[17]

The next portion of the proposed letter clearly showed the influence of the Naval War College on the War Plans Division and Admiral Turner's chain of thought. Although the United States had traditionally opposed war zones, the U.S. Navy had joined the Allies in a war zone in the North Sea against Germany. Like the Naval War College, the war planners did not mention that the sole purpose of the Allied war zone was for mines. However, they did stress that if a war zone had designated routes for neutral shipping, with control points, it could be construed as not interfering greatly with neutral traffic. If a war zone met such conditions, then the war planners postulated that it was acceptable under international law. As a source, they turned to a 1922 international law text by Charles Cheney Hyde, which stated that if a "'belligerent can prove that its interference with the neutral is inconsequential in comparison with the advantage to itself necessarily connected with the defense of its territory, the safety of which is otherwise jeopardized, the excuse is entitled to respectful consideration.'"[18]

The proposed letter then acknowledged that under the current war plan, RAINBOW 5, the Navy had authorized its fleet commanders to create strategical areas for the defense of the Fleet. However, the letter then wanted the secretary of the Navy to declare that he was of the "opinion that, if the United States and its associates are to be enabled to check Japanese aggression against their territory in the Far East Area, two of the principal methods would be the unrestricted attack by submarines and by aircraft on merchant vessels in that area engaged in the supply and support of Japanese armed forces, and in the transport of strategic war materials from the continent of Asia to Japan."[19] In short, the war planners had just redefined their strategical area from being for the defense of the Fleet to being a war zone for unrestricted air and submarine warfare against all shipping.

Obviously, the Navy did not expect the State Department simply to accept that the rules of warfare had changed. To support their case, the war planners repeated the old and most compelling rationale, the impracticality of visit and search. The letter succinctly stated that "the great preponderance of Japanese naval strength over that which would be available to the Associated Powers" made it impossible for submarines and aircraft to conduct traditional visit and search.[20]

Having stated that cruiser warfare was impractical, the naval war planners made a remarkable proposal. Until this point in the letter, the Navy had adhered to the view of Great Britain. But it now proposed to go a step further than the British. Since it was too dangerous to conduct cruiser warfare, the naval war planners did not want to wait for the Japanese to violate international law. Instead, the United States needed to conduct unrestricted submarine warfare *"immediately upon the outbreak of war."*[21]

The naval war planners' intent could not have been plainer. They would not wait for the Japanese to initiate unrestricted warfare. Because of the risks inherent in attempting visit and search, the War Plans Division was boldly seconding the Naval War College's call for unrestricted warfare in the event of war, not as a matter of retaliation.

Once again, this was not a step the State Department would take lightly, so the Navy offered justifications that the United States could offer for its actions in the event of war. The first was retaliation for the numerous atrocities committed by Japan in China. The war planners posited that since China would probably be allied with the United States in the event of war, the United States could simply call upon the "the innumerable unwarranted attacks by Japan against the civilian population and shipping of China" to justify unrestricted warfare.[22]

Another possible justification was to hold Japan responsible for the acts of Germany, since Japan was also a member of the Tripartite Axis. The war planners predicted that in the event of war the United States would probably follow the lead of Great Britain and wage unrestricted warfare against Germany and Italy in retaliation for the German war zones in the Atlantic. Consequently, "there need be no hesitation on the part of the United States and the United Kingdom to extend to Japan the measures which the United Kingdom is now employing against Japan's Axis partners."[23]

Both excuses seem rather flimsy in hindsight, and one imagines that perhaps Turner and the War Plans Division found them flimsy as well. However, it is important to note that military necessity alone was not a sufficient reason for the war planners to justify unrestricted warfare. The fact of the matter was that unrestricted warfare was clearly illegal. As a result, the war planners turned to legal and moral justifications, such as retaliation for atrocities in China or shared guilt as a member of the Axis pact.

The letter concluded by requesting the secretary of state's agreement with the proposal to create a massive war zone in the Far East. In addition to the Far East war zone, the Navy reserved the right to create other war zones in the Western Pacific. In all cases, the war zones would permit unrestricted air and submarine warfare.[24]

Without a doubt, this proposed letter was a remarkable document. For the first time, a decision-making branch of the U.S. Navy had proposed conducting unrestricted warfare in the event of war. The letter illustrates the impact of the Naval War College, even paraphrasing several points straight from Professor Wild's solution; it also shows that the War Plans Division clearly viewed strategical areas not as strategic war zones established for the defense of the Fleet but as war zones for unrestricted air and submarine warfare. Furthermore, despite the British suggestion to the contrary, the war planners were not willing to let the Japanese dictate the nature of the economic war in the Pacific. They were going to conduct unrestricted warfare from the moment hostilities began.

One can only imagine what Secretary of State Cordell Hull's reaction might have been had he actually received this letter. In a startling lapse in an otherwise generally well-researched study, historian Janet Manson believed that Secretary of the Navy Frank Knox had written this letter and had actually sent it.[25] However, it seems clear that Secretary Knox never even saw the proposed letter that he would have been asked to sign.

Instead, Admiral Stark disapproved the proposed letter, sending it back to Rear Admiral Turner for "possible future use."[26] Stark told Turner that his "reason for not approving it was that it seemed better to take the matter up after Japan and the United States are at war, rather than at the present time."[27] Turner jotted this down on a cover memorandum that he attached to the proposed letter before placing it in a file, never to be sent.

The unsent letter would prove to be vastly important. It set up the Navy's rationale for conducting unrestricted warfare in the event of war, and for doing so from the start of hostilities. The letter was also important for another reason: that it remained unsent showed that Admiral Stark and the senior naval leadership had chosen to keep this decision out of the hands of civilian policy makers.

According to Admiral Turner's cover memorandum, Admiral Stark disapproved the proposed letter by the War Plans Division on September 29, 1941. Stark's decision did not mean that he disapproved of the substance of the proposed letter. Three days later, Turner would orally pass along its contents to the prospective chief-of-staff for the submarine force of the Asiatic Fleet, Commander James Fife, as the Navy's policy in the event of war with Japan.

James Fife Jr. had been involved in submarines for many years at this point, having commanded both USS *Nautilus* and the Submarine School in Groton, Connecticut.[28] Furthermore, in 1941 he had probably seen more submerged combat than any other U.S. submariner, although not on U.S. submarines. During the early part of the war, while the United States was a neutral, Fife had served for eight months as an observer with the Royal Navy. Apparently, he did not merely stay on shore to observe, but actually sailed on board British submarines in the Mediterranean. Not only was that "hairy duty," as one U.S. submariner called it afterward, but it could have gotten him and the U.S. Navy into serious trouble had he been captured or killed. Fortunately for Fife and the Navy, he survived his tour with the Royal Navy, and wrote an extremely informative report, which became standard reading throughout the U.S. submarine force before the war.[29]

Fife also earned the admiration and friendship of the rigid and demanding Admiral Hart. When Fife initially visited the Asiatic Fleet in June 1941, after his tour with the British, Admiral Hart had him describe his experiences to a stateroom full of eager listeners. Although Hart gave Fife only one hour to speak, he ended up listening to Fife for two hours, a sign of the admiral's esteem. The next day, Fife and Hart spoke even more about submarines. Hart noted that Fife had applied "an old-timer's ideas and reactions concerning recent developments," something that Hart, who had never quite grown past his experience with submarines in the 1920s, could relate to.[30] Even several months into the war, Hart still felt that Fife's experiences were "the most extensive that I know of," and he highly recommended Fife's abilities and judgment.[31]

As a result of his experiences with the British and his conversations with Admiral Hart, Fife not only understood the role of unrestricted submarine warfare from firsthand experience, he also knew that Hart was deeply interested in the topic. That made Fife the perfect courier to relay the Navy's current policy regarding unrestricted submarine warfare. Shortly before October 1941 Fife was named to be the chief of staff to Captain Walter Doyle, the prospective commander of the Asiatic submarine force. On October 1, Fife met with Rear Admiral Turner specifically to ask whether the Navy would be changing its official policy regarding unrestricted submarine warfare.

When questioned, Turner told Fife that the State Department was "reluctant to make commitments in writing, principally because of its stand during and after World War I against unrestricted warfare."[32] Whether Fife misconstrued Turner's words is unclear, but if Turner said this, he was almost certainly not being candid with Fife, since no records exist to show that the State Department was *ever* consulted about the prospective use of unrestricted warfare. Since the State Department's reaction would undoubtedly be negative, as Stark had already pointed out to Turner, the time to handle the issue would be when the United States was already at war.

Turner did tell Fife that he and Admiral Hart could expect unrestricted warfare almost immediately upon the commencement of hostilities: "Admiral Turner told Commander Fife that he could assure Admiral Hart that within one week of the commencement of hostilities in the Pacific, the Navy Department would issue an order for unrestricted warfare for both aircraft and submarines."[33]

Fife had his answer: The Navy would conduct unrestricted warfare almost immediately upon the outbreak of hostilities. In November Fife ensured that his "conversation was reported to Admiral Hart upon Commander Fife's arrival in Manila."[34] By that point, however, Admiral Hart had already received a letter from Admiral Stark essentially saying the same thing.

REPLYING TO THE BRITISH

In October 1941, having decided not to discuss the matter of unrestricted warfare with the State Department, but having finalized its views on the subject, the Navy finally replied to the British letter of August, explaining the delay and also the U.S. decision to put this matter off until the commencement of hostilities. Naturally, the letter did not reveal the naval leadership's intention to conduct unrestricted warfare from the start of the war. However, the War Plans Division was able to use the draft of its proposed letter for the secretary of the Navy, to write the response to the British Joint Staff. Although the letter was ostensibly written and signed by the U.S. secretary for collaboration, Commander McDowell, because of the close similarities between the unsent secretary of the Navy message and McDowell's eventual response to the British, it seems quite probable that the War Plans Division, or possibly Rear Admiral Turner himself, ghost-wrote the response and McDowell signed it.

The letter began with a brief explanation for the delay in responding. The letter noted that the proposed war zones and unrestricted warfare had been extensively studied by the U.S. Navy's leadership and that Admiral Hart had previously brought up the subject of unrestricted warfare when asking about the nature of the strategical areas as established under the RAINBOW 3 and 5 war plans.[35]

The letter then explained that the U.S. Navy was currently referring to war zones as "strategical areas" instead of using the British phrase "combat zones dangerous to navigation." The letter then cited the definition of a strategical area as given by the war plans, which was explicitly a defensive strategic war zone. Unrestricted warfare, of course, was not explicitly permitted in the war plans.[36]

The next paragraph of the letter clearly stated the new and evolved view of what was meant by a "strategical area": "Under the above concept, it is apparent that it would be the purpose, should circumstances require and justify such action, to wage unrestricted warfare not only by submarines, but also by aircraft. In the opinion of the Chief of Naval Operations, the justification for such action must be clear, but need not necessarily depend upon prior similar action in that area, or in areas related thereto, by an enemy of the United States."[37] Of course, the letter was kept at the low level of the liaison officers between the two staffs, but the message from the U.S. naval leadership was clear: *War zones, although explicitly for the defense of the fleet, will actually be for unrestricted warfare.*

However, the letter refused to formally pledge that the United States would establish a war zone. Although the previous paragraphs made it clear that the United States ultimately planned to establish war zones, "*[u]ntil the United States is at war, it obviously would be impracticable for its Government to adopt any policy other than the one which has heretofore been set forth on numerous occasions. It is, therefore, judged expedient to let final decision wait until the actual outbreak of hostilities.*"[38]

Having said that, the letter then accepted the boundaries proposed by Admiral Hart and Vice Admiral Layton for a potential war zone. The letter to the British justified the use of unrestricted warfare in the proposed war zone because there would be virtually no neutral shipping in that region of the Far East. Most of the language used in this portion of the letter was identical to that in the unsent letter. Admiral Turner and the War Plans Division had found a "possible future use" for their unsent letter.[39]

The letter continued to draw from the unsent secretary of the Navy letter with its description of the need for maritime control stations to control the routes of neutral traffic in order to protect neutral ships from harm. This part of the letter went into greater detail than the unsent letter, since the Allies would obviously have to work together to ensure that such control stations were effective.[40]

The letter concluded with the recommendation that no further action be taken other than to ensure that the appropriate commanders in the Far East—namely, Admiral Hart and Vice Admiral Layton—knew about the decisions that the U.S. naval leadership had reached. Although this paragraph, and other points in the letter, referred to the decisions being made as those of "the Chief of Naval Operations [Admiral Stark] and the [Army] Chief of Staff [General George C. Marshall]," it seems quite probable that while General Marshall may have given his approval to this decision, he was not actively involved in making it.[41]

The letter to the British promised that copies would be sent to the Army War Plans Division, and the commanders-in-chief of the Pacific Fleet and the Asiatic Fleet.[42] The next day Admiral Stark forwarded the letter that he had sent to the British Joint Staff to Admiral Kimmel and Admiral Hart. In his subject line to the fleet commanders, Stark made a subtle but important change. The subject line in the letter from and to the British referred to "Action by Submarines against Merchant Ships," while the subject line of the letter Stark sent to Hart and Kimmel read "Action by submarines against merchant raiders." This was not a major change, and the two admirals could have merely flipped a page to see that the original subject line read "ships" and not "raiders." However, it reflected Stark's belief that virtually all Japanese merchant shipping would not only be under the control of the Japanese military, but also would probably be extremely hostile. His terse message to the two fleet commanders was no less important: "The above enclosure is forwarded for information and guidance. The Chief of Naval Operations anticipates the decision of this important question *promptly upon the outbreak of war* with Japan."[43] The correspondence with the British, the unsent letter for the secretary of the Navy, and Turner's conversation with Commander Fife all pointed to a number of certainties. To begin with, the United States *would* conduct unrestricted warfare within a large Pacific war zone. Just as important, the Navy would declare this war zone almost instantaneously with the beginning of hostilities. Finally, and perhaps most important, since it was quite probable that civilian leadership, either within the State Department or within the Navy's chain of command, would veto this proposal, Admiral Stark chose to keep the civilian leadership uninformed and refused to make any formal guarantees to the British. The die, however, had been cast, and the Navy silently crossed the Rubicon of unrestricted warfare.

PRELUDE TO GENERAL ACCEPTANCE: FINAL REVISION TO THE NEUTRALITY LEGISLATION

As the United States entered the final month of peace before Pearl Harbor, a number of events took place that solidified the U.S. Navy's decision to conduct unrestricted warfare. The first event, although unrelated to the Navy's decision-making process, was a final revision to the nation's neutrality legislation on November 17, 1941. The new act repealed the old prohibitions on traveling into combat areas and allowed the president to arm merchant ships. Consequently, for the first time, the legislation allowed American merchant ships to carry armament and proceed into the U.S.-proclaimed combat areas. Congress approved the measure only after the Roosevelt administration launched a tough political offensive to overcome the isolationist sentiment expressed by groups like America First.[44]

Steven Conn, the Army's chief historian, wrote in 1961 that in his view the neutrality legislation of November 17 "was the decisive step toward American acceptance of unrestricted submarine warfare in World War II."[45] Even though the U.S. Navy's leadership had already decided to conduct unrestricted warfare, Conn's point deserves attention.

By arming merchant ships, the United States was legitimizing the German rationale for unrestricted warfare. Before, the United States had inherently legitimized the German war zone by declaring it a combat area off limits to U.S. ships. But the U.S. combat area also served to constrain unrestricted warfare to the German war zone. Now, however, the United States was giving the Germans an opening to declare that any merchant ship, anywhere in the world, by virtue of being armed, was a legitimate target because attempting visit and search against armed merchant ships was impractical. By legislating the arming of merchant ships, the United States was implicitly stating that its opposition to unrestricted warfare was on its last legs.

Whether the neutrality legislation deserves to be termed a significant factor, let alone a decisive factor, in the U.S. acceptance of unrestricted warfare seems too difficult to gauge accurately. It seems far more important that ten days later, Admiral Stark put the final imprint of peacetime planning for unrestricted warfare by informing Admiral Hart that he would have the authority to create a war zone for unrestricted warfare in the event of hostilities.

THE TWO MESSAGES OF NOVEMBER 27

At the end of November 1941, negotiations between the United States and Japan had reached their last phase, though the American officials did not fully comprehend this. The United States had broken the Japanese diplomatic codes and knew that the Japanese negotiations had reached a critical impasse, but the Americans did not understand how serious the situation was.

Clearly, however, the Americans expected war. On November 27, with war possibly within hours, Admiral Stark issued several dispatches to prepare the Pacific Fleet and the Asiatic Fleet for war. First, he sent a lengthy message to Admiral Hart, specifically telling Hart that he would have the authority to set up strategic areas and to conduct unrestricted submarine warfare upon the outbreak of hostilities.[46]

Admiral Stark's message started directly and to the point:

IF FORMAL WAR EVENTUATES BETWEEN US AND JAPAN
QUOTE INSTRUCTIONS FOR THE NAVY OF THE UNITED
STATES GOVERNING MARITIME AND AERIAL WARFARE
MAY 1941 UNQUOTE WILL BE PLACED IN EFFECT BUT
WILL BE SUPPLEMENTED BY ADDITIONAL INSTRUCTIONS
INCLUDING AUTHORITY TO CINCAF TO CONDUCT
UNRESTRICTED SUBMARINE AND AERIAL WARFARE
AGAINST AXIS SHIPPING WITHIN THAT PART OF THE FAR
EAST AREA LYING SOUTH AND WEST OF A LINE JOINING

LAT 30 NORTH LONG 122 EAST AND LAT 7 NORTH LONG 140
WHICH YOU WILL DECLARE A STRATEGICAL AREA.[47]

The message informed Hart that not only would he be able to create a war zone that encompassed the Philippine Sea and the South China Sea, but also he would be able to conduct unrestricted warfare within that area.

Stark then enjoined Hart, following the RAINBOW 3 and 5 war plans, to fully publicize the war zone once he created it:

IN YOUR PROCLAMATION YOU WILL WARN ALL FRIENDLY,
ENEMY, AND NEUTRAL MERCHANT SHIPS AND AIRCRAFT
TO REFRAIN FROM ENTERING THIS STRATEGICAL AREA
EXCEPT UNDER CERTAIN SPECIFIED CONDITIONS X
YOU WILL STATE THIS STEP IS NECESSARY TO PREVENT
DAMAGE TO SUCH SHIPS OR AIRCRAFT THROUGH NAVAL
AND AIR OPERATIONS AND TO PREVENT SUCH SHIPS OR
AIRCRAFT FROM SUPPORTING HOSTILE ACTION AND TO
PREVENT THEM FROM OBTAINING INFORMATION WHICH
IF TRANSMITTED TO THE ENEMY SHOULD BE SERIOUSLY
DETRIMENTAL TO ARMED FORCES OF THE UNITED STATES.[48]

In short, the war zone would be for unrestricted warfare, but the publicly stated rationale would be that of a strategic area for the defense of the fleet. Although these ideas were not mutually exclusive, Leslie McNemar and the JAG Office might have objected to such an interpretation: strategic areas, after all, were meant to protect the Fleet, but the war zone that Stark was ordering Hart to create was really for the destruction of merchant vessels.

Having ensured that Hart would fully warn all shipping about the war zone, Stark then turned his attention to how to deal with neutral shipping in the area, just as the letter to the British Joint Staff had promised:

THE CONDITIONS UNDER WHICH FRIENDLY OR NEUTRAL
MERCHANT VESSELS MAY ENTER THE STRATEGICAL AREA
WILL BE ONLY THROUGH CERTAIN PRESCRIBED LANES
THAT LEAD TO NAVAL CONTROL STATIONS XX YOU ARE
REQUESTED TO TAKE UP WITH BRITISH AND DUTCH
NAVAL AUTHORITIES THE MATTER OF DEFINING AND
ESTABLISHING THESE LANES AND CONTROL STATIONS.[49]

However, Stark refused to allow Hart to prepare for these war zones in advance, instead swearing him to secrecy:

AVOID DISCLOSING FOR THE PRESENT THESE
INSTRUCTIONS TO WAGE UNRESTRICTED SUBMARINE
AND AIR WARFARE.[50]

Stark undoubtedly had a number of reasons for maintaining silence until the start of hostilities. To begin with, the United States was attempting to maintain its neutral advantage over Germany until the very last minute. Furthermore, the Japanese might not be planning to deal with an enemy conducting unrestricted warfare, and keeping American intentions secret might give American commanders a slight advantage over their adversaries in the opening days of the war. Finally, there is no evidence that Stark had discussed this decision with the civilian leadership, having already stated that the decision regarding unrestricted warfare best awaited the beginning of war. Until faced with the reality of conflict with Japan, Stark probably did not want to have to attempt to justify this decision to a civilian leadership that had been traditionally and staunchly opposed to unrestricted warfare.

Stark added a final note to ensure that Hart would not act rashly in the event of hostilities. Stark ordered Hart to wait for orders if conflict began without a formal declaration of war:

IN CASE HOSTILITIES ENSUE WITHOUT A FORMAL
DECLARATION OF WAR THE SITUATION WILL BE FAR MORE
COMPLEX BUT IT SEEMS PROBABLE THAT APPROXIMATELY
THE SAME PROCEDURE WILL BE FOLLOWED ALTHOUGH
THIS MUST BE DONE ONLY UPON FURTHER ADVICE
FROM CNO.[51]

This portion of the message would take on added significance because Hart would essentially ignore it when the Japanese did initiate hostilities without a declaration of war.

The message informing Hart that he would be able to conduct unrestricted warfare had been for his eyes only. Admiral Kimmel in the Pacific Fleet was not informed, even as a courtesy. About eleven hours later, however, the fleet commanders both received another message. If Hart had not already been jolted by the implications of Stark's previous message, he certainly must have understood how serious the situation was when he received what would be-come known as the famous "war warning" message:

272337 THIS DISPATCH TO BE CONSIDERED WAR WARNING.
NEGOTIATIONS WITH JAPAN LOOKING TOWARD
STABILIZATION OF CONDITIONS IN THE PACIFIC HAVE
LAPSED AND AN AGGRESSIVE MOVE BY JAPAN IS EXPECTED
IN THE NEXT FEW DAYS . . . EXECUTE AN APPROPRIATE
DEFENSIVE DEPLOYMENT PREPARATORY TO CARRYING
OUT THE TASKS ASSIGNED IN WPL 46.[52]

Although historians and naval officers would later argue what this message was meant to say and what the various addressees interpreted it as saying, Admiral Hart, who also had access to the MAGIC intercepts, could tell that war was in the offing.[53] Although he professionally mentioned nothing about his orders to conduct unrestricted warfare, he understood that he had to be prepared to not only sortie the Asiatic Fleet in the event of war but he also had to be ready to create the necessary war zone and conduct unrestricted warfare.

In 1960 and 1961, when Samuel Flagg Bemis researched the decision to conduct unrestricted warfare, he tried to ascertain who gave the go-ahead for Admiral Stark to issue his message to Admiral Hart on November 27. The archivists at the Franklin D. Roosevelt Presidential Library in Hyde Park, New York, were unable to find any record behind Stark's message, perhaps because Bemis stated the wrong date for the message, writing the 26th instead of the 27th. However, the archivists pointed out that Stark, General Marshall, Secretary of State Cordell Hull, Secretary of War Henry Stimson, and Secretary of Navy Frank Knox had met with President Roosevelt on both November 25 and November 28. Although the meeting on November 25 lasted only forty-five minutes, the archivists felt that it was "possible that the order from Admiral Stark . . . was discussed at either or both of these conferences."[54]

However, the historians at the State Department disagreed with this possibility, drawing from the Pearl Harbor investigations, the records of Secretary of State Hull, the diary of Secretary of War Stimson, and other sources available in Hull's papers. Stimson's recollections of the event were probably the most accurate, since he recorded the meeting in his diary, which he referenced when giving testimony for the Pearl Harbor investigations.

As Stimson recalled the meeting of November 25, 1941, President Roosevelt was dwelling upon the situation with Japan. Like his advisers, Roosevelt fully understood that the Japanese often started wars with surprise attacks, and he even guessed that the United States was "'likely to be attacked perhaps (as soon as) Monday [December 1, 1941]."[55] Having recognized that the United States was in all likelihood about to be attacked, Roosevelt wanted to "'maneuver them into firing the first shot without too much danger'" to the United States.[56] Naturally, this was far more easily said than done. Secretary Stimson felt that since the United States had already told Japan that crossing into Thailand would be considered a threat to the United States, the president could use the probable Japanese invasion of Thailand as *casus belli*. Secretary of State Hull, however, also brought up other "'general broad propositions on which the thing should be rested—*the freedom of the seas* and the fact that Japan was in alliance with Hitler and was carrying out his policy of world aggression.'"[57] Hull's recollections of the meeting essentially matched Stimson's.

While no one recollected the discussion of unrestricted warfare, this could have been because by the time of the Pearl Harbor hearings such war zones and unrestricted warfare were taken for granted. This seems unlikely, if only because Secretary of State Hull was still arguing that the United States needed to protect "the freedom of the seas" against the Japanese and the Germans. It also seems highly improbable that a politically astute naval officer such as Admiral Stark would have requested permission to conduct a form of warfare that the U.S. government was still actively opposing in a meeting where the freedom of the seas had just been touted. Based on the testimony and documentation about the meeting, the State Department historians justifiably concluded: "it is highly unlikely that the subjects of 'war zones' or 'strategic zones' or submarine warfare were discussed at the November 24, 25 and 28 meetings, and probably not at the November 21 meeting. Testimony would tend to support a thesis that these conversations were concerned more with the critical situation at hand and the need to bolster our defenses in the event of the likely Japanese attack than with the establishment of any 'war zones.'"[58] It therefore seems probable that Admiral Stark issued the message to Admiral Hart solely on his own authority. In keeping with his earlier letter to Hart and Kimmel, Stark wanted to be able to establish a war zone almost immediately upon the outbreak of hostilities. Furthermore, Stark favored a decentralized command structure that placed as much authority as possible in the hands of his subordinates. With war apparently imminent, Stark properly and characteristically gave Hart confirmation that he would be authorized to create the war zone upon the beginning of war. With this last message, Stark placed the final touches on the decision to conduct unrestricted warfare upon the outbreak of hostilities.

CHAPTER 9

Day of Infamy, Day of Decision

DECEMBER 7, 1941

For the United States, the Second World War started with a surprise attack, one that most naval officers expected. The Japanese, however, surprised virtually everyone with their choice of target. Between 0753 and 0755 on December 7, 1941, Pearl Harbor time, the first Japanese bombs fell on Oahu, bringing the stunned U.S. Pacific Fleet and U.S. Army units in Hawaii straight into battle.

Although U.S. authorities would not know it for some time, the Japanese initiated unrestricted submarine warfare within minutes of the attack on Pearl Harbor. At 0808, Pearl Harbor time, the Japanese submarine *I-26* attacked and sank the merchant ship *Cynthia Olson* approximately 1,200 nautical miles west of Los Angeles and 800 miles east-northeast of Honolulu. Although *Cynthia Olson* was completely unarmed, she could technically be considered a U.S. Army ship, since the Army had chartered her as a merchant transport. However, civilians made up virtually her entire crew, with only two Army enlisted men filling out the ship's complement as a radio operator and a medic. *Cynthia Olson* probably would have disappeared without a trace if another ship, SS *Lurline,* had not received her distress call at 0838 local time (0808, Pearl Harbor time). The distress message declared that *Cynthia Olson* was under attack by a submarine, before all contact with the ship was lost. There were no survivors.[1]

Cynthia Olson's fate remained unknown to decision-makers for quite some time. As so often happens during such eventful days, events occurred simultaneously at Pearl Harbor and across a broad series of time zones. Pearl Harbor's frantic 0758 message read: "AIR RAID PEARL HARBOR THIS IS NOT DRILL." Within a matter of minutes, virtually the entire U.S. government was turned upside down as officials and commanders at every level attempted to rapidly inform and deploy the U.S. armed forces.

In Manila, Marine Corps Lieutenant Colonel William T. Clement woke up

Admiral Hart shortly after 0300, Manila time, to inform him of the attack, which had been in progress for almost half an hour at that point. Hart quickly issued his first orders of the war, informing the entire Asiatic Fleet: "Japan started hostilities, govern yourself accordingly." The dispatch was sent at 0331.[2]

ADMIRAL HART ORDERS UNRESTRICTED WARFARE

Within the next fourteen minutes, Admiral Hart must have run through a number of thoughts before sending his next radio dispatch. He had always planned for his submarines to take a major role in fighting for the Philippines. Shortly before Stark's messages about the Far East war zone and the war warning, Hart had already written to his superior officer that he believed that the Asiatic Fleet had "become a Submarine Fleet, of great power in that type" and that Hart "expected to employ said power with full effectiveness."[3]

Furthermore, although Admiral Hart and Admiral Stark were friends, by November 1941, if not far earlier, Hart had reached the breaking point of frustration with the Navy Department, at one point venting to Stark that "men in other jobs could sleep while the ball continued to pass back and forth between Washington and here, — slowly, — but we can't out here. We have to stay ready, one way or another."[4] By the point Hart wrote this to Stark, he had already made up his mind that he would just issue orders and then inform the Navy Department as a matter of courtesy. Three days earlier, exasperated with Stark and the Navy Department, Hart had written in his diary: "Can't get any considered decisions out of the Department, which scarcely answers any direct questions ever, and now are just making the best guesses that I can, then telling Washington 'unless otherwise ordered will—' I now see that I should have adopted that method months ago—I learned it during the preceding war—and hope its [sic] not too late."[5] At the same time, Hart also knew that Admiral Stark and Rear Admiral Turner planned to conduct unrestricted warfare almost immediately upon the outbreak of hostilities. Over the past year, Hart had watched Washington officials slowly but surely come around to his view that unrestricted warfare was necessary. Only ten days earlier, Stark had informed Hart that he would have authorization to conduct unrestricted warfare when the war began. With or without permission, Hart now meant to force the issue by using that supposedly impending authority.

Although Stark's dispatch of November 27 had told Hart that "IN CASE HOS-TILITIES ENSUE WITHOUT A FORMAL DECLARATION OF WAR" he needed to await "FURTHER ADVICE FROM CNO," Hart evidently decided that the scope of Japan's attack deserved his fullest possible response. At 0345, on his own authority, Admiral Hart issued his next set of orders to the Asiatic Fleet:

SUBMARINES AND AIRCRAFT WILL WAGE UNRESTRICTED WARFARE.[6]

The message was time-stamped "080345," which stood for 0345 on December 8, 1941. It was 0915 on December 7, Pearl Harbor time. In Washington, D.C., it was 1445 on December 7. Within hours, the Asiatic Fleet's submarines were deploying to their wartime patrol positions. The commander, Submarine Force, Asiatic Fleet, issued orders to his submarines, leaving no question that they were to attack any and all Japanese shipping. USS *S-38* was informed that her mission was "UNRESTRICTED ATTACK."[7] About twenty minutes later, USS *S-36* was told to "WAGE UNRESTRICTED WARFARE."[8] Only five hours after the initial attack at Pearl Harbor, the Asiatic Fleet and its submarine force had sortied to conduct unrestricted warfare.

ADMIRAL STARK ORDERS UNRESTRICTED WARFARE

Although Admiral Hart's orders to conduct unrestricted warfare had been out for over three hours before Admiral Stark issued his own orders, Stark's orders have received the most attention from researchers, including Samuel Flagg Bemis and Janet Manson. Unlike Hart's orders, which were only issued to the Asiatic Fleet, Stark's orders affected virtually every unit with submarines and aircraft in the U.S. Navy.

Stark learned about the attack at some time between 1330 and 1400, Washington time, as the first dramatic messages announcing the Pearl Harbor air raid reached Washington, D.C. At the office of the secretary of the Navy, Stark famously confirmed the location to an incredulous Frank Knox, who believed that the target had to be the Philippines: "No sir; this is Pearl."[9]

Shortly thereafter, at 1428, Washington time, Stark telephoned President Roosevelt to confirm the attack. Sitting with the president, and taking notes, was Roosevelt's longtime aide and friend Harry Hopkins. Hopkins's memorandum is probably the only remaining primary source regarding the conversation between Roosevelt and Stark. Unfortunately, Hopkins could only hear Roosevelt's side of the conversation. Hopkins wrote: "At 2:28 Admiral Stark called the President and confirmed the attack, stating that it was a very severe attack and that some damage had already been done to the fleet and that there was some loss of life. He discussed with the President briefly the next step and the President wanted him to execute the agreed orders to the Army and Navy in event of an outbreak of hostilities in the Pacific."[10] The archivists at the Franklin D. Roosevelt Presidential Library at Hyde Park noted that there was no other record of the telephone conversation, which was hardly unusual since almost none of President Roosevelt's phone calls were ever transcribed. However, the archivists at the library, as well as Samuel Flagg Bemis, concluded: "it would appear that President Roosevelt's order to Admiral Stark was given by telephone a few moments after 2:28 P.M. on December 7."[11]

The archivists at the Roosevelt Library also guessed that the agreed orders could have meant the RAINBOW 5 war plan. Although Roosevelt had not officially approved the plan previously, he had told Stark and Marshall to resubmit it in the event of hostilities. At 1500, Washington time, Roosevelt met with Marshall, Stark, Knox, Stimson, and Hull, and verbally approved RAINBOW 5. Upon his return to his office, General Marshall jotted down a quick note that the president had given him verbal permission to place RAINBOW 5 in effect. Although Samuel Eliot Morison later wrote that the Pearl Harbor attack had instantly nullified RAINBOW 5, both Stark and Marshall put the war plan into operation immediately, and it was not officially retired until 1946.[12]

On May 31, 1961, almost twenty years after the event, Rear Admiral Ernest Eller, director of naval history for the U.S. Navy, and Samuel Flagg Bemis questioned Admiral Stark regarding the events of December 7.[13] Stark insisted that he had read his order to conduct unrestricted warfare to the president on the telephone during his conversation at 1428: "Yes, I read those very words to the President."[14] Rear Admiral Eller later wrote that Admiral Stark's "story . . . seems to me to be just about what happened. It was very simple and straightforward."[15]

Although Stark probably discussed the matter with the president at 1428, seventeen minutes before Admiral Hart issued his orders for unrestricted warfare at 0345, Manila time, Stark waited until he had returned from his meeting at the White House to send his message at 1752, Washington time. The message was addressed to virtually every commander who had forces in the Pacific Ocean, including both Admiral Kimmel and Admiral Hart. Stark was short and to the point, just as Hart had been:

EXECUTE AGAINST JAPAN UNRESTRICTED AIR AND
SUBMARINE WARFARE. CINCAF INFORM BRITISH AND
DUTCH. INFORM ARMY.[16]

Just as Stark and Turner had promised, the Navy had started conducting unrestricted warfare almost immediately upon the outbreak of war. It had been just a little under four and a half hours since the first bomb had fallen at Pearl Harbor.

ADMIRAL HART'S ORDER IN THE CONTEXT OF CHRONOLOGY AND SIGNIFICANCE

As the study of the past, history is inevitably a study of events in time. It is vitally important for historians to place events in their proper order. The chronology of relevant events on December 7, 1941, is summarized in the accompanying table:

EVENT	Greenwich (Zulu) Time	Manila Time	Pearl Harbor Time	Washington, D.C., Time
Japan begins hostilities.	1825, December 7, 1941	0225, December 8, 1941	0755, December 7, 1941	1325, December 7, 1941
Japan begins unrestricted submarine warfare by sinking SS *Cynthia Olson*.	1838	0238	0808	1338
Admiral Hart is woken up in Manila.	1900	0300	0830	1400
The president orders Admiral Stark to put in effect the "agreed orders."	1928	0328	0858	1428
Admiral Hart relays war notice to Asiatic Fleet.	1931	0331	0901	1431
Admiral Hart orders unrestricted warfare.	1945	0345	0915	1445
Admiral Stark and General Marshall meet with President Roosevelt.	2000	0400	0930	1500
Admiral Stark orders unrestricted warfare.	2252	0652	1222	1752

As noted earlier, Admiral Hart sent his orders to conduct unrestricted warfare a little less than an hour and a half after the initial attack at Pearl Harbor. Admiral Hart's 0345, Manila time, dispatch certainly was important, but how important? Samuel Flagg Bemis and Janet Manson did not even mention Hart's order, instead focusing on Admiral Stark's message at 1752, Washington time. Only one researcher, J. E. Talbott, writing in 1984, made the critical observation that if Hart issued his order at 0345, then he preceded Admiral Stark's order by almost three hours. Such a difference is certainly important. On the one hand, if Hart's order did precede Stark's, then the order to conduct unrestricted warfare was issued without any formal authorization by the civilian government of the United States. On the other hand, if Stark preceded Hart, then the chief of naval operations, although he had planned in isolation from the civilian leadership, would still have technically fulfilled his duty by awaiting permission from the constitutional commander-in-chief of the U.S. armed forces, President Roosevelt.

So the question comes down to precisely when Hart issued his order and whether or not he preceded Stark. The first official narrative of the Asiatic Fleet submarine force, submitted as a report on April 1, 1942, after the demise of the Asiatic Fleet, stated: "Before the outbreak of hostilities the decision of the Navy Department with regard to conducting commerce war by submarines was to the effect that 'Instructions for the Navy of the United States Governing Maritime and Aerial Warfare, May 1941' would be complied with. It was, however, understood that a directive for unrestricted warfare could be expected within the first week after the outbreak of hostilities. Before noon, Manila time, 8 December, the Commander in Chief, ASIATIC FLEET directed submarines and aircraft to wage unrestricted submarine warfare."[17] If Admiral Hart issued his order "[b]efore noon, Manila time," that certainly would have been acceptable, since Admiral Stark's message would have arrived at 0652, Manila time. The report, however, did not mention Stark's order, instead focusing on Admiral Hart's message.

After the war, the unpublished submarine force administrative history also devoted attention to Admiral Hart's order in a paragraph that implicitly claimed Hart had preceded everyone else in issuing his orders:

At 0345 8 December (0915 7 December Pearl Harbor Time) fourteen
minutes after he had relayed the message "Japan started hostilities, govern
yourself accordingly," CinCAF promulgated the message "Submarines and
aircraft will wage unrestricted warfare."
 . . . [T]he transmission of this order . . . was given on Admiral Thomas C.
Hart's own initiative.[18]

The paragraph went on to describe why Hart felt he could issue the order, by discussing Commander James Fife's visit to Rear Admiral Turner on October 1, 1941, and Turner's verbal assurance that the United States would conduct unrestricted warfare within a week of hostilities. This paragraph was probably added to the administrative history at the behest of then Rear Admiral James Fife, who was one of five submariners named as having served as a consultant to both the operational and administrative histories.[19]

If Fife's account is to be believed, Hart issued his orders only one hour and twenty minutes after the initial bombs had fallen at Pearl Harbor, and over three hours ahead of Admiral Stark. The radio time-date group on Hart's dispatch supports Fife's account, since it is time-dated "080345."[20] The next question a critical researcher should ask, however, is what time zone the message was dated in.

Even in the 1940s, some military units chose to time-date all their messages to Greenwich Mean Time, otherwise known as Zulu time, in order to properly keep track of events. Messages from Washington, D.C., for instance, often carried a Zulu time-date group. Thus, Admiral Stark's 2252, Zulu time, dispatch was sent at 1752, Washington time. If Admiral Hart's 080345 message carried a Zulu time-date group, then he would actually have sent his message at 0345, December 8, in Greenwich; 2245, December 7, in Washington; 1715, December 7, in Pearl Harbor; and 1145, December 8, in Manila. Such a time would concur with the initial report of April 1, 1942, that Hart had sent his message sometime "before noon."

Such a line of thinking is tempting to a historian who would like to believe that Admiral Hart loyally and properly followed his orders to await word from Stark before issuing his own orders. However, numerous sources record that submarines of the Asiatic Fleet received Hart's message at 0345, local time.

Bobette Gugliotta recorded first-person recollections of receiving the message in the darkness of the night on board USS S-39:

It was 0330, 8 December. Pennell's urgent tone of voice snapped Monk's head up. As he read the words of the message, he jumped to his feet, as wide awake as though he were about to hit a home run. "Take this to the captain immediately," he said.

Pennell had been on watch in the machinery spaces and had just made one tour through the boat when Radioman Bill Harris handed him the message that now sent him scrambling up the hatch with all speed, Hendrix at his heels. Picking his way among the bodies on deck, he spied the red hair of his skipper as the clouds parted; it was the last time for a long time that any man on 39 would welcome a bright night. As soon as Coe read the historic words, "Japan has started hostilities, govern yourselves accordingly," he told Hendrix, "Make all preparations to get underway." Pennell was ordered to rouse the sleepers at once and to strip the lifelines, benches, stanchions—items that fell into the unnecessary or personal convenience class . . .

By the time the second message came from CINCAF (Commander-in-Chief Asiatic Fleet), about 15 minutes later, "Submarines and aircraft will wage unrestricted warfare," all personnel and cots were stowed away below. In 11 minutes more, 39 was underway for her patrol area, by 0445 they had rigged ship for dive, which took place at 0700 much to everybody's relief.[21]

Gugliotta, the wife of one of the officers on board S-39, published her history of the old S-boat in 1984. Among her sources was the widow of S-39's captain, James Coe; James Pennell, the sailor who had handed the officer of the deck the message announcing the start of hostilities; and finally, recorded interviews from 1944 with "Monk" Hendrix, the officer of the deck who had initially received the message before alerting the commanding officer. In addition, Gugliotta consulted S-39's war patrol reports.[22]

Another secondary source that supports the 0345, Manila time, time-date group of the message is Carl LaVO's 1994 book about the saga of the sister submarines *Sailfish* and *Sculpin*. Although LaVO's quotation of the Asiatic Fleet dispatches is questionable, he did interview survivors of USS *Sailfish* and *Sculpin* who were on board the boats when the war began. His account, like Gugliotta's, supports the account that the Asiatic Fleet dispatches were sent with local time-date groups:

At exactly 0315 on December 8, the world as they knew it came to an end. A message was flashed to the submarines from Hart's headquarters. *Sailfish* and *Sculpin* signalmen jotted down the startling news: FROM COMMANDER ASIATIC FLEET . . . TO ASIATIC FLEET . . . URGENT . . . BREAK . . . JAPAN HAS COMMENCED HOSTILITIES . . . GOVERN YOURSELVES ACCORDINGLY.

Aboard the *Sailfish,* the order was passed down the conning tower hatch to Bayles, who went to awaken Cassedy, the fiery duty officer. "Cassedy got up and read the message. He half jumped out of his bunk and yelled, 'Hold reveille!'" recounted Bayles. "I went into all the sleeping compartments and turned on the lights and said, 'Wake up! The war has started!' I remember someone in the after battery yelling back, 'Bullshit!'"

. . . As Mumma hurried to the *Sailfish* from the Army-Navy Club, a

second message was received from Hart at 0330: CONDUCT UNRESTRICTED
AIR, SURFACE AND UNDERSEAS WARFARE AGAINST THE EMPIRE OF JAPAN![23]

Since LaVO did not use standard endnotes or footnotes, his source for the message is unclear. His interviews with *Sailfish* crewmen, however, fully support the early-morning nature of the dispatches, even if the times he recorded were early by fifteen minutes.

In 1991 Stanley Weintraub offhandedly mentioned the order in his *Long Day's Journey into War,* a popular history of the events of December 7, 1941, all across the globe. "At 0345," wrote Weintraub, "Hart followed up his war message with a second one. As received by the sub *Sturgeon* it read, 'Submarines and aircraft will wage unrestricted warfare.'"[24] Since Weintraub did not even provide a bibliography, one must infer from his writing that his source for this was USS *Sturgeon's* report of events. Alas, not all of Weintraub's popular history can be taken at face value. Later in the same paragraph he claims that four U.S. submarines were destroyed by the Japanese air raids on Cavite on December 10, 1941, when in reality only USS *Sealion* was lost on that date.[25]

Last but not least was the mention of Hart's order in W. J. Holmes's *Undersea Victory* (1966). Holmes had been one of the fleet intelligence officers at Pearl Harbor and actively involved with crypto-analysis, so he was in a unique position to understand the importance of message traffic time-date groups. Holmes was heavily involved in writing the unpublished administrative and operational history of the Pacific Submarine Force after the war ended, and he used his knowledge from that unpublished history to write *Undersea Victory.* Holmes also cited the messages by Admiral Hart as being in the morning. In an interesting and startling lapse on Holmes's part, however, he cited the wrong time for the dispatches. It seems probable that he was working directly from the unpublished official history because he used virtually the same wording, but through a mistake in either comprehension or editing, he shifted the time of Admiral Hart's message back by fifteen minutes:

> At 0345 on the morning of 8 December, East Longitude date (0915 on 7 December at Pearl Harbor), Admiral Thomas C. Hart, Commander-in-Chief, U.S. Asiatic Fleet, broadcast his command: "JAPAN STARTED HOSTILITIES. GOVERN YOURSELF ACCORDINGLY." Fourteen minutes later he amplified these instructions in a second message: "SUBMARINES AND AIRCRAFT WILL WAGE UNRESTRICTED WARFARE."[26]

Despite Holmes's error in transcribing the time of the dispatch, he obviously believed that Hart had issued his order in the early morning of December 8, fully supporting Fife's account that Hart sent his message at 0345.

The preponderance of evidence indicates that Admiral Hart sent his orders to conduct unrestricted warfare at 0345, Manila time. By doing so, he preempted Admiral Stark by more than three hours. He also singlehandedly reversed U.S. official policy regarding unrestricted warfare.

It may seem surprising that skilled researchers like Samuel Flagg Bemis or Janet Manson failed to notice that Admiral Hart issued his orders well before Admiral Stark, but they are not alone—virtually all historians have overlooked the timing of Hart's order. Gugliotta, LaVO, and Weintraub all mentioned the order and its timing, but failed to remark on its timing relative to Stark's order. Even W. J. Holmes, who had helped write the unpublished administrative history that discussed the topic in terse but informative detail, did not bring the subject up when he wrote *Undersea Victory*.

Interestingly, one historian did notice the timing and properly understood its significance, but he did not fully understand the motivations behind Hart's actions. J. E. Talbott, a historian at the University of California at Santa Barbara, studied the decision to conduct unrestricted submarine warfare and correctly pointed out that "Hart jumped the gun, setting aside the rules on submarine warfare before the Chief of Naval Operations, speaking for the Commander in Chief of the Armed Forces, had authorized him to do so."[27]

Unfortunately, Talbott did not know about Admiral Turner's verbal assurance to Hart via Commander Fife, nor did he mention Stark's written intention to conduct unrestricted warfare almost immediately upon the outbreak of war. Consequently, Talbott depicted Hart's order as an isolated action by a jumpy commander, instead of viewing it as the culmination of a year of strategic, legal, and moral consideration by Navy leadership.

In addition, Talbott altered the chronology of events by misunderstanding the nature of time zones in 1941. At one point he noted that "2:28 P.M. Washington time" was "9:28 A.M. in Pearl Harbor." Since this was the time at which Admiral Stark telephoned President Roosevelt to ask permission to conduct unrestricted warfare, Talbott made the dramatic but erroneous claim that Hart had sent his order "13 minutes before Stark even called Roosevelt to confirm the Pearl Harbor raid."[28] This would be correct if Pearl Harbor and Washington had been offset by five hours, and Manila and Washington had been offset by thirteen and a half hours. However, in 1941, it was Hawaii that had a five-and-a-half-hour offset with Washington, while Manila and Washington were separated by only thirteen hours.[29] Since then, time zones have been changed so that time differences are usually hourly, replacing the confused system of 1941, "when Bangkok and Singapore were twenty minutes apart, and Java was a further ten minutes off Malayan time, and Hawaii was two and a half hours earlier than California time."[30]

Despite Talbott's limited conclusion and his mistaken chronology, he deserves credit as one of the earliest researchers to notice the timing of Admiral Hart's message and to recognize its importance in the context of the broader U.S. decision to conduct unrestricted submarine warfare. Without waiting for permission, Admiral Hart issued his own orders, beginning a long campaign of unrestricted submarine warfare that would not end until Japan surrendered.

CHAPTER 10

Unrestricted Warfare and the Civilian Chain of Command

Within hours of Admiral Stark's message ordering unrestricted warfare, on the evening on December 7, Admiral Turner mentioned the U.S. decision to conduct unrestricted warfare to Admiral Little of the Royal Navy, who was part of the British naval staff in Washington, D.C. Turner explained to Little that the United States had decided to begin unrestricted warfare "in retaliation for the Japanese bombing of open towns in Oahu."[1]

A NAVAL DECISION

Despite Turner's explanation, the events from December 1940 to December 1941 showed that the U.S. Navy had planned to conduct unrestricted warfare no matter what the Japanese did. In 1961, when he had completed his research, Samuel Flagg Bemis emphatically condemned Turner's ex post facto justification as disingenuous:

> However justified unrestricted submarine warfare against Japan might have been because of Japan's attack on Pearl Harbor without declaration of war, in violation of Hague Convention III — not to mention violation of other treaties including the Kellogg-Briand Pact of Paris — *the fact is that the orders of December 7 would have been issued even if there had been a Japanese declaration of war.* The sneak attack on Pearl Harbor only triggered off a command to set up strategic zones in the whole Pacific Ocean and to sink all Japanese ships within sight of that area of naval operations, a command that had already been prepared and sent out, awaiting only the outbreak of war between Japan and the United States.[2]

Not only was Admiral Turner's justification for the decision to conduct unrestricted warfare not entirely truthful, but it belied months of preparation by the U.S. Navy, which occurred even as the commander-in-chief of the U.S.

Army and Navy, President Franklin D. Roosevelt, continued to declare that the United States stood for freedom of the seas in all oceans and at all times.

"ALL FREEDOM . . . DEPENDS ON FREEDOM OF THE SEAS"

Despite the retreat from the concept of absolute freedom of the seas that U.S. neutrality legislation implicitly represented, there can be no doubt that in 1941, the public position of the Roosevelt administration had hardened considerably in regard to Germany and absolute freedom of the seas. In fireside chats, memoranda cleared for public release, and letters to congressional representatives, the president and the State Department both publicly stated their adherence to and strong belief in the Wilsonian paradigm of absolute freedom of the seas.

On May 27, 1941, President Roosevelt addressed the country in a fireside radio chat about the severity of the situation facing Great Britain and the United States. Roosevelt emphasized the number of British ships being sunk in the Atlantic and the current inability of British and American shipyards to replace those losses. He summed up the German threat: "The Axis Powers can never achieve their objective of world domination unless they first obtain control of the seas. This is their supreme purpose today; and to achieve it, they must capture Great Britain. They could then have the power to dictate to the Western Hemisphere."[3]

To justify his administration's policy against Germany, President Roosevelt brought up freedom of the seas, stating: "All freedom—meaning freedom to live, and not freedom to conquer and subjugate other peoples—depends on freedom of the seas. All of American history—North, Central and South American history—has been inevitably tied up with those words, 'freedom of the seas.'"[4] As the president explained, this was hardly a new idea. Since the Quasi-War with France, the United States had traditionally "striven and fought in defense of freedom of the seas—for our own shipping, for the commerce of our sister Republics, for the right of all nations to the use the highways of world trade—and for our own safety."[5] Although modern weapons of war, particularly the submarine, made commerce protection more difficult, the president refused to shrink from defending the right of freedom of the seas: "We shall actively resist his [Hitler's] every attempt to gain control of the seas . . . We reassert the ancient American doctrine of freedom of the seas."[6]

Like Woodrow Wilson, President Roosevelt cast unrestricted submarine warfare as the counterpoint of the traditional U.S. right of freedom of the seas. With his public reassertion of freedom of the seas, he was echoing the stand of

Woodrow Wilson, which was predicated upon the right of commerce to travel on the world's oceans without the threat of attack. It was a theme that he and the State Department would return to again and again.

Even before Roosevelt "reasserted" American freedom of the seas, Secretary of State Cordell Hull was warning of the dire dangers of Nazi control of the oceans. In a speech on October 25, 1940, just before that year's elections, Hull warned: "Should the would-be conquerors gain control of other continents, they would next concentrate on perfecting their control of the seas, of the air over the seas, and of the world's economy; they might then be able with ships and with planes to strike at the communication lines, the commerce and the life of this Hemisphere; and ultimately we might find ourselves compelled to fight on our soil, under our own skies, in defense of our independence and our very lives."[7] A few months later, on January 15, 1941, Hull reprised his warning: "control of the high seas by law-abiding nations is the key to the security of the Western Hemisphere in the present-day world situation."[8]

Absolute freedom of the seas remained an important issue within the Roosevelt administration throughout 1941. Significantly, the president emphasized that unrestricted warfare was antithetical to freedom of the seas. When Roosevelt reported the sinking of SS *Robin Moor* to Congress on June 20, 1941, he did not solely dwell on the fact that the unarmed ship was sunk outside of the German war zone and in clear violation of freedom of the seas. He also specifically pointed out the violation of the 1936 London Submarine Protocol, to which Germany was a signatory:

> The sinking of this American ship by a German submarine flagrantly violated the right of United States vessels freely to navigate the seas subject only to a belligerent right accepted under international law. This belligerent right, as is known to the German Government, does not include the right deliberately to sink a merchant vessel, leaving the passengers and crew to the mercies of the elements. On the contrary the belligerent is required to place the passengers and crew in places of safety . . . The total disregard for the most elementary principles of international law and of humanity brands the sinking of the *Robin Moor* as the act of an international outlaw.[9]

The *Robin Moor* incident only warmed Roosevelt up. When a German U-boat, believing itself to be under attack, fired torpedoes at the U.S. destroyer *Greer,* the president condemned unrestricted submarine warfare in no uncertain terms while continuing to assert freedom of the seas. In his fireside address of

September 11, 1941, Roosevelt focused on the conflict between freedom of the seas and unrestricted warfare. Like Woodrow Wilson before him, Roosevelt depicted the German submarine campaign as an attempt to wrest away basic American rights, and he cast his policy as a traditional and time-honored right:

> It is the Nazi design to abolish the freedom of the seas, and to acquire absolute control and domination of the seas for themselves . . .
>
> Generation after generation, America has battled for the general policy of the freedom of the seas. That policy is a very simple one—but a basic, a fundamental one. It means that no nation has the right to make the broad oceans of the world at great distances from the actual theatre of land war unsafe for the commerce of others.
>
> That has been our policy, proved time and again, in all of our history.
>
> Our policy has applied from time immemorial—and still applies—not merely to the Atlantic but to the Pacific and to all other oceans as well.
>
> *Unrestricted submarine warfare in 1941 constitutes a defiance—an act of aggression—against that historic American policy . . .*
>
> These Nazi submarines and raiders are the rattlesnakes of the Atlantic. They are a menace to the free pathways of the high seas. They are a challenge to our sovereignty. They hammer at our most precious rights when they attack ships of the American flag—symbols of our independence, our freedom, our very life.[10]

More than any other address Roosevelt had given, this fireside chat thoroughly elucidated his views on freedom of the seas and unrestricted warfare. He defined freedom of the seas as the right of merchant shipping to travel without the threat of attack. He stated that freedom of the seas applied to all oceans at all times. He clearly identified unrestricted warfare as the principal menace to freedom of the seas.

A week after the president's address, on September 19, 1941, the assistant to the assistant secretary of state, Carlton Savage, drafted a memorandum describing the U.S. tradition of freedom of the seas. Savage's memorandum described the legal underpinnings of the concept, from Grotius and the Armed Neutrality of 1780, and the long tradition of resorting to arms to defend freedom of the seas, from the Quasi-War with France to the First World War. As expected, the memorandum discussed the attempts to curb submarine warfare since the First World War, focusing on the London Naval Treaty of 1930, the London Submarine Protocol of 1936, and the Nyon Agreement of 1937. Savage extensively quoted President Wilson, Secretary of State Hull, and particularly

President Roosevelt's fireside chats of May 27, 1941, and September 11, 1941. Although brief, the memorandum illustrated the importance that the Roosevelt administration placed upon freedom of the seas, and highlighted the administration's absolute opposition to unrestricted warfare.[11]

Savage's memorandum went all the way to President Roosevelt, who liked it so much that he wanted to send copies to the chairs of the Senate Committee on Foreign Relations and the House Committee on Foreign Affairs. The president also wanted to make the memorandum public. After deleting a page of text implying U.S. hypocrisy in the First World War, Savage gave the new draft to Secretary Hull, who presented it to the president. To Savage's knowledge, the president sent at least one copy of the revised draft to Senator Thomas Connally, chair of the Senate Foreign Relations Committee. Whether or not Savage's memorandum went any further toward public consumption is unclear, but the president's interest in and support for the memorandum were yet another illustration of Roosevelt's public support for a concept of absolute freedom of the seas that utterly denied the acceptability of unrestricted warfare.[12]

The timeframe during which the president was approving and distributing Savage's memorandum was the same time period in which Admiral Turner presented Admiral Stark with a proposed letter to consult the State Department about the possibility of unrestricted warfare in the event of hostilities. It is unclear whether Stark actually saw the Savage memorandum, but given the president's recent speech of September 11, 1941, Stark must have known the Navy's proposal was antithetical to the administration's public position. Given this perspective, Stark's decision to veto the proposed letter is extremely understandable. It may also explain why there is no documented evidence that the Navy ever attempted to consult the civilian leadership of the United States until December 7, 1941.

NO DOCUMENTATION

Based on the documentation within the files of the Navy Department, the Navy made little or no effort to consult the civilian leadership of the United States regarding the propriety of unrestricted warfare. President Roosevelt kept no records of ever having discussed or considered this decision. Other than the Hopkins memorandum of December 7, which does not explicitly refer to unrestricted warfare, there is no documentation at all in Roosevelt's papers at his library in Hyde Park.[13] The three other civilian leaders in the government who should have been most concerned with this decision were Secretary of State Cordell Hull, Secretary of War Henry Stimson, and finally and most certainly, Secretary of the Navy Frank Knox. However, a careful search by archivists through the classified and declassified papers of all three men revealed no record of this decision.[14] Similarly, there was no documentation in the papers of Knox's assistant, successor, and future Secretary of Defense, James V. Forrestal.[15] There was also no documentation of the decision in the historical files of the Joint Chiefs of Staff from the Second World War—not surprising, since only the Navy seemed to be dealing with the decision and the Army was, at most, an indifferent spectator.[16] In fact, Admiral Stark did not even consult his own judge advocate general. While the Navy JAG had issued its opinion of unrestricted warfare during the General Board hearing in April 1941, Stark recalled later that he did not ask for the legal opinions of either "the State Legal Section or the Judge Advocate General of the Navy Department."[17]

Samuel Flagg Bemis's research indicated that the planning for this decision was insulated from the civilian leadership, but Bemis assumed that the final decision to conduct unrestricted warfare ultimately, and properly, rested with the president of the United States. Yet on December 7, 1941, Admiral Hart issued his orders as Stark was finishing his telephone call with the president. From start to finish, the decision to conduct unrestricted warfare remained entirely insulated within the command structure of the U.S. Navy. There is no record of this decision ever being considered or formally accepted by any civilian leaders until Stark's phone call to President Roosevelt at 1428 on December 7.

Despite the lack of documentation, Janet Manson concluded that the decision to conduct unrestricted warfare required "[c]lose cooperation between the Navy, the State Department, and the President."[18] Manson explained the lack of documentation as either a consequence of the decision having been made over a series of telephone conversations, or else perhaps a deliberate act:

> Like many other modern leaders, Roosevelt often preferred to communicate on an oral basis. Certainly, the use of the telephone for important and urgent business has dramatically increased this trend with little, if any, record kept of decisions made or business transacted in this manner. It is possible too that Roosevelt and others who discussed the decision at some point consciously decided to leave no record of discussions because it did represent such a dramatic change in policy. Providing a record of the decision and its rationale would necessarily call attention to its ramifications, in particular the destruction of innocent lives and property.[19]

Although such a wide-ranging conspiracy, involving a president, his secretary of state, and his military advisers, may seem titillating, another scenario seems more likely and plausible.

The lack of documentation in the archives of the president and the secretary of state probably does not indicate deliberate omission, but rather reflects that discussion regarding unrestricted warfare never formally extended beyond the uniformed Navy. The theory of a conspiracy of silence works only if all three parties remained silent, but the Navy kept a great deal of paperwork on file and also sent messages well ahead of the beginning of the war. If the first message regarding this decision had been Stark's "EXECUTE AGAINST JAPAN," then the conspiracy theory might have more weight, but his message of December 7 succeeded a number of letters and his dispatch of November 27 regarding a war zone. Admiral Stark's messages, while classified at the time, entered the realm of history as soon as he sent them.

Furthermore, as noted above, the Roosevelt administration and the State Department had publicly committed themselves to upholding the Wilsonian paradigm of absolute freedom of the seas in all oceans and at all times. Roosevelt, in particular, made this pledge in numerous public statements, particularly the two fireside chats of May 27, 1941, and September 11, 1941. How likely is it that both the president and the State Department were closely cooperating on a decision that was contrary to a position they had publicly espoused?

At the very least, the State Department was not involved in the decision. Although it is conceivable that Cordell Hull may have concurred in this decision before war began, his insistence at the White House in late November 1941 that the United States continue to force the Axis to respect "freedom of the seas" seems to indicate that he would hardly have agreed to a decision that utterly denied freedom of the seas.[20] Furthermore, the Navy's antipathy toward the State Department could hardly have been clearer. It had taken over twenty years for the State Department to approve a new set of *Instructions* for naval warfare. At its hearings in April 1941, the Navy's General Board took it for granted that the State Department would veto any *Instructions* that contained provisions for unrestricted warfare.[21] As noted earlier, a letter had been drafted for the secretary of state, but Rear Admiral Turner's memorandum indicates that it was never sent. The lack of any records relating to this matter in the files of the Department of State seems to bear out the contention that once Admiral Stark vetoed the intended letter, the Navy never again tried to discuss the matter with the State Department.[22] The chief legal adviser to the State Department at the time, Green H. Hackworth, could not remember the issue even being brought up.[23]

In the case of President Roosevelt, the matter is far more nebulous. Although Stark insisted to Rear Admiral E. M. Eller and Samuel Flagg Bemis that he discussed the unrestricted warfare message with Roosevelt on December 7, neither Eller nor Bemis recorded whether or not Stark had ever brought the topic up beforehand. Based on Hopkins's memorandum, Roosevelt's allusion to "the agreed orders" possibly indicates that he and Stark had discussed the matter previously. If Stark and Roosevelt did discuss the matter beforehand, Roosevelt may have chosen to "tacitly" approve unrestricted warfare, just as he had approved RAINBOW 5, contingent upon Stark consulting him upon the outbreak of war.[24]

Another possibility is that Stark informed Roosevelt of his intentions but Roosevelt gave no formal answer. Roosevelt habitually chose to approve potentially controversial plans on an oral basis, with no written notes showing that he had even looked at a document. For instance, Roosevelt never formally approved Plan Dog. Admiral Stark's biographer, B. Mitchell Simpson, speculated that Roosevelt might have used an intermediary to quietly approve Plan Dog, because of "Roosevelt's general penchant for deviousness and with the arm's length treatment he gave the Plan Dog Memorandum . . . He filed the original without even initialing it or otherwise indicating he had read it. One thing is clear: He did not disapprove it."[25] Similarly, Roosevelt may have ingested the idea of unrestricted warfare silently, neither approving nor disapproving it.

There is also the possibility that Stark did not discuss the issue at all with the president before December 7, 1941. Stark sometimes acted behind the president's back in order to give his old friend what later became known as "plausible deniability," in the off chance that something might go wrong. For instance, Stark set up the first American–British–Canadian meeting without first informing Roosevelt that he had sent an invitation to the British and Canadians, although he knew that Roosevelt favored such talks. Consequently, both he and the president could later claim that Stark had acted without the "permission" of his civilian superiors, if isolationists attempted to claim that Stark and Roosevelt were colluding to draw the United States into a war.[26]

All of this is speculation. What is certain is that there is absolutely no documentation that President Roosevelt ever discussed this matter until 1428 on the afternoon of December 7, 1941, when Stark telephoned him. Even then, the only evidence that Roosevelt was involved in the decision is Stark's word. When Eller and Bemis interviewed Stark in 1961, there was little chance that Stark would stand trial for any wartime "offenses," so there was no reason for Stark to lie. Of course, by the time Bemis and Eller interviewed him, Stark was eighty years old. As a number of historians have noted, even over a relatively brief time, one's memories of the past, particularly of traumatic or significant events, are bound to be corrupted by what one believes happened or *should* have happened.[27] Consequently, there is no guarantee that Stark's story was true and correct, in whole or in part. But whether or not President Roosevelt actually approved the orders to conduct unrestricted warfare, as one historian noted, after the Pearl Harbor attack, the president "was in no mood to restrict any line of military action against the Japanese."[28]

Afterward, the decision apparently elicited little or no outrage from the State Department, which seems to have accepted the explanation that unrestricted warfare was undertaken in reprisal for the Japanese sneak attack on Pearl Harbor. By May 1942 the State Department had even accepted that unrestricted warfare was a fact of life in modern warfare. In an attempt to compel all the belligerents to comply with some of the Hague Conventions on land and naval warfare, the State Department prepared a letter and memorandum to the War and Navy Departments outlining the conventions that the United States should request all belligerents to comply with. Among them were the conventions on land warfare, naval bombardment, and the laying of mines.[29] The State Department's Treaty Division, however, conceded that there was no point in requesting compliance with Convention XI of the 1907 Hague Conventions, which discussed the rules of search and seizure on the high seas. Indeed, in a rare show of pragmatism, the State Department officers wrote: "As practically all merchant ships are now used either directly or indirectly in the prosecution of the war and there appears to be no respect shown such vessels by Axis powers, there would appear to be no point in proposing that the provisions of this convention be applied."[30]

And so, with hardly a murmur and despite their strenuous public protestations of the previous year, both the president and the State Department acceded to the Navy's decision to conduct unrestricted warfare.

Regardless of when or if President Roosevelt approved the orders to conduct unrestricted warfare, those orders still violated a ratified treaty of the United States and they came before any reported Japanese unrestricted warfare that demanded such a reprisal. Although it is debatable who had the authority to unilaterally abrogate the London Submarine Protocol of 1936, the protocol was never formally terminated.[31] After the war, the Nuremberg Tribunals determined that despite the actions of the belligerents, the London Submarine Protocol was still in effect, a view confirmed by subsequent publications on maritime law.[32] And although international law implicitly sanctions reprisals, the Navy planned to conduct unrestricted warfare no matter how the war started.[33] Consequently, by formulating and following orders that improperly violated a ratified treaty without any reported enemy actions that permitted such a reprisal, the senior naval officers arguably violated their oaths of office.

Like all officers in the U.S. armed forces since 1868, U.S. naval officers swore to support and defend the Constitution of the United States.[34] As part of that oath, naval officers were sworn to uphold Article VI, Paragraph 2 of the Constitution, which stated:

> This Constitution, and the Laws of the United States which shall be made in Pursuance thereof; and all Treaties made, or which shall be made, under the Authority of the United States, *shall be the supreme Law of the Land;* and the Judges in every state shall be bound thereby, any thing in the Constitution or Laws of any State to the Contrary notwithstanding.[35]

Therefore, U.S. naval officers were sworn to uphold Article 22 of the London Naval Treaty as the supreme law of the United States, comparable in force to the Constitution and laws passed by Congress.

Although some may question the importance or validity of oaths, the oath of U.S. military officers to the U.S. Constitution has been a defining difference between the U.S. military and other militaries around the world throughout time. Instead of swearing allegiance to a monarch, country, populace, or even each other, U.S. military officers and enlisted personnel swear to support and defend the democratic ideals and laws of the United States, embodied in the Constitution. Paul Roush, a military ethics scholar, summed up the absolute importance of the constitutional oath to the American military system:

The inexorable linkage from oath to all subsequent behavior is a fundamental fact of military life. It cannot be otherwise if the nation is to retain the essential character of the relationship between the people (through their elected representatives) and the military. If the linkage goes, so does the trust between the citizen and soldier. A military unconstrained by the provisions of the Constitution is a threat to the civil society.[36]

Unfortunately, as the case of unrestricted warfare demonstrates, the oath carries an inherent conflict: what if it is necessary to break some laws in order to preserve the rest?

This conflict is not new. Perhaps the most famous case of a federal officer choosing to violate the law in order to defend the rest of the Constitution was when President Abraham Lincoln suspended *habeas corpus* during the Civil War in order to imprison Confederate sympathizers suspected of attempting to undermine the Union government. Lincoln defended his actions to a joint session of Congress on July 4, 1861, declaring: "[A]re all the laws but one to go unexecuted, and the Government itself go to pieces, lest that one be violated?"[37] Lincoln clearly believed his actions were warranted by his oath to "preserve, protect and defend" the Constitution, gambling that by violating one law, he could save the rest. Arguably, the U.S. naval officers who formulated the decision to conduct unrestricted warfare in 1941 felt the same way. While the decision to conduct unrestricted warfare may have been an illegal order, the decision was *not* unambiguously immoral.

Let there be no doubt: U.S. unrestricted submarine warfare in the Second World War clearly violated the London Submarine Protocol of 1936 and most naval officers understood that. The U.S. submarine force doctrine, first printed and disseminated in April 1939, plainly stated that unrestricted submarine warfare would only be approved "as a last resort."[38] Prewar submarine commanders like Dick Voge even believed they could be hanged as pirates for conducting unrestricted submarine warfare.[39] Such a consideration caused the Pacific Fleet's naval leaders to issue written authorization to their submarine commanders to conduct unrestricted submarine warfare before sending them out on patrol. It was hoped that if they were captured, the signed orders would exculpate the submarine commander from the charge of piracy.[40] No matter what, as Edward L. Beach wrote after the war: "the old cruiser rules . . . were still technically in effect."[41]

However, the senior naval leadership also knew that unrestricted submarine warfare was absolutely necessary if Japan's war machine was to be stopped. If Japan could operate freely in the Pacific Ocean, unconstrained by economic worries, the United States would have no choice but to concentrate its forces and matériel in the Pacific Ocean, instead of focusing on Europe first. The U.S. naval leadership had no doubts: Europe had to be the top priority, while Japan had to be slowed by some means that did not require the full employment of U.S. forces. Faced with the pressing need to interdict Japanese supplies from the very outbreak of hostilities, but constrained by impractical laws, Admiral Stark, Admiral Hart, and Rear Admiral Turner chose to act decisively and courageously.

Afterward, having seen military necessity trump international law in the case of unrestricted submarine warfare, Samuel Flagg Bemis rhetorically queried: "What good is international law?"[42] While Bemis's cynicism is understandable, perhaps he should have accepted the wisdom of Payson S. Wild Jr. and his colleagues at the U.S. Naval War College, who insisted in 1941: "Clinging to obsolete legal formulae does not make for respect for law. On the contrary, it may hasten the end of the effectiveness of law . . . Law unrelated to the facts is not real law at all."[43] For instance, some laws that have been deliberated over for many years continue to exist because they serve to protect both one's personnel and one's enemies—for example, the Geneva Convention's prohibitions regarding prisoners of war. Sensible international law preserves the rule of law and the order of civilized government.

Unfortunately, the conflict between military necessity and the rule of law will probably continue to be relevant in the future. As long as military officers and national leaders are placed in a position where untold numbers of citizens can possibly be saved by violating international law, a moral quandary will continue to exist. Consequently, even if the decision to conduct unrestricted submarine warfare did not carry historical significance, it would still remain relevant to present and future concerns.

The Victory of Unrestricted Submarine Warfare

The smoke had not even begun to clear over Pearl Harbor when Admiral Hart and Admiral Stark issued their orders to destroy all Japanese shipping. These orders turned out to be more easily transmitted than executed, however. For the first year of the war, the U.S. submarine force was continually hampered by malfunctioning torpedoes, timid commanders, and improper doctrine.

OVERCOMING INTERWAR PROBLEMS

The most vexing and complicated problem facing the U.S. submarine force turned out to be the submariners' own torpedoes. Just before the war began, the Navy's Bureau of Ordnance revealed its top-secret warhead for the Mark XIV steam-driven torpedo: the Mark VI magnetic exploder. By all accounts, the designed weapon was remarkable. The warhead sensed the magnetic field around an enemy ship and was designed to detonate at the point of maximum magnetism directly underneath the target. The resulting detonation of over six hundred pounds of explosive would snap the target's keel like a toothpick.[1]

But unbeknownst to the submariners, as both a cost-saving measure and a misguided effort to maintain secrecy, the Bureau of Ordnance never live-tested the Mark VI warhead. Instead, the Bureau of Ordnance presented the warhead to the U.S. submarine force and claimed the torpedoes would need only one shot to work against a target. As it was, submariners could fire six shots directly at a target, and the torpedoes still would not work. Instead, torpedoes, weighed down by the magnetic exploder, would run too deep, explode prematurely because of the intense magnetic field of the target, or fail to explode if they reached a target. The magnetic exploder was at fault for the first two shortcomings, while faulty contact exploder pins were responsible for the last problem. Consequently, American submariners would pursue daring attacks, only to see their torpedo wakes bubble under a target or prematurely detonate, giving away their position.[2]

Worse than the failure of the U.S. torpedoes was the reaction of the Bureau of Ordnance, which steadfastly insisted that the problem was not the Mark VI exploder but the aim of American submariners. Eventually, submarine force leaders were compelled to carry out their own tests using fishing nets, underwater cliffs, and cherry pickers. At the forefront was the naval officer who became the commander of the Pacific Fleet's Submarine Force from February 1943 until the end of the war, Vice Admiral Charles A. Lockwood. Throughout the war, Lockwood and his staff doggedly pursued the torpedo problem, discovering the depth excursion defect, pulling the magnetic exploder out of service, and eventually determining that the contact exploder was improperly constructed as well. But although Lockwood and his staff eventually fixed the torpedoes, it was a painfully prolonged process. Not until October 1943, over *twenty-one months* after the start of hostilities, could American submariners put to sea and know that their torpedoes would actually work.[3] Even so, a few torpedo problems continued to plague the American submarine force for the rest of the war, including a problem with circular runs that may have been responsible for as many as eight U.S. submarines sunk with all hands.[4]

The torpedo problem was the most serious issue facing the submarine force, but it was hardly the only one. As previously noted, timid commanders and unrealistic tactics forged in the interwar period constrained the submarine force just as much as the terrible torpedoes. When the test of war came, neither the tactics nor the commanders shaped up. Some U.S. submarine commanders simply could not handle the stress of combat. Others were relieved out of hand for lack of aggressiveness. American submariners were forced to reinvent their tactics and learn how to fight *while in combat*—an unenviable task for any combatant. A new breed of younger and more aggressive American sub commanders eventually proved equal to the task.[5]

Without a doubt, the one submarine commander who most instilled aggressiveness and tenacity into the U.S. submarine force was Dudley W. "Mush" Morton. Nicknamed "Mush" after a fellow Kentuckian in the *Moon Mullins* comic strip, Morton had been a football star at the U.S. Naval Academy, graduating in the class of 1930. After being relieved from command of the troubled USS *Dolphin* in 1942, Morton had been on his way out of the submarine force when fate and Captain John H. "Babe" Brown intervened.[6] Brown picked Morton to replace USS *Wahoo*'s first commanding officer, who had not shown the aggressiveness necessary for submarine warfare. At the time, Brown could only explain his decision by pointing to Morton's gridiron performance and his satisfaction with "the way Morton shakes hands."[7]

Starting in January 1943, Morton's ferocity transformed U.S. submarine warfare. He audaciously took *Wahoo* into a Japanese-controlled harbor in Wewak, New Guinea, using only an enlarged almanac map as his chart. Although he was in shallow water, Morton attacked a Japanese destroyer, sinking her at point blank-range with a bow shot. Later in the patrol, he daringly attacked and destroyed an entire convoy, earning *Wahoo* a broomstick for a "clean sweep." Out of torpedoes, and finding another convoy, Morton once more attempted to strike using only his small deck gun. His plan derailed when the convoy's destroyer discovered him and shelled *Wahoo*, which barely escaped.[8] This sort of tenacity and determination inspired the entire submarine force. After the war, Edward L. Beach praised Morton: "more than any other man . . . [he] showed the way to the brethren of the Silent Service."[9]

When Morton was killed in October 1943, after ten months in combat, he had sunk a confirmed total of 19 ships, making him the second-top U.S. submarine ace of the war. He earned four Navy Crosses. His training heavily influenced his executive officer and the future leading U.S. submarine ace of the war, Dick O'Kane, as well as other highly aggressive and successful submarine commanders and officers.[10]

Men like Morton energized the submarine force, but new and reliable equipment was necessary as well. In addition to the improved Mark XIV torpedoes, new types of torpedoes were developed, including the wakeless Mark XVIII electric torpedo and the acoustic Mark XXVII torpedo.[11] In the last years of the war, new types of equipment began to enter the submarine force, giving the Americans even more of an edge over the Japanese. This technological superiority included the new SJ radar and its plan position indicator, the improved Target Bearing Transmitter, and a bathythermograph to find thermal layers, allowing U.S. submarines to evade Japanese sonar.[12]

DECISIVE VICTORY

As a result of the myriad equipment and leadership problems plaguing the U.S. submarine force, American submariners did not get much of a chance to shine during the first year of the war. At the end of 1942, U.S. submarines had only sunk 180 ships in return for 7 American submarines. It was a start, but given that the number of Japanese ships sunk by all U.S. submarines equaled the number of Allied ships sunk by German U-boats in only two months of 1942, it was disappointing.[13]

But even this small start was enough, because the Japanese displayed an attitude regarding their merchant marine that can be only described as staggeringly nonchalant, inept, and incompetent. At the beginning of the war, Japan only had about 6 million tons of merchant shipping, and of that, only 525,000 tons of tankers. And even though Japan went to war over raw materials in Southeast Asia, the Japanese military command saw no inherent contradiction in requisitioning almost two-thirds of Japan's merchant marine solely for military transportation and supplies. Thus, just as the war began, Japanese military leaders had already drastically cut the vital importation of raw materials with which to supply the Japanese war machine and economy. Moreover, Japan's leaders spared little thought to building up Japan's merchant marine. And the ships that were afloat were used so inefficiently that they might as well have been on the bottom: empty merchant ships passed empty merchant ships, heading toward ports the other had just left. If that was not enough, the Japanese Navy ignored the issue of commerce protection, disregarding the lessons of the First World War and interwar Japanese submarine exercises. Consequently, despite the numerous troubles plaguing the U.S. submarine force, the amount of Japanese tonnage sunk in 1942 exceeded the amount constructed.[14]

In 1943 the momentum began to shift even more to the U.S. submarine force thanks to aggressive commanders such as Mush Morton and the correction of the numerous torpedo problems. At the end of 1943, 335 ships had been sunk in exchange for 15 submarines. The Japanese, however, had focused on one important slice of their tonnage that U.S. submarines had not made enough of a dent in—oil tonnage. Admittedly, the Japanese started off the war with pitifully few tankers, but Japan's shipbuilding industry quickly ramped up to supply more. Despite rising success by U.S. submarines, the Japanese *were* able to replace their tanker losses in both 1942 and 1943.[15] One reason why Japan's tanker fleet seemed to remain relatively unscathed was the U.S. torpedo problem: tankers were hard targets to sink, and even being holed by an unexploded torpedo was no great emergency. Indeed, Japanese merchant mariners claimed that "a tanker would not sink if torpedoed."[16] If the Japanese believed their momentary success with tankers was decisive, however, they were completely mistaken: Japan still lost twice as much shipping as it constructed in 1943.[17]

At the start of 1944, Japan's leaders finally began to awaken to the mortal danger they had been in since the beginning of the war. Ironically, Japan's awakening was probably slowed by the miserable performance of American torpedoes, which lulled Japanese naval leaders into a false sense of security regarding the apparent impotence of U.S. submarines. Toward the end of 1943, Japanese naval leaders suddenly "realized that some innovation had come to the American torpedoes . . . [and the] sinking rate of our torpedoed ships suddenly began to increase."[18] The Japanese finally began systematic convoying in March 1944 and attempted to establish and provision an effective antisubmarine force, but it was too little and too late. Even if the resources had been present to create such an effective antisubmarine force, the rest of the Japanese military would have greedily seized those resources, as they did with the few air components of the Japanese antisubmarine effort. Consequently, 1944 turned out to be the halcyon year of the U.S. submarine force. Finally equipped with reliable torpedoes and equipment, as well as experienced crews, U.S. submarines chewed into the Japanese. American submariners sank 603 ships in 1944 at the cost of 19 U.S. submarines. Significantly, the submarine force annihilated the Japanese tanker fleet, quadrupling the number of tankers sunk. By the beginning of 1945, virtually no oil from the oil fields in Southeast Asia, for which Japan had gone to war, was reaching the home islands.[19]

As 1945 went on, American submarines found fewer and fewer targets left to sink. In a quest for what remained of Japanese shipping, Admiral Lockwood approved Operation BARNEY, the invasion of the mined Sea of Japan by submarines specially equipped with anti-mine sonar. But even that once protected haven had little shipping to sink. By the end of the war, Japan had only 700,000 tons of "serviceable" merchant tonnage remaining.[20]

The U.S. submarine force achieved its mission to strangle Japan with devastating efficiency. By the end of the war, U.S. submarines had sunk 1,113 Japanese merchant ships and 201 warships. That amounted to 4,779,902 tons of enemy commerce and 540,192 tons of naval warships. The commerce figures were particularly impressive, since Japan had started the war with only 6,337,000 tons of commercial shipping. In terms of casualties, the Japanese lost virtually their entire prewar merchant marine: out of 122,000 sailors, 27,000 were killed and 89,000 were wounded or "otherwise incapacitated."[21]

But the true effectiveness of the U.S. submarine blockade did not lie at sea. The blockade severely affected the Japanese military throughout the Pacific, as well as the Japanese population on the home islands. In particular, the U.S. unrestricted campaign dramatically reduced the nutritional intake of most Japanese soldiers and civilians. Starvation, and related illnesses such as beriberi, "became the major cause of death among fighting men" in Japan's overseas holdings.[22] On the home islands, the Japanese population felt the pangs of hunger from a very early stage of the war. Even before U.S. bombers destroyed Japanese industrial centers, a large percentage of the Japanese work force suffered from malnutrition and related illnesses. By the end of the war, the food situation was so bad that authorities in Osaka recommended that Japanese civilians add items like acorns, rose leaves, silkworm cocoons, grasshoppers, and even sawdust to their diet. The Japanese government issued dishonest radio bulletins advising the Japanese people that fishbone ash had nutritional value. Even after the surrender, as many as six people a day died from starvation in just one homeless center in Tokyo. In October 1945 the Japanese minister of finance told the United Press that as many as 10 million people would starve to death without immediate U.S. food aid. Although this number was "exaggerated," it reflected Japan's desperate situation. The exact toll on the Japanese military and population due to starvation and privation during and immediately after the war may never be fully known, but the number is probably staggering.[23]

Whatever the exact number of casualties caused by the U.S. submarine campaign, the Japanese had no illusions about the ultimate cause of their defeat. Directly after Japan surrendered, the Japanese cabinet reported to the Diet that "the greatest cause of defeat was the loss of shipping."[24] This was a remarkable admission given the Japanese Navy's extraordinary ineptitude and nonchalance towards antisubmarine warfare. The submarine blockade against Japan was so successful that submarine historian Clay Blair later claimed: "[M]any experts concluded that the invasions of the Palaus, the Philippines, Iwo Jima, and Okinawa, and the dropping of fire bombs and atomic bombs on Japanese cities were unnecessary. They reasoned that despite the fanatical desire of some Japanese to hang on and fight to the last man, the submarine blockade alone would have ultimately defeated that suicidal impulse."[25] Blair's "experts" were perhaps exaggerating the potential windfalls of the submarine campaign, but few people, on either side of the war, could argue that U.S. submarines were devastatingly effective. Mark Parillo, the foremost academic expert on the Japanese merchant marine in the Second World War, wrote: "The submarine had stopped Japan's industrial heart from beating by severing its arteries, and it did so well before the bomber ruptured the organ itself."[26]

The American victory is even more remarkable given the small size of the U.S. submarine force. Including all rear-echelon personnel, the submarine force amounted to only 50,000 officers and men, about 1.6 percent of the entire U.S. Navy personnel. Out of those 50,000, only 16,000 men actually went to sea. Of those 16,000 submariners, 3,500 never returned, amounting to a 22 percent casualty rate, the highest of any combat branch in the U.S. Armed Forces during the Second World War. And yet, despite the high casualty rate and extremely low number of personnel serving in the U.S. submarine force, American submarines sank 55 percent of all Japanese ships in the Second World War.[27] In terms of sheer decisiveness and cost-effectiveness, it is hard to argue with the conclusions of Japanese naval historian Masanori Ito, who wrote: "U.S submarines . . . proved to be the most potent weapon . . . in the Pacific War."[28]

AN UNRESTRICTED WAR

The U.S. submarine victory over Japan was unambiguous. But the victory did not have clearly defined limits of acceptable behavior. If anything, unrestricted submarine warfare sometimes became truly unrestricted.

One oft-repeated maxim of military history is that a military force fights as it trains. The U.S. submarine force had never trained for unrestricted warfare. Without having prepared for the war they ended up fighting, the submarine force had no guidance about the limits of unrestricted warfare. Dick Voge, prewar commander of USS *Sealion*, wrote of his surprise at receiving the unexpected orders to conduct unrestricted submarine warfare: "This directive hadn't been expected. It was as startling as the Japanese attack . . . The submarines were not caught napping—they were ready for war, or as ready as the peace time ships of a peace loving nation can be. But it was a war of their own conception, an orthodox, *an ethical war* that they were prepared to fight . . . Neither by training nor indoctrination were the submarines prepared to wage unrestricted warfare."[29] Dick Voge's words were revealing. He did not expect unrestricted submarine warfare, and he emphasized that it was not the "ethical" form of warfare he had trained for. Although the U.S. submarine force would grow to fully embrace this new mission, the submarine force leaders made little effort at casting the unrestricted war as an "ethical" war.

After the attack at Pearl Harbor, U.S. submariners eagerly accepted their orders to conduct unrestricted warfare. Clay Blair recorded: "There were no moral qualms at Pearl Harbor. 'On the contrary,' Weary Wilkins said later, 'I was cheered by the order.' Said Barney Sieglaff, duty officer on the *Tautog*, 'After the carnage at Pearl Harbor—a sneak attack—who could have moral qualms about killing Japanese? Every ship they had, combat or merchant, was engaged in the war effort one way or the other.'"[30]

Even though the submariners accepted their orders, unrestricted warfare remained technically illegal. Consequently, the very first submarine to depart Pearl Harbor on a war patrol carried written authorization to conduct unrestricted submarine warfare. Although the U.S. submarine force chain of command eventually stopped issuing these letters, the letters emphasized the murky legal and ethical nature of unrestricted warfare.[31] Moreover, neither the U.S. Navy's leadership nor its judge advocate general legally sanctioned the unrestricted war in the Pacific. In April 1944 the Navy reissued its 1941 *Instructions for the Navy of the United States Governing Maritime and Aerial Warfare*, with revisions that had been made during hostilities. Amazingly, despite the fact that American submarines had been conducting unrestricted warfare for almost two and a half years, the 1944 *Instructions* continued to insist that the U.S. Navy and its submarine force were bound by Article 22 of the London Naval Treaty of 1930. A perplexed submariner would have opened the book to the same pages as the 1941 edition to find *that nothing had changed.*[32] In short, American submariners were conducting a form of warfare that was plainly in violation of both international law and their own *Instructions for the Navy of the United States.*

Just as the Navy never "legalized" unrestricted submarine warfare, the submarine force leadership set no limits on unrestricted warfare. The unclear limits on unrestricted submarine warfare were illustrated by an incident in late 1943 concerning one of the top U.S. submarine aces of the war, Lieutenant

Commander Slade D. Cutter. In command of USS *Seahorse,* Cutter followed the letter of his operational orders to sink all Japanese shipping by destroying a number of Japanese sampans that crossed his path. The experience left him disgusted. After sinking three sampans in three days, with no survivors, Cutter swore off sinking the defenseless fishing boats, recalling later: "It was just too much, and I said, 'Goddamn it, I'm not going to do this any more.'"[33]

With the patrol over, Cutter reported to Admiral Lockwood, the commander, Submarine Force, U.S. Pacific Fleet. Cutter asked Lockwood for clarification on what to do about the sampans. Lockwood, usually known for his decisiveness, oddly chose to equivocate, and told Cutter, "Slade, let your conscience be your guide."[34]

The *Pinocchio*-style answer left Cutter to make up his own mind, and he sided with his feeling that sinking the sampans was murder. As he recalled later, with satisfaction, "we never bothered any more. I never fired a gun again."[35]

Cutter epitomized the view many submariners held toward unrestricted warfare, which seemed to regard the only legitimate targets as ships one could sink with torpedoes. Cutter explained his rationale after the war, pointing out that sinking enemy freighters and tankers hurt the Japanese war effort far more than sinking sampans: "Well, when we sank a ship with torpedoes, we were sinking a target, and that hurt the enemy. And I don't think that sinking those fishing boats hurt the enemy. It was just hurting some people, the few fish that they were going to take in to feed some people that were already starving to death or that were hard up. But it wasn't hurting their war effort. I didn't think it would contribute anything to the war effort. If you sink a ship, you do, particularly in the traffic lanes going to Saipan and Southeast Asia down to New Guinea and the Philippines—that hurt."[36] Significantly, Cutter's operational reasoning directly tied into the strategic needs that had prompted U.S. unrestricted warfare in the first place. The U.S. unrestricted war, after all, was meant to cut off Japanese trade, not to slaughter fishermen. But Cutter was forced to come up with this rationale for himself. His chain of command provided little or no guidance.

Other submarine commanders developed their own rationales regarding sampans. Some chose to avoid the fishing craft, whether because of moral qualms or simply because they had bigger fish to fry. Other commanders, however, frequently targeted sampans. In some cases, submarine commanders justified their attacks by evaluating the fishermen as actively aiding the Japanese war effort with their catches. Other submarine commanders felt that any and every Japanese ship sunk ended the war that much sooner. Regardless of the rationale, however, U.S. submarine attacks on sampans left few, if any, survivors.[37]

Based on Slade Cutter's experience with Admiral Lockwood, the differing treatment of Japanese sampans, and the completely unhelpful guidance in the *Instructions for the Navy of the United States,* the exact limits of unrestricted warfare remained ambiguous for submariners throughout the war. Such a state of affairs left individual submarine commanders as the arbiters of the limits of unrestricted warfare. Unsurprisingly, at least one submarine commander chose to take unrestricted submarine warfare to its logical extreme.

THE LOGICAL EXTREME OF UNRESTRICTED SUBMARINE WARFARE

On January 26, 1943, during a dogged and intense action, USS *Wahoo,* under the command of Lieutenant Commander Dudley W. "Mush" Morton, surfaced amid the shipwrecked survivors of the transport *Buyo Maru.* Pausing to recharge batteries, Morton idled in the vicinity of what he estimated to be almost 10,000 Japanese troops who had just abandoned their sinking ship. He ordered his crew to shoot at the survivors and their lifeboats.[38]

Morton's actions have since been discussed, often in passing, in both histories and fiction dealing with submarine warfare during the Second World War. In one sense, Morton's actions were a solitary blemish upon the history of the submarine force and an ugly stain on the reputation of one of the greatest American submariners of the war. At the same time, the incident was emblematic of the ambiguities associated with unrestricted submarine warfare, because Morton rationalized his actions as being entirely consistent with his mission.

As previously noted, Mush Morton was perhaps the most important submarine commander in the U.S. Navy. His executive officer, and the future leading U.S. submarine ace of the war, Dick O'Kane, eulogized Morton as "the captain who shook off the shackles and set the pace" for the entire submarine force.[39] Unfortunately, there was a dark side to Mush Morton's greatness. As Edward L. Beach put it: "Morton felt that the destruction of the Japanese merchant marine was his own private job."[40] Morton did not merely want to sink enemy shipping, however. He also wanted to kill his Japanese adversaries. Throughout *Wahoo,* he posted placards that read "SHOOT THE SUNZA BITCHES." When Morton sailed into Pearl Harbor after his first successful war patrol, not only did he have a broom lashed to his scope to signify a "clean sweep," but he also had a pennant that read "SHOOT THE SUNZA BITCHES" dangling aft of his periscopes.[41] The submarine force was generally aggressive about sinking merchant ships, but Morton's focus on actually shooting Japanese was unusual, since most submarine commanders avoided surface gunfire when possible.[42]

On January 26, 1943, Morton's hatred meshed with his mission of unrestricted submarine warfare. Dick O'Kane later recalled that Morton's justification was directly tied to *Wahoo's* mission to interdict enemy personnel and supplies: "Dick . . . the army bombards strategic areas, and the air corps uses area-bombing so the ground forces can advance. Both bring civilian casualties. Now without other casualties, I will prevent these soldiers from getting ashore, for every one who does can mean an American life."[43] Under the logic of unrestricted warfare, inanimate goods and soldiers on board ship were lawful targets because upon reaching shore they would directly aid the enemy war effort. Just as *Wahoo* prevented Japanese supplies and personnel from reaching their destination by sinking transports and merchant ships, Morton chose to ensure that the troops in the water would not be of any further assistance to the Japanese war machine.

Morton's rationale had a chilling logic to it. Even sixty years later, naval personnel used the rationale of unrestricted submarine warfare to justify Morton's actions. One Navy commentator wrote:

> This controversy seems to hinge on one major point: the "defenseless survivor" status of the troops . . . [but] the individual soldier was just as defenseless and powerless to prevent the *Wahoo's* attack while in his bunk on board ship as he was in the boats . . .
> . . . These men still constituted a threat, one that could not be mitigated, and therefore needed to be eliminated. Anything less would have been a dereliction of duty. That left Morton with one choice, the same choice that he had when he first sighted the ship: kill them.[44]

Another Navy writer pointed out that "if indeed the survivors were headed ashore to regain the fight, it can be argued that they were still combatants engaged in the larger context of battle."[45] Morton apparently believed so. His actions were the logical extreme of unrestricted submarine warfare.

However, Morton did *not* attack defenseless Japanese troops. He actually shot at friendly prisoners of war. The *Buyo Maru* survivors were not part of "Hirohito's crack Imperial Marine outfit" but rather British Indian prisoners of war from the 2nd Battalion, 16th Punjab Regiment, captured in the fall of Singapore. There *were* some Japanese troops in the water, but they were mostly garrison troops from the 26th Field Ordnance Depot.[46] That Morton shot at friendly prisoners of war generally remained unknown for over fifty years, until James F. DeRose learned of the story of the *Buyo Maru* from the Japanese Diet Library for his history of Morton and the submarine force, *Unrestricted Warfare* (2000).[47]

Fortunately, the Americans' aim and numerical perception was as poor as their identification skills. Morton and his crew claimed there were 10,000 soldiers in the water and Morton wrote: "We destroyed all the boats and most of the troops."[48] Such claims led Edwin Hoyt to pen that "hundreds, perhaps thousands of" the survivors were killed.[49] The actual number was much lower. A total of 1,126 men had been embarked on the *Buyo Maru* and some were undoubtedly killed when the transport sank. But between the torpedo attack, Morton's gunfire, fighting between the two sets of soldiers in the water, and drownings, only 195 Indian troops and 87 Japanese soldiers died.[50]

At the time, Morton's actions were greeted by silence from the submarine force leadership. Perhaps it was because Morton's patrol had been otherwise so spectacularly successful that the submarine force did not wish to impugn the reputation of its only shining star. After all, for a service that had seen a heartbreaking year of torpedo failures and skipper timidity, Mush Morton's success was a breath of desperately needed fresh air. More likely, however, it was the fact that Morton's patrol took place while the Pacific Fleet Submarine Force was undergoing a temporary leadership gap. The previous ComSubPac, Rear Admiral Robert English, had been killed in an airplane accident shortly after *Wahoo* went on patrol, and his successor, Rear Admiral Charles A. Lockwood, did not assume command until after *Wahoo* had returned to Pearl Harbor to a hero's welcome. During that time, Captain "Babe" Brown temporarily filled in as ComSubPac, but he hardly could have been expected to challenge the actions of the very man whom he had handpicked to command *Wahoo*.[51]

Decades later, however, Clay Blair condemned Morton's actions as "cold-blooded murder and repugnant."[52] That Morton was never censured, Blair asserted, represented "tacit approval from the submarine high command."[53] Of course, Blair noted that the submarine force leadership never issued any policy statements regarding shipwrecked troops or other survivors, which meant "whether other skippers should follow Morton's example was left up to the individual. Few did."[54]

Morton's "massacre" should rightly be labeled as a direct consequence of the decision to conduct unrestricted submarine warfare. Although Mush Morton might well have shot at the survivors of *Buyo Maru* even if he had sunk the troop ship in compliance with cruiser rules of warfare, it seems more likely that he felt the submarine force's mission of unrestricted warfare authorized his actions. Moreover, as far as Morton's *Instructions for the Navy of the United States* were concerned, he was already guilty of gross violations of international law. As one later commentator wrote: "Don't forget that unrestricted warfare itself ran contrary to international law . . . While Morton's actions were illegal (outside international law), they were nowhere near as straightforward or as serious as the crimes committed at My Lai or Son Thang."[55] Having metaphorically thrown the rules of naval warfare "overboard," as Dick Voge later phrased it, the U.S. Navy should not have been surprised when one of its commanders chose to take his mission to its logical extreme.

The Navy's refusal to change its *Instructions for the Navy of the United States,* as well as Admiral Lockwood's unhelpful clarification of the limits of unrestricted submarine warfare, created the conditions for an extreme form of unrestricted submarine warfare. Admittedly, Morton's actions occurred before the Navy reissued the *Instructions* and Admiral Lockwood assumed command of Pacific Fleet's submarine force. But by refusing to explicitly address the legality and limits of unrestricted submarine warfare, the U.S. Navy and its submarine force inculcated an unhealthy command climate of moral ambiguity that permitted incidents like the *Buyo Maru* massacre.

After the war, Rear Admiral Richard Voge devoted five pages to defending the decision to conduct unrestricted warfare, in the official operational history of the U.S. submarine force in the Second World War. His arguments underscored the ambiguous legality and morality of unrestricted warfare. Even though the decision had been necessary to defeat Japan, it was still outlawed by international law. More than that, noncombatants had been killed, ashore and afloat.

The U.S. decision to conduct unrestricted warfare did not just mean Japanese noncombatant casualties in the Second World War, however. If anything, the success of U.S. unrestricted submarine warfare opened the door for future unrestricted warfare in other maritime conflicts.

THE END OF ABSOLUTE FREEDOM OF THE SEAS

Due in no small measure to U.S. unrestricted submarine warfare, the Second World War resulted in an Allied victory. But the decision held unintended consequences, such as Mush Morton's "massacre." More important, U.S. unrestricted warfare in the Second World War ended the noncombatant nature of merchant ship sailors and the Wilsonian paradigm of absolute freedom of the seas. Referring to the decision after the Second World War, historian Samuel Flagg Bemis melodramatically wrote: "The Freedom of the Seas sank beneath the Ocean."[56]

One can understand Bemis's distress. After all, every paradigm of freedom of the seas stipulated that any merchant ship, even if a belligerent, was still a noncombatant vessel and therefore could not be sunk without warning.[57] Treaties such as the Washington Submarine Treaty of 1922, the London Naval Treaty of 1930, and the London Submarine Protocol of 1936 all supported this universal view of the noncombatant nature of merchant ships by requiring submarines to conduct cruiser warfare.[58] As a result, despite the events of the First World War, merchant sailors were still considered to be noncombatants as the Second World War began.

By the end of the Second World War, however, sinking a merchant ship without warning and leaving its sailors to drown hardly seemed controversial. Decades after the Second World War, Clay Blair wrote that merchant marine sailors "were not innocent civilian bystanders . . . seamen manning merchant ships were as much warriors as were the German submariners."[59] Although Blair was discussing Allied merchant sailors, his description could be applied to all merchant marine sailors.

Ironically, the United States, which had once gone to war to defend the noncombatant status of merchant ship sailors, belligerent or neutral, was the nation that ultimately redefined the status of these sailors. Until the U.S. decision, unrestricted submarine warfare remained illegal and constrained to acts of reprisal.[60] By conducting unrestricted submarine warfare without provocation, the United States implicitly legitimized the entire German unrestricted submarine campaign and irrevocably tore away the noncombatant status of civilian sailors. Henceforth, civilian sailors on merchant ships would be legitimate targets.

RESURGENCE OF THE INTERWAR PARADIGM

Despite the experience of the Second World War, the paradigm of the interwar treaties has not yet died. After the war, the Nuremberg tribunal insisted that the 1936 London Submarine Protocol was still in effect. In fact, without any new treaties to override it, the protocol is still in effect today, as illustrated by the *San Remo Manual on International Law Applicable to Armed Conflicts at Sea.* Created by a nongovernmental group under the sponsorship of the Institute of Humanitarian Law, the *San Remo Manual* is the most recent attempt to codify belligerent and neutral rights in time of war. One of its provisions states that submarines are bound to the same rules regarding merchant ships as aircraft and surface ships. In the explanatory notes, the legal and naval experts who drafted the manual specifically note that the London Submarine Protocol of 1936 is still in effect: submarines must carry out cruiser rules of warfare by visiting, searching, and capturing merchant ships. As if the attempts of the *San Remo Manual* to turn back the clock were not astonishing enough, even more astonishing is the date when the *San Remo Manual* was released: *1994,* almost five decades after the Second World War.[61]

To be fair, the *San Remo Manual* does set conditions under which belligerent merchant ships may be attacked as military targets. Among the activities that would result in a loss of noncombatant status are the following:

(b) acting as an auxiliary to an enemy's armed forces, e.g. carrying troops or replenishing warships . . .

(d) sailing under convoy of enemy warships or military aircraft;

(e) refusing an order to stop or actively resisting visit, search or capture;

(f) being armed to an extent that they could inflict damage to a warship; this excludes light individual weapons for the defence of personnel, e.g. against pirates, and purely deflective systems such as 'chaff';

or

(g) otherwise making an effective contribution to military action, e.g., carrying military materials.[62]

In the case of neutral merchant ships, the rules are very similar, except for the clause regarding armament. No matter what, however, a belligerent has to confirm that the neutral ship is actively supporting the military effort of an enemy before treating it as a military target.[63]

The legal and naval experts who helped draft the manual noted that the provision regarding armed merchant ships was difficult to draft. Some drafters wanted to permit merchant ships to be able to carry defensive weapons, but the naval experts countered that most defensive weapons could be turned to offensive purposes.[64] Eventually, the drafters agreed to ban everything but small arms, which could be used to repel pirates: "[I]n light of modern weapons, it is impossible to determine, if it ever was possible, whether the armament on merchant ships is to be used offensively or defensively. It is unrealistic to expect enemy forces to be able to make that determination. *Enemy merchant ships which are armed to the extent that they could damage any warship, including a submarine, may be attacked on sight.*"[65] At last, over seventy years after the end of the First World War, the recommendations of the U.S. Navy had finally been incorporated into a code of international law: armed merchant ships are legitimate military targets that can be attacked without warning.

And yet the rules are hardly practical. In the case of unarmed merchant ships, would a nuclear submarine commander actually give up his greatest asset, stealth, in order to carry out the rules of visit, search, and capture? Moreover, although modern nuclear submarines are larger and carry more personnel than their diesel-electric predecessors, few submarines can spare the crew to man a prize.

Submarines are not the only type of platform that may have problems with the *San Remo Manual*. In a peculiar explanatory note, the *San Remo Manual* admits that it "*was*" impossible for fixed-wing aircraft to conduct visit and search.[66] Unfortunately, the *San Remo Manual* does not explain how this particular situation has changed, if at all. Since most modern militaries hardly use seaplanes, it seems safe to say that it is still impossible for fixed-wing aircraft to conduct visit and search.

Regardless of what the *San Remo Manual* of 1994 says, unrestricted submarine warfare is here to stay. While acknowledging that the London Submarine Protocol is still technically the law of the land, Samuel Flagg Bemis wrote that the protocol is law "only in the thinnest stratosphere of reality."[67] During the Nuremberg trials, Fleet Admiral Chester W. Nimitz declared that the United States would probably wage unrestricted submarine warfare in future naval wars, based on its success in the Pacific War.[68] After Nimitz's testimony, another naval officer, Lieutenant Commander William H. Barnes, argued that "commerce and trade are now so identified with military power in total warfare that merchant ships, armed or unarmed, are in effect warships to be attacked and sunk without warning."[69]

A PACIFIC WAR WITHOUT UNRESTRICTED SUBMARINE WARFARE

Did history have to turn out this way? To answer such a question requires posing the counterfactual question: What would have happened if the United States had not immediately conducted unrestricted submarine warfare on December 7, 1941?

Although the policymakers in Washington probably did not know it as they issued their orders, Japan had already begun unrestricted submarine warfare within minutes of the Pearl Harbor attack, by sinking the unarmed merchant ship *Cynthia Olson*. In hindsight, this attack did not matter since the United States had planned to conduct unrestricted warfare no matter what the Japanese did. If the United States had not planned to conduct unrestricted warfare, the sinking of *Cynthia Olson* would certainly have been sufficient cause for the United States to declare unrestricted submarine warfare in reprisal for the Japanese action.[70]

What if Japan had *not* immediately conducted unrestricted submarine warfare and the United States had not planned unrestricted warfare? The published submarine force doctrine gives a hint of how the U.S. submarine force might have acted in a war bound by treaty limitations. Due to the threat of armed merchant ships, the submarine force doctrine prohibited submarines from even attempting visit and search against a merchant ship found alone. The doctrine did allow surprise attacks on merchant ships traveling in convoys or clearly armed merchant ships, as well as enemy troopships.[71] Ironically, this doctrine would have been ideal for the Japanese, because Japanese naval authorities made no consistent or concerted effort at forming convoys or providing convoy protection until March 1944. Since this would have meant that most ships would have traveled alone, and hence would not have been legitimate targets for unrestricted submarine warfare or even attempts at cruiser warfare, prewar U.S. submarine doctrine would have allowed a number of merchant ships to slip by.[72] Furthermore, the Japanese might have figured out that American doctrine prohibited attacks against single unarmed merchant ships, and exploited this weakness. In short, under the restrictive rules of the U.S. submarine force prewar doctrine, commerce warfare might have been virtually impossible.

If the Japanese supply lines had remained generally untouched, then the war in the Pacific might have been quite different. U.S. Marines and Army units would have made amphibious landings against well-supplied enemy islands. As it was, landings against Japanese garrisons at Tarawa and Iwo Jima were costly enough without giving Japanese troops the advantage of relatively uninterrupted supply lines. If unrestricted submarine warfare had not severed the supply lines of the Japanese war machine, the war in the Pacific might have stretched on far longer, and might never have been decisively resolved. It seems highly improbable that the American people or their political and military leadership would have accepted this state of affairs.

This is as far, however, as this counterfactual exercise can reasonably go. History is filled with contingencies that could have created an entirely different chain of events. What if submarines had been successfully abolished after the First World War? What if the interwar treaties had been drafted to prohibit armed merchant ships? What if the United States had stood up for its neutral rights, as in the First World War, instead of implicitly legitimizing German unrestricted warfare in a combat area? What if the recommendations of the General Board had been carried out and the *Instructions for the Navy of the United States* had included more specific injunctions against unrestricted warfare? What if the United States had somehow avoided war with Japan, thus negating the entire need for an economic war of attrition in the Far East? Exactly how history might have turned out if any one of these possibilities occurred simply beggars the imagination.

It seems safe to say, however, that the United States would eventually have waged unrestricted submarine warfare against Japan. Given the strategic realities facing the United States and the capabilities of the U.S. Navy in 1941, the total defeat of Japan hinged upon winning an economic campaign of attrition. To win such a campaign against the naval might of Japan required the use of unrestricted submarine warfare. While the U.S. decision to conduct unrestricted submarine warfare did not necessarily have to happen on December 7, 1941, or in the manner that it did, it would eventually have happened.

Conclusion

With the passage of so many years since the Second World War, it may be difficult to understand how unrestricted submarine warfare could have been considered so controversial and despicable before the United States entered the war. And yet, the United States did go to war in 1917 over unrestricted submarine warfare, and during two subsequent decades national and military leaders repeated numerous high-minded statements that nothing could be more foreign to the American notion of freedom of the seas than unrestricted warfare. But within one day, the United States abruptly turned about from that position and waged a determined and pitiless maritime war against Japan that ended only in the destruction of Japan's merchant marine. For that reason alone, the U.S. decision to conduct unrestricted submarine warfare remains an important moment in history.

Understandably, the deaths of civilian mariners have not received the attention they deserve. After all, the Second World War targeted and killed civilians on a scale never before seen in history, with a body count of at least 40 million civilians. That number is at least twice as many as the number of soldiers killed in all nations. Compared with the massive number of civilians killed during the Nazi Holocaust, the Japanese conquest of China and Southeast Asia, or the merciless war in Eastern Europe, the deaths caused by the unrestricted submarine warfare may seem insignificant.[1]

But the unrestricted submarine campaigns were arguably among the most dangerous of all the campaigns in the Second World War. The unarmed British merchant marine lost almost 33,000 sailors out of 185,000 who went to sea, a 17 percent fatality rate that proportionally exceeded the fatality rates of any of the British armed services. As noted previously, the Japanese merchant marine was essentially annihilated. Among the submariners, three-quarters of German U-boat sailors never returned, and one out of five U.S. submariners remained on "eternal patrol." While the actual numbers of those killed may seem relatively low, those who did fight in these campaigns had far lower chances of survival than many of their counterparts in other parts of the Second World War.[2]

The true cost of U.S. unrestricted submarine warfare, however, did not lie at sea. Rather, its greatest impact lay ashore, where untold numbers of Japanese soldiers and civilians suffered and died from malnutrition and starvation. The U.S. submarine campaign so successfully interdicted food supplies to the home islands that during the period immediately after the Japanese surrender, the Japanese people relied upon American food shipments to survive. The American unrestricted submarine campaign not only starved Japan of food, but also denied it the materials necessary to make war. Submarine torpedoes sank valuable supplies seized in Southeast Asia, preventing the Japanese military and people from obtaining the very foundations of industry and energy supplies. The dire conditions in Japan at the end of the war are proof of unrestricted submarine warfare's massive impact on Japan and on the course of the Second World War.

The conditions for unrestricted submarine warfare were created during the interwar period by impractical and poorly written naval treaties. One may argue whether outlawing armed merchant ships would have prevented unrestricted submarine warfare in the Second World War. The failure to prohibit armed merchant ships made cruiser warfare impossible, however. The impossibility of cruiser warfare and U.S. neutrality legislation, which ensured the United States would not stand up for its neutral rights, paved the path for German unrestricted submarine warfare. German unrestricted submarine warfare, in turn, though condemned by U.S. leaders like President Roosevelt, created a strategic environment in which U.S. unrestricted submarine warfare seemed permissible.

But the U.S. decision to conduct unrestricted submarine warfare was ultimately predicated on strategic rationale: Japan simply could not wage war without a steady flow of supplies to the home islands and its outlying Pacific outposts. Although the failure of international law and German unrestricted submarine warfare made U.S. unrestricted submarine warfare more permissible, it was the strategic realities of 1941 that made U.S. unrestricted submarine warfare necessary.

Throughout the interwar period, the only Americans who seriously considered the strategic necessity of submarine warfare in any form were the officers of the U.S. Navy. Unlike their civilian counterparts, who considered the question of submarine warfare from an emotional and legal viewpoint, U.S. naval officers professionally studied the issue strategically and realistically. This state of affairs, in which naval officers were the sole evaluators of the strategic necessity for submarine warfare, stretched into the Second World War. Indeed, the chief of naval operations developed Plan Dog, which became the U.S. national military strategy in the Second World War and necessitated unrestricted submarine warfare against Japan.

Given Germany's failure regarding unrestricted submarine warfare in both the First World War and the Second World War, the U.S. unrestricted submarine campaign may not have seemed a wise choice for strategists. But in reality, the two campaigns were fundamentally different. The U.S. campaign consciously exploited Japan's inability to replace its merchant marine, while the Germans found themselves fighting in vain against the phenomenal industrial capability of the United States. Germany also suffered from superior Allied aerial and naval antisubmarine measures, the limited capabilities of German U-boats, and the German Navy's poor geographic position, which required U-boats to brave either the perilous North Sea or the Bay of Biscay. American submarines, in contrast, enjoyed a relatively safe transit to their operating areas, inferior Japanese antisubmarine efforts, and a versatile submarine design that permitted U.S. submarines to conduct long-range patrols for extended periods. Even more important, the United States did not rely solely on the unrestricted submarine campaign to achieve its strategic goals. Rather, the U.S. unrestricted submarine war was just one part of a much larger and cohesive strategy that overwhelmed Japan's defenses.[3]

But while the American strategic decision-making process of the Second World War led to Allied victory, the military's dominance over strategy allowed the Navy to essentially implement unrestricted submarine warfare on its own. The decision to conduct unrestricted warfare was made almost entirely divorced from the civilian chain of command. Just as the U.S. Constitution makes ratified international treaties the supreme law of the land, it also mandates that the military is subservient at all times to the will of the civilian government and populace. In short, while military leaders can formulate, recommend, and carry out policy, it is not their duty or even privilege to make policy.[4] That Admiral Stark and his subordinates developed and implemented a strategy that directly conflicted with the repeated public statements of the president and the State Department should be troubling to any observer of the American civil-military relationship.

Despite the troubling manner in which the United States embarked on unrestricted submarine warfare, the numerous obstacles the U.S. submarine force had to overcome, and the toll that unrestricted submarine warfare took on noncombatants, it is undeniable that unrestricted submarine warfare played a decisive role in defeating Japan. Indeed, unrestricted submarine warfare's impact went far beyond the economic holding action envisioned by Plan Dog, but instead significantly contributed to the overall ORANGE strategy to advance across the Pacific and encircle Japan. As Edward S. Miller concluded: "The old concept of blockade by surface vessels could not have been made effective until late in the war. The decision for undersea predation magnified the success of one of the Orange Plan's most basic prescriptions."[5]

On December 7, 1941, the naval leadership of the United States finalized a decision that had been in process of formulation since the end of the First World War. It was not made on a whim or in reprisal. The U.S. decision to conduct unrestricted submarine warfare reflected the failure of twenty years of international law regarding submarines, thirty years of planning for an ORANGE blockade, and one final year of strategic planning and ethical debate within the U.S. naval service. It was a difficult decision made for strategic reasons that annulled the cherished notions of noncombatant status for civilian mariners and their cargoes. The leaders who made the decision, however, boldly gambled that by forsaking absolute freedom of the seas and recognizing the gritty realities of warfare in the Second World War, they might win a world in which the seas were not at the mercy of the Axis powers. That gamble ultimately paid off.

NOTES

For the ease of other researchers, my citations follow the example of the National Archives citation guide. The breakdown of a citation will normally be:

Document title (normally author to recipient, subject, and date); Folder title (in the case of the State Department records, sometimes just the decimal file number of the document); Box number and title (if any); Subseries; Series title; Subgroup; Record Group (RG) or Personal Paper collection; Archives name and location.

So that researchers will not have to sift through hundreds of notes to find the first citation of a certain source, each chapter stands alone in terms of citations. A researcher need only turn to the beginning of a chapter, not the entire study, to find the full citation for a given source.

The following abbreviations are used for frequently cited archives:

NABW   National Archives Building, Washington, D.C.

NACP   National Archives at College Park, College Park, Md.

NHC   Naval Historical Center

INTRODUCTION

1. This dispatch has often been misquoted as "Execute unrestricted air and submarine warfare against Japan." The correct wording can be seen on two copies of the dispatch, both preserved on microfilm: CNO to CinCPac, Com Panam, CinCAF, Pacific Northern, Pacific Southern, Hawaiian Naval Coastal Frontiers, 072252, December 7, 1941; Operation Orders, December 7, 1941–April 2, 1942; Operations Orders; Box 37; Reel 2; Military Files Series 1; Map Room Army and Navy Messages, December 1941–May 1942; Map Room Files of President Roosevelt, 1939–1945; available on microfilm.

2. Until June 8, 1947, Hawaii was in its own time zone, which was offset from Greenwich Mean Time by ten and a half hours, except for two periods, once in 1933 and again from 1942 to 1945, when Hawaii switched to daylight savings time or war time. Washington, D.C., during this time period was five hours offset from Greenwich Mean Time. For further information, see Thomas G. Shanks, *The American Atlas: Expanded Fifth Edition, U.S. Longitudes & Latitudes, Time Changes and Time Zones* (San Diego: ACS

Publications, 1990), inside front cover, 77, and 107. Similarly, Manila was offset from Greenwich Mean Time by eight hours from 1937 until May 1, 1942. See Thomas G. Shanks, *The International Atlas: Revised Third Edition, World Longitudes & Latitudes, Time Changes and Time Zones* (San Diego: ACS Publications, 1991), 294. Oddly enough, this meant that Pearl Harbor was off from Washington by five and a half hours in 1941, as opposed to only five hours in the present day. Manila was offset from Washington by thirteen hours.

3. Samuel Flagg Bemis, *A Diplomatic History of the United States,* 4th ed. (New York: Henry Holt, 1955), 875.

4. Janet M. Manson, *Diplomatic Ramifications of Unrestricted Submarine Warfare, 1939–1941,* Contributions in Military Studies, No. 104 (New York: Greenwood Press, 1990), 1. Reviewers criticized Manson for this assertion. For instance, see Manfred Jonas, review of *Diplomatic Ramifications of Unrestricted Submarine Warfare, 1939–1941,* by Janet Manson, *American Historical Review* 97, no. 2 (April 1992): 548–549.

5. Manson, *Diplomatic Ramifications of Unrestricted Submarine Warfare,* 6–13, 103–126.

CHAPTER I

1. Samuel Flagg Bemis, *A Diplomatic History of the United States,* 4th ed. (New York: Henry Holt, 1955), 875.

2. Hugo Grotius, *The Free Sea,* trans. Richard Hakluyt, edited and with an introduction by David Armitage, Natural Law and Enlightenment Classics (Indianapolis: Liberty Fund, 2004), 10. Emphasis added.

3. Grotius, *The Free Sea,* 34. For all of Grotius's theoretical argument about the seas, read the fifth chapter of *Mare Liberum.* See Grotius, *The Free Sea,* 20–37. David Armitage helpfully sums up Grotius's argument in his detailed and well-written introduction, ibid., xiv–xvii.

4. Armitage, introduction to Grotius, *The Free Sea,* xvii–xx.

5. Ibid., xiii.

6. Ibid., xiii–xiv.

7. Stephen C. Neff, *The Rights and Duties of Neutrals: A General History* (Manchester: Manchester University Press, 2000), 12, 16. See also W. Arnold-Foster, *The New Freedom of the Seas* (London: Methuen, 1942), 14–15.

8. Neff, *The Rights and Duties of Neutrals,* 29–32. See also Arnold-Foster, *The New Freedom of the Seas,* 15–19; Bemis, *A Diplomatic History of the United States,* 26.

9. Neff, *The Rights and Duties of Neutrals,* 32–34. See also Arnold-Foster, *The New Freedom of the Seas,* 36–37, 41–43.

10. Arnold-Foster, *The New Freedom of the Seas,* 22–23, 33–35.

11. Ibid., 19. See also Bemis, *A Diplomatic History of the United States,* 26.

12. Bemis, *A Diplomatic History of the United States,* 25–26. The congressional committee that drafted the Plan of 1776 included such notable Americans as John Adams, John Dickinson, Benjamin Franklin, Benjamin Harrison, and Robert Morris.

13. Ibid., 29.

14. Ibid., 38–41. See also Captain G. J. Meyers, Maritime Rights in Time of War (ONI)

Sea Supremacy vs. Freedom of the Sea, from Monthly Information Bulletin, Office of Naval Intelligence, January 1929; XLAI, 1930–1934; Box 88, XLAI-XLFG; Intelligence and Technical Archives, RG 8; Archival Records, U.S. Naval War College, Newport, R.I., 26. See also Carlton Savage, Assistant to the Assistant Secretary of State, to the Secretary of State, September 19, 1941, 700.00112 Freedom of the Seas/102, Enclosure: The American Doctrine of Freedom of the Seas, Draft 1; 700.00112 Freedom of the Seas/100—700.00116/447; Box 1770, From: 700:00112 Freedom of the Seas, To: 700.00116 M.E./203; Decimal File, 1940–44; General Records of the Department of State, RG 59; National Archives at College Park, College Park, Md. (hereafter cited as NACP), 1. See also Carlton Savage, Assistant to the Assistant Secretary of State, to the Secretary of State, September 19, 1941, 700.00112 Freedom of the Seas/102, Enclosure: The American Doctrine of Freedom of the Seas, Draft 2; 700.00112 Freedom of the Seas/100—700.00116/447; Box 1770, From: 700:00112 Freedom of the Seas, To: 700.00116 M.E./203; Decimal File, 1940–44; General Records of the Department of State, RG 59; NACP, 1.

15. Bemis, *A Diplomatic History of the United States,* 39–40. For a briefer but similar paraphrasing of these principles, see also Neff, *The Rights and Duties of Neutrals,* 71. See also Carlton Savage, Assistant to the Assistant Secretary of State, to the Secretary of State, September 19, 1941, 700.00112 Freedom of the Seas/102, Enclosure: The American Doctrine of Freedom of the Seas, Draft 1, 1. See also Carlton Savage, Assistant to the Assistant Secretary of State, to the Secretary of State, September 19, 1941, 700.00112 Freedom of the Seas/102, Enclosure: The American Doctrine of Freedom of the Seas, Draft 2, 1.

16. Bemis, *A Diplomatic History of the United States,* 39–40.

17. Neff, *The Rights and Duties of Neutrals,* 71–72. See also Bemis, *A Diplomatic History of the United States,* 40–41; Arnold-Foster, *The New Freedom of the Seas,* 19–20. See also Carlton Savage, Assistant to the Assistant Secretary of State, to the Secretary of State, September 19, 1941, 700.00112 Freedom of the Seas/102, Enclosure: The American Doctrine of Freedom of the Seas, Draft 1, 2. See also Carlton Savage, Assistant to the Assistant Secretary of State, to the Secretary of State, September 19, 1941, 700.00112 Freedom of the Seas/102, Enclosure: The American Doctrine of Freedom of the Seas, Draft 2, 2.

18. Neff, *The Rights and Duties of Neutrals,* 97–99. See also Arnold-Foster, *The New Freedom of the Seas,* 19–30; Bemis, *A Diplomatic History of the United States,* 335–336.

19. Bemis, *A Diplomatic History of the United States,* 120–121, 163–170, 176–179, 335–336. See also Arnold-Foster, *The New Freedom of the Seas,* 22–29.

20. Bemis, *A Diplomatic History of the United States,* 336–337. See also Larry Gara, *The Presidency of Franklin Pierce,* American Presidency Series (Lawrence: University Press of Kansas, 1991), 135–136. To state that historians have generally derided Pierce's administration is to put it mildly. Even other presidents scorned him. Historian Nathan Miller ranked Pierce as the fourth worst president, after Nixon, Harding, and Buchanan, and just ahead of Andrew Johnson, for his lack of "the character, the broad vision, and the political skills to meet [the] challenge [of his times]." See Nathan Miller, *Star-Spangled Men: America's Ten Worst Presidents* (New York: Scribner's, 1998), 151–172.

21. Bemis, *A Diplomatic History of the United States,* 335–336. See also Gara, *The Presidency of Franklin Pierce,* 138–139; Neff, *The Rights and Duties of Neutrals,* 98–99.

22. Bemis, *A Diplomatic History of the United States,* 335–336. See also Gara, *The Presidency of Franklin Pierce,* 138–139; Neff, *The Rights and Duties of Neutrals,* 98–99.

23. Bruce L. Felknor, ed., *The U.S. Merchant Marine at War, 1775–1945* (Annapolis: Naval Institute Press, 1998), 101.

24. For a brief discussion of the catastrophic effect of Confederate raiders like *Alabama* on the U.S. merchant marine, see Felknor, *The U.S. Merchant Marine at War, 1775–1945,* 101. For the diplomatic attempts in the late nineteenth century, see Arnold-Foster, *The New Freedom of the Seas,* 36–37. Among the great powers that voted against the American proposal at the Second Hague Conference were Great Britain, France, Russia, and Japan. See also Bemis, *A Diplomatic History of the United States,* 431, 596.

25. Neff, *The Rights and Duties of Neutrals,* 127–142. See also Bemis, *A Diplomatic History of the United States,* 431, 596; Arnold-Foster, *The New Freedom of the Seas,* 39–59.

26. Patrick Devlin, *Too Proud to Fight: Woodrow Wilson's Neutrality* (London: Oxford University Press, 1974), 156–172. See also Bemis, *A Diplomatic History of the United States,* 597–604; Arnold-Foster, *The New Freedom of the Seas,* 44–59; Neff, *The Rights and Duties of Neutrals,* 136–142.

27. Devlin, *Too Proud to Fight,* 180–186, 191–198. See also Neff, *The Rights and Duties of Neutrals,* 146–159; Bemis, *A Diplomatic History of the United States,* 598–603; Arnold-Foster, *The New Freedom of the Seas,* 44–51.

28. Devlin, *Too Proud to Fight,* 188–191, 198–216. See also Neff, *The Rights and Duties of Neutrals,* 159–161; Bemis, *A Diplomatic History of the United States,* 601–604; Arnold-Foster, *The New Freedom of the Seas,* 51–59.

29. Devlin, *Too Proud to Fight,* 156–172. See also Arnold-Foster, *The New Freedom of the Seas,* 61–64; Carlton Savage, Assistant to the Assistant Secretary of State, to the Secretary of State, September 19, 1941, 700.00112 Freedom of the Seas/102, Enclosure: The American Doctrine of Freedom of the Seas, Draft 1, 5–8. See also Carlton Savage, Assistant to the Assistant Secretary of State, to the Secretary of State, September 19, 1941, 700.00112 Freedom of the Seas/102, Enclosure: The American Doctrine of Freedom of the Seas, Draft 2, 5–7.

30. Devlin, *Too Proud to Fight,* 170–172. See also Neff, *The Rights and Duties of Neutrals,* 146–162.

31. Devlin, *Too Proud to Fight,* 158–159. See also Neff, *The Rights and Duties of Neutrals,* 36–37.

32. Devlin, *Too Proud to Fight,* 158–159, 283, 319–343, 416, 472–483. See also Neff, *The Rights and Duties of Neutrals,* 161; Bemis, *A Diplomatic History of the United States,* 604–609. For more sources on why submarines could not possibly conduct cruiser warfare, see Planning Section Memorandum No. 68, Subject: Submarine Warfare; 420–15 1919; Box 108; Subject File 420–15; General Board, Subject File 1900–1947; General Records of the Department of the Navy (hereafter cited as GR Navy), RG 80; National Archives Building, Washington, D.C. (hereafter cited as NABW), 1–3. See also Lieutenant H. G. Rickover, "International Law and the Submarine," U.S. Naval Institute *Proceedings* 61, no. 9 (September 1935): 1218–1219.

33. Devlin, *Too Proud to Fight,* 410–418. Merchant ships sank only 5 of the 175 Ger-

man submarines sunk by the British. See also Bemis, *A Diplomatic History of the United States*, 606. For more sources on why armed merchant ships made it impossible for submarines to conduct even "warfare in accordance with cruiser rules," see Planning Section Memorandum No. 68, Subject: Submarine Warfare, 3–4. See also Rickover, "International Law and the Submarine," 1218–1219.

34. Janet M. Manson, *Diplomatic Ramifications of Unrestricted Submarine Warfare, 1939–1941*, Contributions in Military Studies, No. 104 (New York: Greenwood Press, 1990), 7–13. See also Devlin, *Too Proud to Fight*, 618–622, 626–635; Neff, *The Rights and Duties of Neutrals*, 162; Bemis, *A Diplomatic History of the United States*, 609–610.

35. Devlin, *Too Proud to Fight*, 410–430, 629–639, 642–671. See also Bemis, *A Diplomatic History of the United States*, 606, 609–615; Arthur S. Link, ed., *The Papers of Woodrow Wilson*, vol. 41: *January 24–April 6, 1917* (Princeton: Princeton University Press, 1983), 108–112, 118–125, 519–527. See also Neff, *The Rights and Duties of Neutrals*, 162.

36. Link, ed., *The Papers of Woodrow Wilson*, 41:520. Emphasis added.

37. Woodrow Wilson, quoted in Margaret MacMillan, *Paris 1919: Six Months That Changed the World* (New York: Random House, 2001), 495.

38. Bemis, *A Diplomatic History of the United States*, 618, 875. See also Neff, *The Rights and Duties of Neutrals*, 164. See also Carlton Savage, Assistant to the Assistant Secretary of State, to the Secretary of State, September 19, 1941, 700.00112 Freedom of the Seas/102, Enclosure: The American Doctrine of Freedom of the Seas, Draft 1, 6–8. Notably, references to the double standard of the United States in time of peace and war in the First World War were deleted from the final and approved draft of Savage's memorandum. See also Carlton Savage, Assistant to the Assistant Secretary of State, to the Secretary of State, September 19, 1941, 700.00112 Freedom of the Seas/102, Enclosure: The American Doctrine of Freedom of the Seas, Draft 2, 6–7.

39. MacMillan, *Paris 1919*, 177–178.

40. Julian S. Corbett, *The League of Nations and Freedom of the Seas* (London: Oxford University Press, 1918), 6–7.

41. Ibid., 8–9.

CHAPTER 2

1. "The Submarine in Trade Warfare: Staff Presentation," Naval War College, Newport, Rhode Island, August 4, 1941; Submarine in Trade Warfare 8/4/41; Box 34, Study—Utilization; NWC Presentations, Studies, etc. (Series II-B); Strategic Plans Division Records; Records of the Office of the Chief of Naval Operations, RG 38; NACP, 14.

2. Ibid.

3. Geoffrey Till, *Maritime Strategy and the Nuclear Age* (London: Macmillan, 1982), 36–38.

4. "The Submarine in Trade Warfare: Staff Presentation," Naval War College, August 4, 1941, 23.

5. Ibid., 24. See also U.S. Naval Attaché, American Embassy, 5, Rue de Chaillot, Paris, France, to the Director of Naval Intelligence, Subject: Disarmament Conference, trend of thought on, March 8, 1926; 438–1 1925–1926; Box 171; Subject File 438–1; General Board, Subject File 1900–1947; GR Navy, RG 80; NABW, 3.

6. "The Submarine in Trade Warfare: Staff Presentation," Naval War College, August 4, 1941, 24–25.

7. Planning Section Memorandum No. 68, Subject: Submarine Warfare; 420–15 1919; Box 108; Subject File 420–15; General Board, Subject File 1900–1947; GR Navy, RG 80; NABW, 5.

8. Ibid., 9.

9. Ibid., 6–8. See also Carlton Savage, Assistant to the Assistant Secretary of State, to the Secretary of State, September 19, 1941, 700.00112 Freedom of the Seas/102, Enclosure: The American Doctrine of Freedom of the Seas, Draft 1, 5–8. See also Carlton Savage, Assistant to the Assistant Secretary of State, to the Secretary of State, September 19, 1941, 700.00112 Freedom of the Seas/102, Enclosure: The American Doctrine of Freedom of the Seas, Draft 2, 5–7.

10. Planning Section Memorandum No. 68, Subject: Submarine Warfare, 9–11.

11. Ibid., 11.

12. Force Commander, U.S. Naval Forces Operating in European Waters, to the Secretary of the Navy (Operations), Subject: Submarine Warfare—Planning Section Memorandum concerning, December 9, 1918; 420–15 1919; Box 108; Subject File 420–15; General Board, Subject File 1900–1947; GR Navy, RG 80; NABW.

13. Planning Committee to the Chief of Naval Operations, Subject: Abolition of Submarines, January 18, 1919; 420–15 1919; Box 108; Subject File 420–15; General Board, Subject File 1900–1947; GR Navy, RG 80; NABW, 1–2.

14. Ibid., 2. "Out of 189 surface naval vessels lost by Great Britain during the war, 62 were due to submarines, 40 to mines, 30 in action, 2 to torpedo boats, 4 blown up accidentally, and 51 lost by wreck, collision, or use as block ships."

15. Ibid. The tonnage figure cited by the three captains was quite accurate. Five years after the war, some sources believed the amount of total tonnage sunk to be 12,850,814 gross tons, although later sources believe the figure could have been as low as 12,026,324 gross tons. Since most of these sinkings were actually carried out by U-boat deck guns, giving the attacked vessels more time for hands to abandon ship, the estimated death toll seems reasonable as well. See Clay Blair, *Hitler's U-Boat War: The Hunters, 1939–1942* (New York: Random House, 1996), 20.

16. Planning Committee to the Chief of Naval Operations, Subject: Abolition of Submarines, January 18, 1919, 2.

17. Orientation Lecture on International Law, issued December 16, 1938; Orientation Lecture on International Law, December 16, 1938; Box 86, Nos. 2197-IL2–2201; Publications, RG 4; Archival Records, U.S. Naval War College, Newport, R.I., 18–19. Professor Wilson had been teaching at the Naval War College since 1900.

18. Planning Committee to the Chief of Naval Operations, Subject: Abolition of Submarines, January 18, 1919, 3–4.

19. Ibid., 4.

20. Gary E. Weir, *Building American Submarines, 1914–1940*, Contributions to Naval History, No. 3 (Washington, D.C.: NHC, 1991), 29. Land would go on to become the chief of the Bureau of Construction and Repair, as well as the chairman of the U.S. Maritime Commission during the Second World War.

21. Commander E. S. Land, USN, to the Force Commander, Subject: Prohibition of construction of Submarines, January 6, 1919; 420–15 1919; Box 108; Subject File 420–15; General Board, Subject File 1900–1947; GR Navy, RG 80; NABW.

22. Commander E. S. Land, USN, to the Force Commander, Subject: Prohibition of construction of Submarines, January 6, 1919, Enclosure (a); 420–15 1919; Box 108; Subject File 420–15; General Board, Subject File 1900–1947; GR Navy, RG 80; NABW, [1].

23. Ibid.

24. Ibid.

25. Ibid., [3].

26. Ibid., [4].

27. Ibid., [5].

28. Commander E. S. Land, USN, to the Force Commander, Subject: Prohibition of construction of Submarines, January 6, 1919, Enclosure (b); 420–15 1919; Box 108; Subject File 420–15; General Board, Subject File 1900–1947; GR Navy, RG 80; NABW, [2].

29. William M. McBride, *Technological Change and the United States Navy, 1865–1945* (Baltimore: Johns Hopkins University Press, 2000), 47. For more information about the General Board in this time period, see Gerald E. Wheeler, *Admiral William Veazie Pratt, U.S. Navy: A Sailor's Life* (Washington, D.C.: Naval History Division, Department of the Navy, 1974), 174–176.

30. Rear Admiral Charles J. Badger, Senior Member Present, General Board, to the Secretary of the Navy, Subject: Rights of neutral merchant vessels in the light of developments during this war, March 27, 1919; 438 1915–1921; Box 168; Subject File 438; General Board, Subject File 1900–1947; GR Navy, RG 80; NABW, 3–6.

31. Ibid., 5.

32. Ibid., 4.

33. Ibid., 6.

CHAPTER 3

1. Yücel Güçlü, "The Nyon Arrangement of 1937 and Turkey," *Middle Eastern Studies* 38, no. 1 (January 2002): 55–57.

2. Ibid., 55.

3. Ibid., 55–59. See also Carlton Savage, Assistant to the Assistant Secretary of State, to the Secretary of State, September 19, 1941, 700.00112 Freedom of the Seas/102, Enclosure: The American Doctrine of Freedom of the Seas, Draft 1; 700.00112 Freedom of the Seas/100—700.00116/447; Box 1770, From: 700:00112 Freedom of the Seas, To: 700.00116 M.E./203; Decimal File, 1940–44; General Records of the Department of State, RG 59; NACP, 9. See also Carlton Savage, Assistant to the Assistant Secretary of State, to the Secretary of State, September 19, 1941, 700.00112 Freedom of the Seas/102, Enclosure: The American Doctrine of Freedom of the Seas, Draft 2; 700.00112 Freedom of the Seas/100—700.00116/447; Box 1770, From: 700:00112 Freedom of the Seas, To: 700.00116 M.E./203; Decimal File, 1940–44; General Records of the Department of State, RG 59; NACP, 8.

4. Güçlü, "The Nyon Arrangement of 1937 and Turkey," 59–61. See also Carlton Savage, Assistant to the Assistant Secretary of State, to the Secretary of State, September 19,

1941, 700.00112 Freedom of the Seas/102, Enclosure: The American Doctrine of Freedom of the Seas, Draft 1, 9. See also Carlton Savage, Assistant to the Assistant Secretary of State, to the Secretary of State, September 19, 1941, 700.00112 Freedom of the Seas/102, Enclosure: The American Doctrine of Freedom of the Seas, Draft 2, 8.

5. Güçlü, "The Nyon Arrangement of 1937 and Turkey," 61–63. See also Carlton Savage, Assistant to the Assistant Secretary of State, to the Secretary of State, September 19, 1941, 700.00112 Freedom of the Seas/102, Enclosure: The American Doctrine of Freedom of the Seas, Draft 1, 9–10. See also Carlton Savage, Assistant to the Assistant Secretary of State, to the Secretary of State, September 19, 1941, 700.00112 Freedom of the Seas/102, Enclosure: The American Doctrine of Freedom of the Seas, Draft 2, 8–9.

6. Güçlü, "The Nyon Arrangement of 1937 and Turkey," 66–67.

7. Winston S. Churchill, *The Second World War: The Gathering Storm* (Boston: Houghton Mifflin, 1948), 248.

8. Margaret MacMillan, *Paris 1919: Six Months That Changed the World* (New York: Random House, 2001), 177–178.

9. Ibid.

10. Woodrow Wilson quoted in Carlton Savage, Assistant to the Assistant Secretary of State, to the Secretary of State, September 19, 1941, 700.00112 Freedom of the Seas/102, Enclosure: The American Doctrine of Freedom of the Seas, Draft 1, 8. See also Carlton Savage, Assistant to the Assistant Secretary of State, to the Secretary of State, September 19, 1941, 700.00112 Freedom of the Seas/102, Enclosure: The American Doctrine of Freedom of the Seas, Draft 2, 7. Based on this answer, under the logic that all members of the League of Nations were obligated to "maintain the right" without resort to neutrality, Senator Henry Cabot Lodge and his Republican colleagues had every reason to believe that the League of Nations would deprive Congress of its power to declare war.

11. The text of the Washington Naval Treaty of 1922, including supplemental treaties, is included as Appendix 1 of Emily O. Goldman, *Sunken Treaties: Naval Arms Control between the Wars* (University Park: Pennsylvania State University Press, 1994), 274–294. The broad outlines of the treaty are also discussed in William M. McBride, *Technological Change and the United States Navy, 1865–1945* (Baltimore: Johns Hopkins University Press, 2000), 140–141, 163. See also Samuel Flagg Bemis, *A Diplomatic History of the United States,* 4th ed. (New York: Henry Holt, 1955), 693–695.

12. Philip C. Jessup, *Elihu Root,* vol. 2: *1905–1937* (Hamden, Conn.: Archon Books, 1964), 447.

13. Lieutenant H. G. Rickover, "International Law and the Submarine," U.S. Naval Institute *Proceedings* 61, no. 9 (September 1935): 1219.

14. Jessup, *Elihu Root,* 2:453.

15. Ibid., 2:454–455.

16. Goldman, *Sunken Treaties,* 293–294.

17. Rickover, "International Law and the Submarine," 1219–1220.

18. Goldman, *Sunken Treaties,* 294. Emphasis added.

19. Ibid.

20. Rickover, "International Law and the Submarine," 1220.

21. William Ledyard Rodgers, Vice Admiral, USN (Ret.), *Greek and Roman Naval*

Warfare: A Study of Strategy, Tactics, and Ship Design from Salamis (480 B.C.) to Actium (31 B.C.) (Annapolis: Naval Institute Press, 1964), 5.

22. Ibid., 5–6.

23. Rear Admiral William L. Rodgers, "Suggestions as to Changes in the International Law for Maritime War," reprinted from *American Journal of International Law* 17, no. 1 (January 2, 1923); 438 1923 to March 30; Box 168; Subject File 438; General Board, Subject File 1900–1947; GR Navy, RG 80; NABW, 3. Aside from the reports Rodgers wrote for the General Board, this 1923 article best illustrates Rodgers's views regarding freedom of the seas and unrestricted warfare in 1922.

24. Ibid., 11.

25. Minutes of the Tenth Meeting of the Advisory Committee, January 6, 1922; 438–1 1921–1922; Box 170; Subject File 438–1; General Board, Subject File 1900–1947; GR Navy, RG 80; NABW, 1–16. See also Rickover, "International Law and the Submarine," 1223.

26. Minutes of the Tenth Meeting of the Advisory Committee, January 6, 1922; 438–1 1921–1922; Box 170; Subject File 438–1; General Board, Subject File 1900–1947; GR Navy, RG 80; NABW, 1–16. See also: Rickover, "International Law and the Submarine," 1223.

27. Admiral W. L. Rodgers, Senior Member Present, General Board, to the Secretary of the Navy, Subject: Limitation of Armaments. Part IV: Draft of relating to war on commerce, January 7, 1922; 420–15 1923–1924; Box 109; Subject File 420–15; General Board, Subject File 1900–1947; GR Navy, RG 80; NABW, 2.

28. "An Attempt to Interpret the Treaty entered into to make more effective the Rules adopted by Civilized Nations for the Protection of the Lives of Neutrals and Noncombatants at Sea in time of war," February 13, 1922; 438 22; Box 168; Subject File 438; General Board, Subject File 1900–1947; GR Navy, RG 80; NABW, 10.

29. Ibid., 1.

30. Ibid., 1–2.

31. Ibid., 3.

32. Ibid., 11–14.

33. Ibid., 4–6, 8.

34. Ibid., 6.

35. Ibid., 7.

36. Ibid., 9.

37. Ibid., 10.

38. Ibid., 9.

39. Ibid., 14. Apparently Rear Admiral Rodgers and the General Board did not favor legislating alcohol, either.

40. Ibid., 9.

41. Ibid., 14.

42. Ibid., 15.

43. "The Submarine in Trade Warfare: Staff Presentation," Naval War College, Newport, R.I., August 4, 1941; Submarine in Trade Warfare 8/4/41; Box 34, Study—Utilization; NWC Presentations, Studies, etc. (Series II-B); Strategic Plans Division Records; Records of the Office of the Chief of Naval Operations, RG 38; NACP, 14–15.

44. Rickover, "International Law and the Submarine," 1220.

45. Jessup, *Elihu Root,* 2:456.

46. Ibid., 2:457.

47. Ibid., 2:457.

48. For a brief discussion of the failed 1927 Geneva Naval Conference, see William F. Trimble, "Admiral Hilary P. Jones and the 1927 Geneva Naval Conference," *Military Affairs* 43, no. 1. (February 1979): 1–4.

49. "Treaty Series, No. 845, Maritime Neutrality, Convention between the United States and other American Republics," U.S. Government Printing Office, Washington, D.C.: 1932; 438 1929; Box 169; Subject File 438; General Board, Subject File 1900–1947; GR Navy, RG 80; NABW, 2–3.

50. Ibid., 3.

51. Samuel Flagg Bemis, Lecture Outline for History 32, Yale University, on Development of Belligerent Maritime Systems Affecting American Rights and Interests; Folder 778, U.S. Navy, Naval War College, 1958–1959; Box 64, U.S. Navy, Naval War College, 1933–1962; Series II: Organization and Project Files, 1918–1969; Papers of Samuel Flagg Bemis, Manuscript Group No. 74; Manuscripts and Archives, Yale University Library, 5.

52. McBride, *Technological Change and the United States Navy,* 163. Unlike many naval officers, Pratt held views that were in accord with those of his president, Herbert Hoover. See John R. M. Wilson, "The Quaker and the Sword: Herbert Hoover's Relations with the Military," *Military Affairs* 38, no. 2 (April 1974): 43–44. See also Henry H. Adams, *Witness to Power: The Life of Fleet Admiral William D. Leahy* (Annapolis: Naval Institute Press, 1985), 65–66; Gerald E. Wheeler, *Admiral William Veazie Pratt, U.S. Navy: A Sailor's Life* (Washington, D.C.: Naval History Division, Department of the Navy, 1974), 293–311.

53. Secretary Stimson, quoted in Solution of a Situation, issued December 3, 1938; Solution of a Situation II—Inter. Law, December 3, 1938; Box 86, Nos. 2197-IL2–2201; Publications, RG 4; Archival Records, U.S. Naval War College, Newport, R.I., 10.

54. Senator Robinson, quoted in ibid., 10–11. Sen. Joseph T. Robinson is usually remembered for being Senate majority leader during the early part of President Franklin D. Roosevelt's presidency. The most ardent defender of Roosevelt's court-packing scheme, he died of a heart attack during the debates over the court-packing legislation, and the scheme died with him.

55. Article 22 of the London Naval Treaty of 1930, quoted in ibid., 11. See also Goldman, *Sunken Treaties,* 317.

56. Digest of the Department of State, quoted in ibid., 12. See also Goldman, *Sunken Treaties,* 317.

57. Rickover, "International Law and the Submarine," 1221.

58. Samuel Flagg Bemis, Lecture Outline for History 32, 5.

59. McBride, *Technological Change and the United States Navy,* 172–175.

60. William Phillips, Acting Secretary of State, to President Franklin D. Roosevelt, March 20, 1936; Dept. of State Jan–Aug 1936; Box 4, OF 20 Department of State; Official File; Franklin D. Roosevelt Presidential Library, Hyde Park, NY, 2–3. A printed version of this letter, as well as other correspondence related to this topic, is included in *Foreign Relations of the United States: Diplomatic Papers, 1936,* 5 vols., vol. 1: *General, The British Commonwealth* (Washington, D.C.: U.S. Government Printing Office, 1953), 160–164.

61. Among the other nations that signed the London Submarine Protocol of 1936 were minor but important powers, such as Turkey, Sweden, Norway, Switzerland, and Mexico, as well as nautically impotent signatories like the Vatican City State, Afghanistan, and Nepal. See *Foreign Relations of the United States: Diplomatic Papers, 1930*, 3 vols., vol. 1 (Washington, D.C.: U.S. Government Printing Office, 1945), 131. See also "The Submarine in Trade Warfare: Staff Presentation," Naval War College, August 4, 1941, 16–17.

62. Carlton Savage, Assistant to the Assistant Secretary of State, to the Secretary of State, September 19, 1941, 700.00112 Freedom of the Seas/102, Enclosure: The American Doctrine of Freedom of the Seas, Draft 1, 9–10. See also Carlton Savage, Assistant to the Assistant Secretary of State, to the Secretary of State, September 19, 1941, 700.00112 Freedom of the Seas/102, Enclosure: The American Doctrine of Freedom of the Seas, Draft 2, 8–9. See also Güçlü, "The Nyon Arrangement of 1937 and Turkey," 53–70. See also Stephen C. Neff, *The Rights and Duties of Neutrals: A General History* (Manchester: Manchester University Press, 2000), 181.

63. Edwin Borchard and William Potter Lage, *Neutrality for the United States* (1937), quoted in "The Submarine in Trade Warfare: Staff Presentation," Naval War College, August 4, 1941, 17.

64. Norman Polmar and Thomas B. Allen, *Rickover: Controversy and Genius: A Biography* (New York: Simon & Schuster, 1982), 74–85.

65. Rickover, "International Law and the Submarine," 1219.

66. Ibid., 1221.

67. Ibid., 1223.

68. Ibid.

69. Ibid., 1226–1227.

70. Ibid., 1227.

CHAPTER 4

1. Claude A. Swanson, Secretary of the Navy, to the General Board of the Navy, Subject: U.S. Neutrality Laws, December 13, 1934; 438 1933–; Box 170; Subject File 438; General Board, Subject File 1900–1947; GR Navy, RG 80; NABW, 1–6.

2. Claude A. Swanson, Secretary of the Navy to the Chief of Naval Operations, the Judge Advocate General, and the President, Naval War College, Subject: U.S. Neutrality Laws, November 28, 1934; 438 1933–; Box 170; Subject File 438; General Board, Subject File 1900–1947; GR Navy, RG 80; NABW.

3. Rear Admiral Claude C. Bloch, Judge Advocate General, to the Secretary of the Navy, Subject: U.S. Neutrality Laws, re: proposed revision of, December 7, 1934; 438 1933–; Box 170; Subject File 438; General Board, Subject File 1900–1947; GR Navy, RG 80; NABW, 7.

4. Ibid., 8.

5. Ibid., 8.

6. Ibid., 8–9.

7. Rear Admiral Frank H. Clark, Chairman General Board, to the Secretary of the Navy, Subject: U.S. Neutrality Laws, December 15, 1934; 438 193–; Box 170; Subject File 438; General Board, Subject File 1900–1947; GR Navy, RG 80; NABW, 2.

8. Ibid.

9. Ibid., 3.

10. Rear Admiral E. C. Kalbfus, President, Naval War College, to Secretary of the Navy, Subject: U.S. Neutrality Laws, December 17, 1934; XLAI, 1934–1939; Box 88, XLAI-XLFG; Intelligence and Technical Archives, RG 8; Archival Records, U.S. Naval War College, Newport, R.I., 3.

11. Rear Admiral E. C. Kalbfus, President, Naval War College to Secretary of the Navy, Subject: U.S. Neutrality Laws, December 22, 1934; XLAI, 1934–1939; Box 88, XLAI-XLFG; Intelligence and Technical Archives, RG 8; Archival Records, U.S. Naval War College, Newport, R.I., 7. Additional copy at 438 1933–; Box 170; Subject File 438; General Board, Subject File 1900–1947; GR Navy, RG 80; NABW, 7.

12. Ibid., 7–8.

13. Claude A. Swanson, Secretary of the Navy, to Cordell Hull, Secretary of State, December 15, 1934; 438 1933–; Box 170; Subject File 438; General Board, Subject File 1900–1947; GR Navy, RG 80; NABW. See also Claude A. Swanson, Secretary of the Navy, to Cordell Hull, Secretary of State, December 28, 1934; 438 1933–; Box 170; Subject File 438; General Board, Subject File 1900–1947; GR Navy, RG 80; NABW.

14. Public Resolution-No.67–74th Congress, S.J. Res. 173, Joint Resolution, printed in *Neutrality Laws,* ed. Elmer A. Lewis (Washington, D.C.: U.S. Government Printing Office, 1951), 1–5. For the complex evolution of the 1935 neutrality legislation, see Wayne S. Cole, *Roosevelt and the Isolationists, 1932–1945* (Lincoln: University of Nebraska Press, 1983), 163–186.

15. Cole, *Roosevelt and the Isolationists,* 166.

16. Walter Lippman, "Today and Tomorrow: The Approaching War and American Policy," *New York Herald Tribune,* August 8, 1935; 438 1933–; Box 170; Subject File 438; General Board, Subject File 1900–1947; GR Navy, RG 80; NABW.

17. Ibid.

18. Ibid.

19. Ibid.

20. Ibid.

21. Robert A. Divine, *The Illusion of Neutrality* (Chicago: University of Chicago Press, 1962), 334–335.

22. Cole, *Roosevelt and the Isolationists,* 321–330. For the text of the 1939 Neutrality Act, see Public Resolution-No.54–76th Congress, Chapter 2–2nd Session, H.J. Res. 306, Joint Resolution, printed in *Neutrality Laws,* ed. Elmer A. Lewis, 18–27.

23. Admiral Harold R. Stark, Acting Secretary of the Navy, to the Chairman, General Board, Subject: Proposed Neutrality Act, October 3, 1939; 438 1933–; Box 170; Subject File 438; General Board, Subject File 1900–1947; GR Navy, RG 80; NABW.

24. R. S. Crenshaw, Director War Plans Division, to the Chief of Naval Operations, Subject: H.J. Res. 306—Neutrality Act of 1939, September 29, 1939; 438 1933–; Box 170; Subject File 438; General Board, Subject File 1900–1947; GR Navy, RG 80; NABW, 1.

25. Ibid., 1–2.

26. Office of the Judge Advocate General, Department of the Navy, Memorandum,

Subject: Proposed Neutrality Legislation, September 29, 1939; 438 1933–; Box 170; Subject File 438; General Board, Subject File 1900–1947; GR Navy, RG 80; NABW.

27. Rear Admiral Edward C. Kalbfus to Admiral Harold R. Stark, October 7, 1939; XLAI, 1939–1941; Box 88, XLAI-XLFG; Intelligence and Technical Archives, RG 8; Archival Records, U.S. Naval War College, Newport, R.I.

28. Rear Admiral Edward C. Kalbfus, President of the U.S. Naval War College, to the Secretary of the Navy, Subject: Proposed Neutrality Act, October 10, 1939; XLAI, 1939–1941; Box 88, XLAI-XLFG; Intelligence and Technical Archives, RG 8; Archival Records, U.S. Naval War College, Newport, R.I.

29. Rear Admiral W. R. Sexton, Chairman General Board, to the Secretary of the Navy, Subject: Proposed Neutrality Act, October 9, 1939; 438 1933–; Box 170; Subject File 438; General Board, Subject File 1900–1947; GR Navy, RG 80; NABW, 1.

30. Ibid., 2–3.

31. Ibid., 3.

32. Ibid., 1.

33. Ibid.

34. Ibid.

35. Ibid., 2.

36. Ibid.

37. Ibid., 4.

38. Ibid., 4–5.

39. Ibid., 5.

40. For an appraisal of the beliefs of the isolationists, their actions regarding neutrality legislation, and the attempts of internationalists to stop them, see Cole, *Roosevelt and the Isolationists,* 163–186, 223–262, 310–330, 409–455.

41. President Franklin Roosevelt, quoted in "The Submarine in Trade Warfare: Staff Presentation," Naval War College, Newport, Rhode Island, August 4, 1941; Submarine in Trade Warfare 8/4/41; Box 34, Study—Utilization; NWC Presentations, Studies, etc. (Series II-B); Strategic Plans Division Records; Records of the Office of the Chief of Naval Operations, RG 38; NACP, 20.

42. Ibid., 20–21.

43. The use of the phrase "unrestricted warfare" rather than "unrestricted submarine warfare" is deliberate. For while German U-boats conducted the vast majority of unrestricted attacks on Allied merchant ships, German aircraft and surface raiders, such as *Scharnhorst* and *Gneisenau,* also carried out unrestricted warfare.

44. For instance, see Selig Adler, *The Isolationist Impulse: Its Twentieth-Century Reaction* (Westport, Conn.: Greenwood Press, 1957), 265.

45. Samuel Flagg Bemis, Lecture Outline for History 32, Yale University, on Development of Belligerent Maritime Systems Affecting American Rights and interests; Folder 778, U.S. Navy, Naval War College, 1958–1959; Box 64, U.S. Navy, Naval War College, 1933–1962; Series II: Organization and Project Files, 1918–1969; Papers of Samuel Flagg Bemis, Manuscript Group No. 74; Manuscripts and Archives, Yale University Library, 6.

46. Janet M. Manson, *Diplomatic Ramifications of Unrestricted Submarine Warfare,*

1939–1941, Contributions in Military Studies, No. 104 (New York: Greenwood Press, 1990), 70–72, 111, 119. Hitler's orders to avoid shooting at potential American destroyers were not lifted until December 1941.

47. Clay Blair, *Hitler's U-Boat War: The Hunters, 1939–1942* (New York: Random House, 1996), 295–296, 405. In the case of the *Astral,* the sinking was actually treated as a mystery for many years after the war because the German U-boat commander, the famous Wolfgang Lüth, was certain he had sunk a British tanker of similar displacement. For some reason, although he recorded her loss, Clay Blair did not describe *Astral* as being sunk before the war, oddly naming *Sagadahoc* as "the third American merchant ship to fall victim to U-boats before the United States entered war." Since *Astral* was sunk a day before *Sagadahoc,* this must be an error.

48. Ibid., 360–361, 370, 375. A German torpedo hit *Kearny,* killing 11 U.S. sailors and injuring 22 more, but her crew saved the ship and she limped back to Iceland for repairs. See also Manson, *Diplomatic Ramifications of Unrestricted Submarine Warfare,* 138–146.

49. Manson, *Diplomatic Ramifications of Unrestricted Submarine Warfare,* 69–70, 83–84, 118–119.

50. See Alastair Mars, *British Submarines at War: 1939–1945* (Annapolis: Naval Institute Press, 1971), 70–71, 92. Although the British decisions were technically acts of "reprisal," Mars noted that the policy "became more one of expediency than of considerations in international law" (92). On April 9, 1940, the British War Cabinet issued orders that all German ships were to be sunk on sight in the Danish Sound. Two days later, the cabinet extended this war zone up the coast of Norway, up to 10 miles from the port of Bergen. In July 1940 the Royal Navy created similar war zones in the Mediterranean, extending 30 miles around Italy and Libya. Due to the high amount of neutral shipping in the Mediterranean, the British did not start conducting general unrestricted warfare throughout the Mediterranean (with some safe zones around Turkey and Spain) until November 21, 1942. See also Peter Padfield, *War beneath the Sea: Submarine Conflict during World War II* (New York: John Wiley & Sons, 1995), 78–79, 131, 267, 482, 483, 495; Stephen C. Neff, *The Rights and Duties of Neutrals: A General History* (Manchester: Manchester University Press, 2000), 182–184.

51. "The Submarine in Trade Warfare: Staff Presentation," Naval War College, August 4, 1941, 17.

52. Ibid., 18.

53. Ibid., 26.

54. Ibid., 28–29.

55. Ibid., 30.

56. Captain O. M. Reed, Memorandum for the Director, War Plans Division, Subject: Prize Crews and Armed Guards, October 27, 1941; WPL-46 Letters (1939–1945); Box 147J, WPL-46—WPL-46-PC; Part III: OP-12B, War Plans and Related Correspondence; Plans, Strategic Studies, and Related Correspondence (Series IX); Strategic Plans Division Records; Records of the Office of the Chief of Naval Operations, RG 38; NACP.

57. W. J. Holmes, *Undersea Victory: The Influence of Submarine Operations on the War in the Pacific* (Garden City: Doubleday, 1966), 46–47.

CHAPTER 5

1. Minutes of the Tenth Meeting of the Advisory Committee, January 6, 1922; 438–1 1921–1922; Box 170; Subject File 438–1; General Board, Subject File 1900–1947; GR Navy, RG 80; NABW, 6–7.

2. Ibid., 7. Eleven out of the thirteen sunken battleships were pre-dreadnought–type battleships, easily susceptible to torpedo hits. The five battleships sunk by submarines were all the pre-dreadnought type. Clay Blair claimed that German U-boats sank as many as 10 Allied battleships and 18 heavy and light cruisers. See Clay Blair, *Hitler's U-Boat War: The Hunters, 1939–1942* (New York: Random House, 1996), 18.

3. Minutes of the Tenth Meeting of the Advisory Committee, January 6, 1922, 7.

4. Ibid., 3.

5. Ibid., 5–6.

6. Michael Vlahos, *The Blue Sword: The Naval War College and the American Mission, 1919–1941*, U.S. Naval War College Historical Monograph Series, No. 4 (Newport: Naval War College Press, 1980), 163.

7. Edward S. Miller, *War Plan Orange: The U.S. Strategy to Defeat Japan, 1897–1945* (Annapolis: Naval Institute Press, 1991), 21–38.

8. Vlahos, *The Blue Sword,* 118.

9. Miller, *War Plan Orange,* 28–38, 363–369.

10. Mark P. Parillo, *The Japanese Merchant Marine in World War II* (Annapolis: U.S. Naval Institute Press, 1993), 32–35. See also Clay Blair, Jr., *Silent Victory: The U.S. Submarine War against Japan* (Philadelphia: J. B. Lippincott, 1975), 17; John W. Dower, *Embracing Defeat: Japan in the Wake of World War II* (New York: W.W. Norton/New Press, 1999), 91. Before Pearl Harbor, Japan imported 31 percent of its rice, 92 percent of its sugar, 58 percent of its soybeans, and 45 percent of its salt from Korea, Formosa, and China.

11. Randy Papadopoulos, "Between Fleet Scouts and Commerce Raiders: Submarine Warfare Theories and Doctrines in the German and U.S. Navies, 1935–1945," unpublished TMs, possession of author, 13.

12. Statement of Admiral Thomas C. Hart, March 4, 1937, "Characteristics of Submarines," *Hearings before the General Board of the Navy, 1917–1950* (hereafter cited as *General Board*), 94.

13. Gary E. Weir, *Building American Submarines, 1914–1940,* Contributions to Naval History, No. 3 (Washington, D.C.: NHC, 1991), 38. For Admiral Hart's role, see James Leutze, *A Different Kind of Victory: A Biography of Admiral Thomas C. Hart* (Annapolis: Naval Institute Press, 1981), 66–67.

14. Commander Charles A. Lockwood Jr., Submarine Officers' Conference Memorandum, May 10, 1939; 420–15 1939; Box 113; Subject File 420–15; General Board, Subject File 1900–1947; GR Navy, RG 80; NABW, 1–2.

15. Keith Wheeler, *War under the Pacific,* Time-Life World War II Series (Alexandria, Va.: Time-Life Books, 1980), 40, 46. Robert H. English and Charles A. Lockwood would both become commander submarines Pacific. Ralph W. Christie would become commander submarines Southwest Pacific. Charles W. Styer would become commander submarines Atlantic.

16. Weir, *Building American Submarines,* 40–43.

17. Testimony of Rear Admiral H. E. Yarnell, July 15, 1930, "General Characteristics and Design of Future Submarines," *General Board,* 296. One board member, Admiral Day, opposed Yarnell's opinion. He presciently remarked, "If trouble comes in the Pacific our prospective opponent has always started operations by attacking before a declaration of war. If he hits us he is going to hit either the Canal Zone or Hawaii. That is the point of having somebody there" (286).

18. Testimony of Admiral W. V. Pratt, May 27, 1930, "Testimony of Commander-in-Chief, U.S. Fleet, in Regard to Needs of the Fleet," *General Board,* 181.

19. Rear Admiral Thomas C. Hart, Commander Control Force, to the Chief of Naval Operations, Subject: Results of Study of Submarine Warfare in Conference at Submarine Base, New London, and Recommendations on Submarine Design, March 31, 1931; 420–15 1931–1933; Box 111; Subject File 420–15; General Board, Subject File 1900–1947; GR Navy, RG 80; NABW, 1.

20. Ibid., 2.

21. Ibid., 2–3.

22. Ibid., 15–16.

23. Even after the war had begun, Hart believed that American submarines were far too spacious and comfortable on the inside. See Admiral Thomas C. Hart to Admiral Harold R. Stark, March 17, 1942; Hart, T. C. ADM Correspondence; Box 12; Series III: Subject Files; Papers of Admiral H. R. Stark; Operational Archives Branch; NHC; Washington, D.C., 3.

24. Submarine Officers' Conference to the Chief of Naval Operations, Subject: Submarine Officers' Conference to discuss submarine characteristics for new construction (188 to 193), December 16, 1935; 420–15 1936; Box 112; Subject File 420–15; General Board, Subject File 1900–1947; GR Navy, RG 80; NABW, 2.

25. Admiral Claude C. Bloch, Commander-in-Chief, United States Fleet, to Chief of Naval Operations, Subject: Submarines—Employment of in a Pacific War, May 11, 1938; 420–15 1938; Box 112; Subject File 420–15; General Board, Subject File 1900–1947; GR Navy, RG 80; NABW, 1–4.

26. Rear Admiral C. S. Freeman, Commander Submarine Force, to Chief of Naval Operations, Subject: Submarines—Employment of in a Pacific War, July 27, 1938; 420–15 1938; Box 112; Subject File 420–15; General Board, Subject File 1900–1947; GR Navy, RG 80; NABW, 1.

27. Ibid., 1.

28. Statement by Admiral Mark L. Bristol, July 15, 1930, "General Characteristics and Design of Future Submarines," *General Board,* 268.

29. John Alden, *The Fleet Submarine in the U.S. Navy: A Design and Construction History* (Annapolis: Naval Institute Press, 1979), 10.

30. Statement by Admiral Thomas C. Hart, March 4, 1937, "Characteristics of Submarines," *General Board,* 95. See also Norman Friedman, *U.S. Submarines through 1945: An Illustrated Design History* (Annapolis: Naval Institute Press, 1995), 292.

31. Alden, *The Fleet Submarine in the U.S. Navy,* 24–35.

32. Ibid., 18.

33. Statement by Admiral Thomas C. Hart, March 4, 1937, "Characteristics of Submarines," *General Board,* 95–98. See also Alden, *The Fleet Submarine in the U.S. Navy,* 18–19, 36–39.

34. Testimony of Rear Admiral Harry E. Yarnell, July 8, 1930, "Main Engines and Necessary Auxiliaries for the U.S.S. *V-8* and U.S.S. *V-9,*" *General Board,* 253–266.

35. Alden, *The Fleet Submarine in the U.S. Navy,* 38–39.

36. Friedman, *U.S. Submarines through 1945,* 191–193.

37. Testimony of Rear Admiral Emory S. Land, Rear Admiral Samuel M. Robinson, Captain G. J. Meyers, and Commander C. R. Hyatt, May 26, 1933, "Characteristics of New Submarines," *General Board,* 64–75.

38. Letter of Rear Admiral Samuel M. Robinson, February 12, 1935, read on February 15, 1935, "Proposed Military Characteristics of Submarines," *General Board,* 36–41. See also Friedman, *U.S. Submarines through 1945,* 203; Alden, *The Fleet Submarine in the U.S. Navy,* 65–68.

39. Testimony of Rear Admiral H. G. Bowen, March 4, 1937, "Characteristics of Submarines," *General Board,* 108–110. See also Friedman, *U.S. Submarines through 1945,* 203–204; Alden, *The Fleet Submarine in the U.S. Navy,* 72.

40. Alden, *The Fleet Submarine in the U.S. Navy,* 101–108.

41. Testimony of Captain H. S. Howard et al., March 27, 1930, "Submarines *V-7* (SC3), *V-8* (SC4) and *V-9* (SC5)—Plans For," *General Board,* 74–106.

42. Ibid., 121. See also Friedman, *U.S. Submarines through 1945,* 187.

43. Letter by Rear Admiral H. R. Stark, February 15, 1935, "Proposed Military Characteristics of Submarines 182–187," *General Board,* 31–32. See also Friedman, *U.S. Submarines through 1945,* 200–202; Alden, *The Fleet Submarine in the U.S. Navy,* 65–66.

44. Friedman, *U.S. Submarines through 1945,* 180, 210. A "hot run" occurred when a torpedo's motor started while the torpedo was secured and stationary, and ran until the motor's governor cut in or the torpedo used up its fuel.

45. Testimony of Commander Ralph W. Christie, Commander Charles A. Lockwood, et al., October 15, 1937, "Characteristics of Submarines," *General Board,* 332–335. See also Alden, *The Fleet Submarine in the U.S. Navy,* 74, 101–108; Friedman, *U.S. Submarines through 1945,* 204–206.

46. Testimony of Lieutenant Commander J. W. Paige and Rear Admiral Emory S. Land, May 26, 1933, "Characteristics of New Submarines," *General Board,* 75. Statement by Admiral Thomas C. Hart, March 4, 1937, "Characteristics of Submarines," *General Board,* 94–97. "Cruiser" submarines *Argonaut, Narwhal,* and *Nautilus* carried two 6-inch guns, and *Dolphin* carried a 4-inch gun.

47. Testimony of Rear Admiral W. R. Furlong, November 9, 1939, "Submarine Characteristics—Building Program 1941," *General Board,* 363.

48. Testimony of Commander Charles A. Lockwood, October 15, 1937, "Characteristics of Submarines," *General Board,* 335–337. Testimony of Commander Charles A. Lockwood, May 24, 1938, "Characteristics of Submarines," *General Board,* 66. Lockwood not only wanted a large 5-inch gun, he wanted it placed forward of the conning tower, because although the gun "is a defensive weapon, sir, [sometimes] the defense may consist of taking the offensive."

49. Alden, *The Fleet Submarine in the U.S. Navy,* 93–94.

50. NS402: Junior Officer Submarine Practicum Distinguished Speaker Lecture by Rear Admiral Maurice Rindskopf, speech presented to students at the U.S. Naval Academy, January 28, 2003. Talking about fire control, Admiral Rindskopf recalled, "We used a device called an 'Is-Was' to shoot torpedoes. It was called an 'Is-Was' because when you got an answer that *is* where he *was.*"

51. Letter by and Testimony of Rear Admiral H. R. Stark, February 15, 1935, "Proposed Military Characteristics of Submarines 182–187," *General Board,* 32–35. Testimony of Commander R. W. Christie and Lieutenant E. K. Walker, May 24, 1938, "Characteristics of Submarines," *General Board,* 65–66. See also Friedman, *U.S. Submarines through 1945,* 194–197.

52. Friedman, *U.S. Submarines through 1945,* 195.

53. Testimony of Commander R. H. English, March 6, 1936, "Characteristics of Submarines," *General Board,* 12–32. See also Alden, *The Fleet Submarine in the U.S. Navy,* 48.

54. Report of J. H. Brown, September 11, 1930, in Statement of Commander C. R. Hyatt, September 22, 1930, "General Characteristics and Design of Future Submarines," *General Board,* 372–374. See also Testimony of Commander R. H. English, March 6, 1936, "Characteristics of Submarines," *General Board,* 33; Alden, *The Fleet Submarine in the U.S. Navy,* 48.

55. Testimony of Lieutenant Commander L. F. Small and Commander R. H. English, March 4, 1937, "Characteristics of Submarines," *General Board,* 113. Although most fleet submarines carried air conditioning, S-boats never carried it, and they maintained absolutely hellish conditions throughout their service in the Second World War. See Vice Admiral Charles A. Lockwood, *Sink 'Em All: Submarine Warfare in the Pacific* (New York: E. P. Dutton, 1951), 36, 49–50. See also Alden, *The Fleet Submarine in the U.S. Navy,* 48.

56. Rear Admiral C. S. Freeman to Chief of Naval Operations, Subject: Submarines—Employment of in a Pacific War, July 27, 1938, 2.

57. Friedman, *U.S. Submarines through 1945,* 227.

58. Testimony of Commander A. S. Carpender, March 6, 1936, "Characteristics of Submarines," *General Board,* 22.

59. Admiral Joseph M. Reeves was a pioneer with the use of naval air power. He was the first naval aviator to earn flag rank, although he was not a pilot but a flight observer. Among Admiral Reeves's other claims to fame was his invention of a crude football helmet while playing for the U.S. Naval Academy football team. It was the first recorded protective headgear worn by a football player. See Thomas Wildenberg, *All the Factors of Victory: Admiral Joseph Mason Reeves and the Origins of Carrier Airpower* (Washington, D.C.: Brassey's, 2003). See also Jack Sweetman, *The U.S. Naval Academy: The Illustrated History,* 2nd ed., revised by Thomas Cutler (Annapolis: Naval Institute Press, 1995), 129, 131.

60. Admiral J. M. Reeves, Commander-in-Chief, U.S. Fleet, to Chief of Naval Operations, Subject: Employment of BLUE Submarines—Orange War, January 20, 1936, Enclosure: A Study on the Initial Employment of the BLUE Submarine Force in an ORANGE War, December 1935; Series III; Strategic Plans Division Records; Records of the Office of the Chief of Naval Operations, RG 38; available on microfilm, 1–2.

61. Ibid., 10–11; original emphasis.

62. Rear Admiral C. S. Freeman to Chief of Naval Operations, Subject: Submarines—Employment of in a Pacific War, July 27, 1938, 1.

63. Current Doctrine, Submarines, 1939, U.S.F. 25, Revised, prepared by Commander Submarine Force, April 1939; NRS 1977–86, Current Tactical Orders and Doctrine—Submarines, 1939–1944; Microfilm Reel; Operational Archives, NHC, Washington D.C., 2.

64. Ibid., 7.

65. Ibid., 11.

66. Ibid.; emphasis added.

67. Ibid., 12.

68. Ibid., 2.

69. Testimony of Commander E. E. Hazlett, October 15, 1937, "Characteristics of Submarines," *General Board*, 337.

70. Lieutenant H. G. Rickover, "International Law and the Submarine," U.S. Naval Institute *Proceedings* 61, no. 9 (September 1935): 1213–1227. See also Commander E. E. Hazlett Jr., "Submarines and the London Treaty," U.S. Naval Institute *Proceedings* 62, no. 12 (December 1936): 1690–1694; Lieutenant J. C. Hubbard, "Future Uses of Submarines," U.S. Naval Institute *Proceedings* 62, no. 12 (December 1936): 1721–1726.

71. Current Doctrine, Submarines, 1939, U.S.F. 25, Revised, April 1939, 17; emphasis added.

72. W. J. Holmes, *Undersea Victory: The Influence of Submarine Operations on the War in the Pacific* (Garden City: Doubleday, 1966), 47–48.

73. Ibid., 48. The U.S. Navy was not the only navy to be fooled by prewar antisubmarine warfare capabilities. The Royal Navy was similarly lulled into a false sense of security by its faith in sonar and air power. See Holger H. Herwig, "Innovation Ignored: The Submarine Problem, Germany, Britain, and the United States, 1919–1939," in *Military Innovation in the Interwar Period,* ed. Williamson Murray and Allan R. Millett (Cambridge: Cambridge University Press, 1996), 245–248.

74. In the first case, the commanding officer of USS *Sailfish* relieved himself of command rather than face sonar-equipped destroyers. See Carl LaVO, *Back from the Deep: The Strange Story of the Sister Subs Squalus and Sculpin* (Annapolis: Naval Institute Press, 1994), 89–90. In the second case, the first commanding officer of USS *Seahorse* allowed numerous contacts to go by rather than take the chance of attacking a contact with sonar-equipped escorts. See Captain Slade D. Cutter, interviewed by Paul Stillwell, *The Reminiscences of Captain Slade D. Cutter, U.S. Navy (Retired),* vol. 1 (Annapolis: U.S. Naval Institute, 1985), 149–155.

75. Holmes, *Undersea Victory,* 47.

76. Ibid.

77. Cutter, *The Reminiscences of Captain Slade D. Cutter,* 1:172–173.

78. Holmes, *Undersea Victory,* 48.

79. Papadopoulos, "Between Fleet Scouts and Commerce Raiders," 16–17.

80. Ibid., 18–19.

81. Ibid.

82. Current Doctrine, Submarines, 1939, U.S.F. 25, Revised, April 1939, 26.

83. Holmes, *Undersea Victory,* 48.

84. Rear Admiral Thomas Withers, "The Preparation of the Submarines Pacific for War," U.S. Naval Institute *Proceedings* 76, no. 1 (April 1950): 387.

85. Ibid., 389.

86. Ibid., 387–388.

87. Ibid., 387.

88. Ibid., 392.

89. Cutter, *The Reminiscences of Captain Slade D. Cutter,* 1:178–179. The night surface approach on *California* ended when the battleship suddenly turned her searchlights onto the submarine, revealing that *California* had a brand-new technological advantage—radar.

90. Ibid., 1:177. "The angle on the bow is the angle between the fore-and-aft axis of the ship and the line that runs from the submarine to the ship."

91. Captain W. E. Doyle, Commander Submarines, U.S. Asiatic Fleet, USS *Sargo* (SS188), Flagship, Manila, P.I., Operation Order No. 2–41, December 2, 1941; Asiatic Fleet Op. Order 2–41, Ser: 001, 2 Dec 41; Box 292, Servron 12 1945 to SubLant Jun 43; Plans, Orders, & Related Documents; Records Relating to Naval Activity During World War II; Records of the Office of the Chief of Naval Operations, RG 38; NACP, 2.

92. Ibid., 2.

93. Papadopoulos, "Between Fleet Scouts and Commerce Raiders," 14.

94. "Submarine Operational History World War II, Prepared by Commander Submarine Force, U.S. Pacific Fleet, Volume 1 of 4"; Submarines Pacific Fleet, Operational History, Vol. 1 of 4; Box 357, Submarines, Pacific Flt-History—Bulletins, Submarine Vol. II, 1945; Type Commands; World War II Command File; Operational Archives Branch, NHC, Washington, D.C., 2, 7. As the source for his quotation Voge cited: "*Principles of International Law* by T. J. Lawrence—7th Edition. D.C. Heath and Co."

95. Ibid., 1–2; emphasis added.

96. Ibid., 4.

97. Papadopoulos, "Between Fleet Scouts and Commerce Raiders," 20–21. Captain Edward L. Beach, the famous Second World War submariner and author, told the story to Papadopoulos. Papadopoulos cited Beach as the submarine communications officer, but this would have been impossible, since Beach was still at Submarine School in New London when Pearl Harbor was attacked on December 7, 1941. See Edward L. Beach, *Salt and Steel: Reflections of a Submariner* (Annapolis: Naval Institute Press, 1999), 59–60.

98. "Submarine Operational History World War II," 1.

99. U.S. fleet submarines arguably were vastly superior to German U-boats as commerce raiders. As Clay Blair argues throughout his history of the German U-boat war, the mainstay submarine of the U-boat force, the Type VIIC, had been designed as a small commerce raider, but it turned out not to have the range, endurance, or requisite weaponry to make it truly effective. See Blair, *Hitler's U-Boat War: The Hunters,* 423. See also Herwig, "Innovation Ignored," 239–241.

CHAPTER 6

1. B. Mitchell Simpson III, *Admiral Harold R. Stark: Architect of Victory, 1939–1945* (Columbia: University of South Carolina Press, 1989), 62–82. A copy of the November

12, 1940, draft of Stark's memorandum, which went to President Roosevelt, is on file at the Franklin D. Roosevelt Presidential Library. See Admiral Harold R. Stark, Chief of Naval Operations, to Secretary of the Navy, Memorandum for the Secretary, November 12, 1940; Navy Department: "Plan Dog"; Box 4, Marshall, George C.: 4/15/42–1944 thru Outline Plans for Specific Operations: Azores; President's Secretary File Safe File; Franklin D. Roosevelt Presidential Library, Hyde Park, NY. Copies of the different drafts of the memorandum, including the ultimate draft that was accepted as the national defense policy for the United States, are in Steven T. Ross, ed., *American War Plans, 1919–1941*, vol. 3: *Plans to Meet the Axis Threat, 1939–1940* (New York: Garland Publishing, 1992), 223–301.

2. Joint Planning Committee to Joint Board, Subject: National Defense Policy for the United States, December 21, 1940; Plan Dog; Box 85; Series XIII: Pearl Harbor Investigations; Papers of Admiral H. R. Stark; Operational Archives Branch; NHC; Washington, D.C., cover letter.

3. Ibid., 16.

4. Ibid., cover letter.

5. Edward S. Miller, *War Plan Orange: The U.S. Strategy to Defeat Japan, 1897–1945* (Annapolis: Naval Institute Press, 1991), 269–270.

6. Joint Planning Committee to Joint Board, Subject: National Defense Policy for the United States, December 21, 1940, 3.

7. Ibid., 4.

8. Ibid., 15.

9. Ibid., 8. This strategy against Japan remained unchanged in every version of Plan Dog, from Stark's original draft, through the draft that went to the President, and eventually the revised draft that became the national defense policy for the United States. For this section in the original draft, see Ross, ed., *American War Plans, 1919–1941*, 3:263–264. For this section in the revised draft, see Admiral Harold R. Stark, Chief of Naval Operations, to Secretary of the Navy, Memorandum for the Secretary, November 12, 1940; Navy Department: "Plan Dog"; Box 4, Marshall, George C.: 4/15/42–1944 thru Outline Plans for Specific Operations: Azores; President's Secretary File Safe File; Franklin D. Roosevelt Presidential Library, Hyde Park, NY, 14. See also Ross, *American War Plans, 1919–1941*, 3:238. For another copy of the final revision of Plan Dog, see ibid., 3:277–301.

10. Joint Planning Committee to Joint Board, Subject: National Defense Policy for the United States, December 21, 1940, 8.

11. Miller, *War Plan Orange*, 21–38.

12. Bemis, "Submarine Warfare in the Strategy of American Defense and Diplomacy," 36.

13. Miller, *War Plan Orange*, 352.

14. Ibid., 268–269.

15. Vice Admiral George Carroll Dyer, USN (Ret.), *The Amphibians Came to Conquer: The Story of Admiral Richmond Kelly Turner*, 2 vols. (Washington, D.C.: U.S. Department of the Navy, U.S. Government Printing Office, 1972), 26.

16. Miller, *War Plan Orange*, 215.

17. Dyer, *The Amphibians Came to Conquer,* 157–160, 162–165.

18. Miller, *War Plan Orange,* 269–271.

19. WPL-44, Naval Basic War Plan—Rainbow No. 3, U.S. Navy, December 1940; Box 33, WPL-44; WPL Series; War Plans Division; Strategic Plans Division Records; Records of the Office of the Chief of Naval Operations, RG 38; NACP, 23.

20. Ibid., 24, 27.

21. WPL-42, Naval Basic War Plan—Rainbow No. 1, U.S. Navy, July 1940; Box 32, WPL-42; WPL Series; War Plans Division; Strategic Plans Division Records; Records of the Office of the Chief of Naval Operations, RG 38; NACP, 45.

22. WPL-44, Naval Basic War Plan—Rainbow No. 3, U.S. Navy, December 1940, 42; original emphasis.

23. Ibid.

24. Ibid.

25. Ibid., 24.

26. James Leutze, *A Different Kind of Victory: A Biography of Admiral Thomas C. Hart* (Annapolis: Naval Institute Press, 1981), 89–90.

27. Ibid., 170–230.

28. Admiral Thomas C. Hart to Admiral Harold R. Stark, Memo re Substance of "Rainbow 3," January 18, 1941; War Plans; Box 86; Series XIII: Pearl Harbor Investigations; Papers of Admiral H. R. Stark; Operational Archives Branch; NHC; Washington, D.C., 3.

29. Admiral Harold R. Stark, Chief of Naval Operations, to Commander-in-Chief, U.S. Asiatic Fleet, Subject: Instructions concerning the preparation of the U.S. Asiatic Fleet for war under "RAINBOW No. 3," February 7, 1941; War Plans; Box 86; Series XIII: Pearl Harbor Investigations; Papers of Admiral H. R. Stark; Operational Archives Branch; NHC; Washington, D.C., 3–4. Also located at WPL-46 Letters (1939–1945); Box 147J, WPL-46—WPL-46-PC; Part III: OP-12B War Plans and Related Correspondence; Plans, Strategic Studies, and Related Correspondence (Series IX); Strategic Plans Division Records; Records of the Office of the Chief of Naval Operations, RG 38; NACP.

30. Ibid.

31. Admiral James O. Richardson, Commander-in-Chief, U.S. Fleet, and Rear Admiral Husband E. Kimmel, prospective Commander-in-Chief, Pacific Fleet, to Chief of Naval Operations, Subject: WPL 44—Advance Copy, January 28, 1941; WPL-46 Letters (1939–1945); Box 147J, WPL-46—WPL-46-PC; Part III: OP-12B War Plans and Related Correspondence; Plans, Strategic Studies, and Related Correspondence (Series IX); Strategic Plans Division Records; Records of the Office of the Chief of Naval Operations, RG 38; NACP, 6; original emphasis.

32. "Proposed Code of Laws of Maritime War," July 15, 1922; G.B. Study No. 438— July 15, 1922 Proposed Code of Laws of Maritime War; Box 168; Subject File 438; General Board, Subject File 1900–1947; GR Navy, RG 80; NABW.

33. General Board Hearing on Proposed Amendment of Rules for Maritime Warfare, April 30, 1941; G.B. Study No. 425-May 15, 1941, Amendment of Rules for Maritime Warfare; Box 133; Subject File 425; General Board, Subject File 1900–1947; GR Navy, RG 80; NABW, 1.

34. Orientation Lecture on International Law, issued December 16, 1938, 9–11.

35. Ibid.

36. Director, War Plans Division to Director, Central Division, Subject: "Instructions for the Navy of the United States governing Maritime Warfare" and "Rules for Aircraft in War," October 24, 1939; Folder 777, U.S. Navy, Naval War College—papers, 1933–1960; Box 64, U.S. Navy, Naval War College, 1933–1962; Series II: Organization and Project Files, 1918–1969; Papers of Samuel Flagg Bemis, Manuscript Group No. 74; Manuscripts and Archives, Yale University Library.

37. Orientation Lecture on International Law, issued December 16, 1938, 9–11.

38. Director, War Plans Division to Director, Central Division, Subject: "Instructions for the Navy of the United States governing Maritime Warfare" and "Rules for Aircraft in War," October 24, 1939.

39. General Board Hearing on Proposed Amendment of Rules for Maritime Warfare, April 30, 1941, 1.

40. *Instructions for the Navy of the United States Governing Maritime and Aerial Warfare, April 1940;* 425 1940; Box 133; Subject File 425; General Board, Subject File 1900–1947; GR Navy, RG 80; NABW, 12. See also *Tentative Instructions for the Navy of the United States Governing Maritime and Aerial Warfare, May 1941* (Washington, D.C.: U.S. Government Printing Office, 1941), 14.

41. *Instructions for the Navy of the United States Governing Maritime and Aerial Warfare, April 1940,* 2.

42. Judge Advocate General to Chairman General Board, Subject: Revision of "Instructions for the Navy of the United States Governing Maritime Warfare," August 15, 1940; 425 1940; Box 133; Subject File 425; General Board, Subject File 1900–1947; GR Navy, RG 80; NABW, 12.

43. Ibid., 12, 14.

44. Ibid., 14–15.

45. Chairman General Board to Secretary of the Navy, Subject: Revision of "Instructions for the Navy of the United States Governing Maritime Warfare," October 31, 1940; 425 1940; Box 133; Subject File 425; General Board, Subject File 1900–1947; GR Navy, RG 80; NABW.

46. Legal Adviser, Department of State, to Department of the Navy, Subject: "Draft Instructions for the Navy of the United States Governing Maritime and Aerial Warfare," January 28, 1941; Folder 777, U.S. Navy, Naval War College—papers, 1933–1960; Box 64, U.S. Navy, Naval War College, 1933–1962; Series II: Organization and Project Files, 1918–1969; Papers of Samuel Flagg Bemis, Manuscript Group No. 74; Manuscripts and Archives, Yale University Library, 7. See also James Forrestal, Acting Secretary of the Navy, to Secretary of State, March 6, 1941, 811.30/209 PS/01; Decimal File 811.30/209 PS/01; Box 3774, From: 811.25 Spiropolos, Gust Petter, To: 811.304 Barry/3; Decimal File, 1940–44; General Records of the Department of State, RG 59; NACP.

47. Rear Admiral R. E. Ingersoll, Acting Chief of Naval Operations, to All Ships and Stations, Subject: Tentative Instructions for the Navy of the United States Governing Maritime Warfare, February 1941, February 28, 1941; 425 1940; Box 133; Subject File 425; General Board, Subject File 1900–1947; GR Navy, RG 80; NABW.

1. Admiral Edward C. Kalbfus, Memorandum of Reminiscences at U.S. Naval War College, January 15, 1954; ADM E. C. Kalbfus: Correspondence, 1953–1954; Box No. 1; Series No. 1; Papers of Admiral Edward C. Kalbfus, Manuscript Group 50; Archival Records, U.S. Naval War College, Newport, R.I., 1–3.

2. Ibid., 3–8.

3. Directive for International Law Course, issued January 3, 1941; Directive for International Law Course, Sr., Jr. Classes of 1941; Box 95, Nos. 2261-DD-2268-B; Publications, RG 4; Archival Records, U.S. Naval War College, Newport, R.I., 1.

4. Charles Loebbaka, "Northwestern University Provost Emeritus Payson Wild Dies at Age 92," *Northwestern News,* February 24, 1998; available online at: http://www .northwestern.edu/univ-relations/media/news-releases/*archives97–98/*obits/wildbo-obit .html (accessed January 27, 2005). After thirteen years as a professor at Harvard, Wild went to Northwestern University, where he eventually became dean of faculties and provost. As a provost emeritus, he died in February 1998, at ninety-two years of age.

5. Orientation Lecture on International Law, issued December 16, 1938; Orientation Lecture on International Law, December 16, 1938; Box 86, Nos. 2197-IL2–2201; Publications, RG 4; Archival Records, U.S. Naval War College, Newport, R.I., 18–19.

6. Professor George Grafton Wilson, Professor of International Law, Harvard University, to Admiral Hilary P. Jones, USN, General Board, Navy Department, Washington, D.C., May 2, 1925; 438 1924–1925; Box 168; Subject File 438; General Board, Subject File 1900–1947; GR Navy, RG 80; NABW.

7. Directive for International Law Course, issued January 3, 1941, 1.

8. Ibid., 6.

9. Ibid., 3; original emphasis.

10. Ibid., 11; original emphasis. Another copy of the major situation is located at A16–3(28)(Jan–Apr); Box 59; 1940–1941—Confidential; Formerly Security-Classified General Correspondence of the CNO/Secretary of the Navy, 1940–1947; GR Navy, 1798–1947, RG 80; NACP. Finally, a copy of the major situation is also enclosed in Frank Knox, Secretary of the Navy, to Chairman, General Board, Serial No. 154, April 4, 1941; G.B. Study No. 425-May 15, 1941, Amendment of Rules for Maritime Warfare; Box 133; Subject File 425; General Board, Subject File 1900–1947; GR Navy, RG 80; NABW.

11. Ibid., 2, 11–13.

12. Memorandum for Commander in Chief, U.S. Fleet, March 1, 1941; A16–3(28) (Jan–Apr); Box 59; 1940–1941—Confidential; Formerly Security-Classified General Correspondence of the CNO/Secretary of the Navy, 1940–1947; GR Navy, 1798–1947, RG 80; NACP. This memorandum is also enclosed in Frank Knox to the Chairman, General Board, Serial No. 154, April 4, 1941.

13. Memorandum on Annex D Major Situation, March 1, 1941; A16–3(28)(Jan–Apr); Box 59; 1940–1941—Confidential; Formerly Security-Classified General Correspondence of the CNO/Secretary of the Navy, 1940–1947; GR Navy, 1798–1947, RG 80; NACP, 1. This memorandum is also enclosed in Frank Knox to the Chairman, General Board, Serial No. 154, April 4, 1941.

14. Ibid., 2.

15. Ibid., 8–9.

16. Ibid., 9.

17. Ibid., 9–10.

18. Ibid., 12–13.

19. Ibid., 18–19.

20. Memorandum for the President, March 7, 1941; XLAI, 1939–1941; Box 88, XLAI-XLFG; Intelligence and Technical Archives, RG 8; Archival Records, U.S. Naval War College, Newport, R.I., 1.

21. Ibid., 2.

22. Ibid., 1–3.

23. Admiral Harold R. Stark to Rear Admiral E. C. Kalbfus, Serial No. 06013, March 15, 1941; A16–3(28)(Jan–Apr); Box 59; 1940–1941—Confidential; Formerly Security-Classified General Correspondence of the CNO/Secretary of the Navy, 1940–1947; GR Navy, 1798–1947, RG 80; NACP.

24. Rear Admiral E. C. Kalbfus to Admiral Harold R. Stark, Subject: Opnav Serial No. 03413, comments on, March 20, 1941; A16–3(28)(Jan–Apr); Box 59; 1940–1941—Confidential; Formerly Security-Classified General Correspondence of the CNO/Secretary of the Navy, 1940–1947; GR Navy, 1798–1947, RG 80; NACP.

25. Ibid., 1–2. See also Frank Knox to the Chairman, General Board, Serial No. 154, April 4, 1941. For the copy of the letter with the handwritten "WPL-44" see Rear Admiral E. C. Kalbfus to Admiral Harold R. Stark, Subject: Opnav Serial No. 03413, comments on, BuNav Copy, March 20, 1941; A16–3(28)(Jan–Apr); Box 59; 1940–1941—Confidential; Formerly Security-Classified General Correspondence of the CNO/Secretary of the Navy, 1940–1947; GR Navy, 1798–1947, RG 80; NACP, 2.

26. Captain F. L. Lowe to Commander L. S. Fiske, Memorandum for Commander Fiske, March 31, 1941; A16–3(28)(Jan–Apr); Box 59; 1940–1941—Confidential; Formerly Security-Classified General Correspondence of the CNO/Secretary of the Navy, 1940–1947; GR Navy, 1798–1947, RG 80; NACP, 1.

27. Ibid., 1.

28. Ibid., 2.

29. Ibid., 1.

30. Ibid., 1–2.

31. Ibid., 2; emphasis added.

32. Rear Admiral Royal E. Ingersoll to Frank Knox, Subject: Opnav Serial No. 03413, comments on, April 1, 1941; A16–3(28)(Jan–Apr); Box 59; 1940–1941—Confidential; Formerly Security-Classified General Correspondence of the CNO/Secretary of the Navy, 1940–1947; GR Navy, 1798–1947, RG 80; NACP. See also Frank Knox to Chairman, General Board, Serial No. 154, April 4, 1941.

33. General Board Hearing on Proposed Amendment of Rules for Maritime Warfare, April 30, 1941; G.B. Study No. 425-May 15, 1941, Amendment of Rules for Maritime Warfare; Box 133; Subject File 425; General Board, Subject File 1900–1947; GR Navy, RG 80; NABW, 1.

34. Chairman General Board to Secretary of the Navy, Subject: Proposed Amendment

of Rules for Maritime Warfare, Serial No. 154X, April 24, 1941; A16–3(28)(Jan–Apr); Box 59; 1940–1941—Confidential; Formerly Security-Classified General Correspondence of the CNO/Secretary of the Navy, 1940–1947; GR Navy, 1798–1947, RG 80; NACP, 1–2.

35. Ibid., 2, 4.

36. Ibid., 4.

37. Rear Admiral A. P. Fairfield, General Board, to Rear Admiral Kalbfus, President, Naval War College, April 21, 1941; G.B. Study No. 425-May 15, 1941, Amendment of Rules for Maritime Warfare; Box 133; Subject File 425; General Board, Subject File 1900–1947; GR Navy, RG 80; NABW.

38. Chairman General Board to Judge Advocate General, Subject: Proposed Amendment to "Instructions for the Navy of the United States Governing Maritime Warfare," April 25, 1941; A16–3(28)(Jan–Apr); Box 59; 1940–1941—Confidential; Formerly Security-Classified General Correspondence of the CNO/Secretary of the Navy, 1940–1947; GR Navy, 1798–1947, RG 80; NACP. Also located at G.B. Study No. 425-May 15, 1941, Amendment of Rules for Maritime Warfare; Box 133; Subject File 425; General Board, Subject File 1900–1947; GR Navy, RG 80; NABW.

39. Samuel F. Bemis, "Submarine Warfare in the Strategy of American Defense and Diplomacy, 1915–1945," December 15, 1961, unpublished TMs; Folder 785, U.S. Navy, Naval War College Paper, 1961; Box 65, U.S. Navy, Naval War College, 1961; Series II: Organization and Project Files, 1918–1969; Papers of Samuel Flagg Bemis, Manuscript Group No. 74; Manuscripts and Archives, Yale University Library, 25–26.

40. General Board Hearing on Proposed Amendment of Rules for Maritime Warfare, April 30, 1941, 1.

41. Ibid., 14–15.

42. Ibid., 18–19.

43. Ibid., 10–11.

44. Ibid., 19. *Navicert* stood for "navigational certificate." These were issued by the British during the First World War and allowed merchants to ship certain cargoes without fear of harassment during passage. See Paul G. Halpern, "World War I: The Blockade," in *Naval Blockades and Seapower: Strategies and Counter-Strategies, 1805–2005*, ed. Bruce A. Elleman and S. C. M. Paine, Cass Series: Naval Policy and History (London: Routledge, 2006), 98.

45. General Board Hearing on Proposed Amendment of Rules for Maritime Warfare, April 30, 1941, 5.

46. Ibid., 5–6.

47. Ibid., 15.

48. Ibid., 17–18.

49. Ibid., 16–17.

50. Ibid., 16.

51. Ibid.

52. Ibid., 17. One presumes that Mr. McNemar was referring to the commander-in-chief of a combatant fleet, such as the commander-in-chief of the Asiatic Fleet or the commander-in-chief of the U.S. Fleet, not the president of the United States, who is constitutionally appointed commander-in-chief of the armed forces. At one point during

the war, President Roosevelt proposed to eliminate the title of commander-in-chief for the various fleets, partially to eliminate confusion and probably for his own ego. Admiral King forestalled this attempt. See Thomas B. Buell, *Master of Sea Power: A Biography of Fleet Admiral Ernest J. King* (Boston: Little, Brown, 1980), 243.

53. General Board Hearing on Proposed Amendment of Rules for Maritime Warfare, April 30, 1941, 17.

54. Ibid., 18–19.

55. Ibid., 19; emphasis added.

56. Ibid., 18.

57. Ibid., 20.

58. Ibid., 21–23.

59. Ibid., 23. Compare to "An Attempt to Interpret the Treaty entered into to make more effective the Rules adopted by Civilized Nations for the Protection of the Lives of Neutrals and Noncombatants at Sea in time of war," February 13, 1922; 438 22; Box 168; Subject File 438; General Board, Subject File 1900–1947; GR Navy, RG 80; NABW, 9.

60. General Board Hearing on Proposed Amendment of Rules for Maritime Warfare, April 30, 1941, 23.

61. Ibid.

62. Ibid., 28–29.

63. Ibid., 23.

64. Chairman General Board to Secretary of the Navy, Subject: Rules for Maritime Warfare, Serial No. 154, May 15, 1941; A16-3(28)(May–Dec); Box 60; 1940–1941—Confidential; Formerly Security-Classified General Correspondence of the CNO/Secretary of the Navy, 1940–1947; GR Navy, 1798–1947, RG 80; NACP, 1. Also located at 425 January–June 1941; Box 134; Subject File 425; General Board, Subject File 1900–1947; GR Navy, RG 80; NABW.

65. Ibid., 2; emphasis added.

66. Ibid., 3.

67. Ibid., 3–4; emphasis added.

68. Ibid., 8.

69. Enclosure (B) of Chairman General Board to Secretary of the Navy, Subject: Rules for Maritime Warfare, Serial No. 154, May 15, 1941, Proposed Letter of Information Concerning Maritime Warfare; 425 January–June 1941; Box 134; Subject File 425; General Board, Subject File 1900–1947; GR Navy, RG 80; NABW, 1–2.

70. Ibid., 2–3.

71. Bemis, "Submarine Warfare in the Strategy of American Defense and Diplomacy," 27. Bemis quoted from a letter between Turner and the director, Central Division, dated May 21, 1941. Unfortunately, this letter is no longer filed where Bemis cited it, in the appropriate folder A16-3(28); 1940–1941—Confidential; Formerly Security-Classified General Correspondence of the CNO/Secretary of the Navy, 1940–1947; GR Navy, 1798–1947, RG 80; NACP.

72. Chief of Naval Operations to Secretary of the Navy, Subject: Rules for Maritime Warfare, December 10, 1941; A16-3(28)(May–Dec); Box 60; 1940–1941—Confidential; Formerly Security-Classified General Correspondence of the CNO/Secretary of the

Navy, 1940–1947; GR Navy, 1798–1947, RG 80; NACP. Also located at 425 January–June 1941; Box 134; Subject File 425; General Board, Subject File 1900–1947; GR Navy, RG 80; NABW.

CHAPTER 8

1. WPL-46, Naval Basic War Plan—Rainbow No. 5, U.S. Navy, May 1941; WPL-46 Rainbow 5: Working Copy #3; Box 147J, WPL-46—WPL-46-PC; Part III: OP-12B War Plans and Related Correspondence; Plans, Strategic Studies, and Related Correspondence (Series IX); Strategic Plans Division Records; Records of the Office of the Chief of Naval Operations, RG 38; NACP, 58.

2. Ibid. Compare to WPL-44, Naval Basic War Plan—Rainbow No. 3, U.S. Navy, December 1940; Box 33, WPL-44; WPL Series; War Plans Division; Strategic Plans Division Records; Records of the Office of the Chief of Naval Operations, RG 38; NACP, 42.

3. WPL-46, Naval Basic War Plan—Rainbow No. 5, U.S. Navy, May 1941, 58.

4. Admiral Harold R. Stark, Chief of Naval Operations, to Admiral Thomas C. Hart, Commander-in-Chief, U.S. Asiatic Fleet, USS *Houston,* July 3, 1941; Director, War Plans Division 1937–1941, Special File #1; Box 20; Series VII: Subject File; Personal Papers of Admiral Richmond Kelly Turner; Operational Archives Branch; NHC; Washington, D.C., 3.

5. Admiral E. J. King, Commander-in-Chief Atlantic Fleet, to Chairman, General Board, Subject: Priorities in 2-Ocean Navy Building Program, July 30, 1941; 420–2 1941–1942; Box 63; Subject File 420–2; General Board, Subject File 1900–1947; GR Navy, RG 80; NABW, 5.

6. Ibid., 4.

7. James Leutze, *A Different Kind of Victory: A Biography of Admiral Thomas C. Hart* (Annapolis: Naval Institute Press, 1981), 179–182, 186.

8. Admiral Thomas C. Hart, Commander-in-Chief, U.S. Asiatic Fleet to Chief of Naval Operations, Subject: PLENAPS, and associated correspondence—Forwarding of., August 7, 1941, Enclosure (A) PLENAPS; US-UK-Dutch Conversations Singapore-1941; Box 118, Miscellaneous—U.S.–U.K.; Anglo-American Cooperation, 1938–1944 (Series VII); Strategic Plans Division Records; Records of the Office of the Chief of Naval Operations, RG 38; NACP, 8.

9. Commander R. D. Coleridge, Royal Navy, and Major R. F. G. Jayne, Joint Secretaries, British Joint Staff Mission in Washington, to Commander L. R. McDowell, U.S. Secretary for Collaboration, Navy Department, Washington, D.C., Subject:- Action by Submarines against Merchant Ships, August 21, 1941; WPL-46 Letters (1939–1945); Box 147J, WPL-46—WPL-46-PC; Part III: OP-12B War Plans and Related Correspondence; Plans, Strategic Studies, and Related Correspondence (Series IX); Strategic Plans Division Records; Records of the Office of the Chief of Naval Operations, RG 38; NACP, 1.

10. Ibid.

11. Ibid.

12. Ibid., 1–2.

13. Ibid.

14. Rear Admiral Richmond K. Turner, Memo for War Plans Files, September 29, 1941; WPL-46 Letters (1939–1945); Box 147J, WPL-46—WPL-46-PC; Part III: OP-12B

War Plans and Related Correspondence; Plans, Strategic Studies, and Related Correspondence (Series IX); Strategic Plans Division Records; Records of the Office of the Chief of Naval Operations, RG 38; NACP, 1.

15. Ibid.

16. Ibid.

17. Ibid., 2.

18. Hyde quoted in ibid.

19. Ibid., 2–3.

20. Ibid., 3.

21. Ibid.; emphasis added.

22. Ibid.

23. Ibid.

24. Ibid., 3–4.

25. Janet M. Manson, *Diplomatic Ramifications of Unrestricted Submarine Warfare, 1939–1941*, Contributions in Military Studies, No. 104 (New York: Greenwood Press, 1990), 154–155.

26. Rear Admiral Richmond K. Turner, Memo for War Plans Files, September 29, 1941, Cover Memorandum.

27. Ibid.

28. Clay Blair Jr., *Silent Victory: The U.S. Submarine War against Japan* (Philadelphia, J. B. Lippincott, 1975), 82.

29. Captain Slade D. Cutter, interviewed by Paul Stillwell, *The Reminiscences of Captain Slade D. Cutter, U.S. Navy (Retired),* vol. 1 (Annapolis: U.S. Naval Institute, 1985), 254.

30. Admiral Thomas C. Hart, "ADM T. C. Hart Private Diary December 29, 1940–December 26, 1941"; Diary of Admiral Thomas C. Hart, December 29, 1938–June 12, 1960; Personal Papers of Admiral Thomas C. Hart; Operational Archives Branch; NHC; Washington, D.C., Entries of June 14 and 15, 1941.

31. Admiral Thomas C. Hart to Admiral Harold R. Stark, March 17, 1942; Hart, T. C. ADM Correspondence; Box 12; Series III: Subject Files; Papers of Admiral H. R. Stark; Operational Archives Branch; NHC; Washington, D.C., 1.

32. "U.S. Naval Administration in World War II: Submarine Commands, Volume I"; Submarines, All Commands Administrative History, Vol. 1 of 3; Box 354, Service Squadrons S-12—Submarines-all commands Admin History Vol. 1 of 3; Type Commands; World War II Command File; Operational Archives Branch, NHC, Washington, D.C., 114.

33. Ibid.

34. Ibid.

35. Commander L. R. McDowell, U.S. Secretary for Collaboration, to Commander The Hon. R. D. Coleridge, R.N., and Major R. F. G. Jayne, D.S.O., Joint Secretaries to the British Joint Staff Mission in Washington, Subject: Action by Submarines against Merchant Ships, October 20, 1941; WPL-46 Letters (1939–1945); Box 147J, WPL-46—WPL-46-PC; Part III: OP-12B War Plans and Related Correspondence; Plans, Strategic Studies, and Related Correspondence (Series IX); Strategic Plans Division Records; Records of the Office of the Chief of Naval Operations, RG 38; NACP, 1.

36. Ibid., 1.

37. Ibid., 2.

38. Ibid.; emphasis added.

39. Ibid.

40. Ibid., 3.

41. Ibid.

42. Ibid.

43. Chief of Naval Operations to Commander in Chief, U.S. Pacific Fleet, and Commander in Chief, U.S. Asiatic Fleet, Subject: Action by submarines against merchant raiders, October 21, 1941 (emphasis added); WPL-46 Letters (1939–1945); Box 147J, WPL-46—WPL-46-PC; Part III: OP-12B War Plans and Related Correspondence; Plans, Strategic Studies, and Related Correspondence (Series IX); Strategic Plans Division Records; Records of the Office of the Chief of Naval Operations, RG 38; NACP.

44. Wayne S. Cole, *Roosevelt and the Isolationists, 1932–1945* (Lincoln: University of Nebraska Press, 1983), 446–455. For the text of the revision, see Public Law 294–77th Congress, Chapter 472–1st Session, H.J. Res. 237, Joint Resolution, printed in *Neutrality Laws,* ed. Elmer A. Lewis (Washington, D.C.: U.S. Government Printing Office, 1951), 31.

45. Stetson Conn, Chief Historian, Office of the Chief of Military History, Department of the Army, to Samuel Flagg Bemis, June 27, 1961; Folder 780, U.S. Navy—Naval War College—1961 Jan–Jun; Box 64, U.S. Navy, Naval War College, 1933–1962; Series II: Organization and Project Files, 1918–1969; Papers of Samuel Flagg Bemis, Manuscript Group No. 74; Manuscripts and Archives, Yale University Library.

46. OpNav to CinCAF, 271422, November 28, 1941; Box 4, Decodes of Confidential and Secret Dispatches, Sept. 1941–Apr. 1942; Records Relating to the Asiatic Fleet and the Asiatic Defense Campaign 1933–1942; NHC; Records of the Office of the Chief of Naval Operations, RG 38; NABW. The time-date group of the message is "271422," which indicates the message was probably sent at 0352 Pearl Harbor Time, 27 November / 0922 Washington Time, 27 November / 1422 Zulu Time, 27 November / 2222 Manila Time, 27 November. This presumes that messages from Washington carried a Zulu time-date group.

47. Ibid.

48. Ibid.

49. Ibid.

50. Ibid.

51. Ibid.

52. OpNav to CinCPac and CinCAF, 272337, November 28, 1941; Box 4, Decodes of Confidential and Secret Dispatches, Sept. 1941–Apr. 1942; Records Relating to the Asiatic Fleet and the Asiatic Defense Campaign 1933–1942; NHC; Records of the Office of the Chief of Naval Operations, RG 38; NABW. The time-date group indicates that this message was probably sent at 1307 Pearl Harbor Time, 27 November/1837 Washington Time, 27 November/2337 Zulu Time, 27 November/0737 Manila Time, 28 November.

53. Unlike Pearl Harbor, Manila was equipped with a PURPLE decoding machine, which gave Hart access to the same intelligence as Washington. MAGIC was the code

name for decoding operations that decoded Japanese message traffic. See Leutze, *A Different Kind of Victory,* 207.

54. Herman Kahn to Samuel Flagg Bemis, May 31, 1961; Folder 780, U.S. Navy—Naval War College—1961 Jan-Jun; Box 64, U.S. Navy, Naval War College, 1933–1962; Series II: Organization and Project Files, 1918–1969; Papers of Samuel Flagg Bemis, Manuscript Group No. 74; Manuscripts and Archives, Yale University Library.

55. Secretary of War Henry Stimson quoted in Mr. Nuermberger to George H. Dengler, Subject: Request from Professor Bemis of Yale University, November 9, 1961; Folder 781, U.S. Navy—Naval War College—1961 Jul-Dec; Box 64, U.S. Navy, Naval War College, 1933–1962; Series II: Organization and Project Files, 1918–1969; Papers of Samuel Flagg Bemis, Manuscript Group No. 74; Manuscripts and Archives, Yale University Library, 1.

56. Ibid.

57. Secretary of War Henry Stimson quoted in ibid.; emphasis added.

58. Ibid., 4.

CHAPTER 9

1. *I-26*'s commander, Yokota Minoru, attacked the wooden steamer with a combination of deck guns and, eventually, torpedoes. The crew abandoned ship, and were last seen alive the next day by another Japanese submarine, *I-19*, which passed along some supplies in a rare act of mercy. Although Yokota allowed the crew to abandon ship, he still left them to the mercy of the seas in lifeboats, directly in contravention of the London Submarine Protocol. Consequently, the sinking of *Cynthia Olson* was undoubtedly an act of unrestricted submarine warfare. *Cynthia Olson* radioed her location as: 33°42' north latitude, 145°29' west longitude. See Burl Burlingame, *Advance Force—Pearl Harbor: The Imperial Navy's Underwater Assault on America* (Kailua: Pacific Monographs, 1992), 153–154, 175–178. See also Rear Admiral E. M. Eller to Samuel Flagg Bemis, May 5, 1961; Folder 780, U.S. Navy—Naval War College—1961 Jan-Jun; Box 64, U.S. Navy, Naval War College, 1933–1962; Series II: Organization and Project Files, 1918–1969; Papers of Samuel Flagg Bemis, Manuscript Group No. 74; Manuscripts and Archives, Yale University Library, 1. See also Rear Admiral E. M. Eller to Samuel Flagg Bemis, June 9, 1961; Folder 780, U.S. Navy—Naval War College—1961 Jan-Jun; Box 64, U.S. Navy, Naval War College, 1933–1962; Series II: Organization and Project Files, 1918–1969; Papers of Samuel Flagg Bemis, Manuscript Group No. 74; Manuscripts and Archives, Yale University Library, 1.

2. Admiral Thomas C. Hart, Commander in Chief, Asiatic Fleet, "Narrative of Events, Asiatic Fleet Leading up to War and from 8 December 1941 to 15 February 1942," June 11, 1942; Hart, Thomas C. ADM Narrative of Events, Asiatic Fleet, Leading up to War and from 8 Dec 1941 to 15 Feb 1942 No Ser.; Box 1726, Individual Personnel, Gower to Hay; WWII Action and Operational Reports; Records Relating to Naval Activity during World War II; Records of the Office of the Chief of Naval Operations, RG 38; NACP, 36. See also "U.S. Naval Administration in World War II: Submarine Commands, Volume I"; Submarines, All Commands Administrative History, Vol. 1 of 3; Box 354, Service Squadrons S-12—Submarines-all commands Admin History Vol. 1 of 3; Type Commands; World War II Command File; Operational Archives Branch, NHC, Washington, D.C., 114.

3. Admiral Thomas C. Hart to Admiral Harold R. Stark, November 20, 1941; Hart, T. C. ADM Correspondence; Box 12; Series III: Subject Files; Papers of Admiral H. R. Stark; Operational Archives Branch; NHC; Washington, D.C., 1.

4. Ibid., 3.

5. Admiral Thomas C. Hart, "ADM T. C. Hart Private Diary Dec. 29. 1940–Dec. 26. 1941"; Diary of Admiral Thomas C. Hart, Dec. 29, 1938–June 12, 1960; Personal Papers of Admiral Thomas C. Hart; Operational Archives Branch; NHC; Washington, D.C., Entry of November 17, 1941.

6. CinCAF to Asiatic Fleet, Commander 16th Naval District, 080345, December 8, 1941; Box 4, Decodes of Confidential and Secret Dispatches, Sept. 1941–Apr. 1942; Records Relating to the Asiatic Fleet and the Asiatic Defense Campaign 1933–1942; NHC; Records of the Office of the Chief of Naval Operations, RG 38; NABW.

7. ComSubAsiatic Flt to Sub 143, 080712, December 8, 1941; Box 4, Decodes of Confidential and Secret Dispatches, Sept. 1941–Apr. 1942; Records Relating to the Asiatic Fleet and the Asiatic Defense Campaign 1933–1942; NHC; Records of the Office of the Chief of Naval Operations, RG 38; NABW.

8. ComSubAsiatic Flt to Sub 141, 080731, December 8, 1941; Box 4, Decodes of Confidential and Secret Dispatches, Sept. 1941–Apr. 1942; Records Relating to the Asiatic Fleet and the Asiatic Defense Campaign 1933–1942; NHC; Records of the Office of the Chief of Naval Operations, RG 38; NABW.

9. Gordon W. Prange, in collaboration with Donald M. Goldstein and Katherine V. Dillon, *At Dawn We Slept: The Untold Story of Pearl Harbor* (New York: McGraw-Hill, 1981), 527.

10. Harry Hopkins, memorandum of December 7, 1941, quoted in Herman Kahn to Samuel Flagg Bemis, May 3, 1961; Folder 780, U.S. Navy—Naval War College—1961 Jan–Jun; Box 64, U.S. Navy, Naval War College, 1933–1962; Series II: Organization and Project Files, 1918–1969; Papers of Samuel Flagg Bemis, Manuscript Group No. 74; Manuscripts and Archives, Yale University Library, 1.

11. Ibid.

12. Herman Kahn to Samuel Flagg Bemis, May 25, 1961; Folder 780, U.S. Navy—Naval War College—1961 Jan–Jun; Box 64, U.S. Navy, Naval War College, 1933–1962; Series II: Organization and Project Files, 1918–1969; Papers of Samuel Flagg Bemis, Manuscript Group No. 74; Manuscripts and Archives, Yale University Library, 1–2. See also Stetson Conn, Chief Historian, Office of the Chief of Military History, Department of the Army, to Samuel Flagg Bemis, June 27, 1961; Folder 780, U.S. Navy—Naval War College—1961 Jan–Jun; Box 64, U.S. Navy, Naval War College, 1933–1962; Series II: Organization and Project Files, 1918–1969; Papers of Samuel Flagg Bemis, Manuscript Group No. 74; Manuscripts and Archives, Yale University Library. See also Edward S. Miller, *War Plan Orange: The U.S. Strategy to Defeat Japan, 1897–1945* (Annapolis: Naval Institute Press, 1991), 271, 314.

13. Samuel Flagg Bemis to Rear Admiral E. M. Eller, June 3, 1961; Folder 780, U.S. Navy—Naval War College—1961 Jan–Jun; Box 64, U.S. Navy, Naval War College, 1933–1962; Series II: Organization and Project Files, 1918–1969; Papers of Samuel Flagg Bemis, Manuscript Group No. 74; Manuscripts and Archives, Yale University Library.

14. Samuel F. Bemis, "Seminar and Panel Discussion—Prof. Bemis—Submarine Warfare," November 1, 1961, unpublished TMs; Box 65, U.S. Navy, Naval War College, 1961; Series II: Organization and Project Files, 1918–1969; Papers of Samuel Flagg Bemis, Manuscript Group No. 74; Manuscripts and Archives, Yale University Library. Also available in Box 3, Columbia University Oral Histories; Privileged Manuscript Collection; Operational Archives Branch, NHC, Washington, D.C., 14.

15. Rear Admiral E. M. Eller to Samuel Flagg Bemis, June 9, 1961, 1–2.

16. CNO to CinCPac, Com Panam, CinCAF, Pacific Northern, Pacific Southern, Hawaiian Naval Coastal Frontiers, 072252 December 7, 1941; Operation Orders, December 7, 1941–April 2, 1942; Operations Orders; Box 37; Reel 2; Military Files Series 1; Map Room Army and Navy Messages, December 1941–May 1942; Map Room Files of President Roosevelt, 1939–1945; available on microfilm.

17. Commander, Submarines, U.S. Asiatic Fleet, to Commander in Chief, U.S. Fleet and Chief of Naval Operations, Subject: War Activities Submarines, U.S. Asiatic Fleet, December 1, 1941–April 1, 1942, April 1, 1942; Asiatic Fleet, 1941–1945; Box 1; Papers of Admiral Thomas C. Hart; Operational Archives Branch; NHC; Washington, D.C., 11–12.

18. "U.S. Naval Administration in World War II: Submarine Commands, Volume I," 114.

19. Ibid., ii–iii.

20. CinCAF to Asiatic Fleet, Commander 16th Naval District, 080345, December 8, 1941.

21. Bobette Gugliotta, *Pigboat 39: An American Sub Goes to War* (Lexington: University Press of Kentucky, 1984), 88.

22. Ibid., 214–216.

23. Carl LaVO, *Back from the Deep: The Strange Story of the Sister Subs* Squalus *and* Sculpin (Annapolis: Naval Institute Press, 1994), 87.

24. Stanley Weintraub, *Long Day's Journey into War: December 7, 1941* (Dutton: Truman Talley Books, 1991), 257.

25. Ibid., 257–258. It is possible that Weintraub confused the loss of *Sealion*, *S-36*, *Shark*, and *Perch*, all from the Asiatic Fleet during the period of December 10, 1941, to March 3, 1942, with the solitary loss of *Sealion* on December 10, 1941. All the same, it is a revealing error.

26. W. J. Holmes, *Undersea Victory: The Influence of Submarine Operations on the War in the Pacific* (Garden City: Doubleday, 1966), 19. Compare this to the corresponding passage in the unpublished administrative history, "U.S. Naval Administration in World War II: Submarine Commands, Volume I," 114.

27. J. E. Talbott, "Weapons Development, War Planning and Policy: The U.S. Navy and the Submarine, 1917–1941," *Naval War College Review* 37, no. 3 (May–June 1984): 66.

28. Ibid., 66.

29. Thomas G. Shanks, *The American Atlas: Expanded Fifth Edition, U.S. Longitudes & Latitudes, Time Changes and Time Zones* (San Diego: ACS Publications, 1990), inside front cover, 77, 107. See also Thomas G. Shanks, *The International Atlas: Revised Third*

Edition, World Longitudes & Latitudes, Time Changes and Time Zones (San Diego: ACS Publications, 1991), 294.

30. Weintraub, *Long Day's Journey into War,* 667.

CHAPTER 10

1. Record of a conversation between Admiral Little and Rear Admiral Turner, USN, on December 7, 1941, December 8, 1941; Sea Frontier Commands; Box 69, Ponape—Sea; Miscellaneous Subject File (Series III); Strategic Plans Division Records; Records of the Office of the Chief of Naval Operations, RG 38; NACP, 3.

2. Samuel Flagg Bemis, Memorandum on Nimitz's Affidavit; Folder 778, U.S. Navy, Naval War College, 1958–1959; Box 64, U.S. Navy, Naval War College, 1933–1962; Series II: Organization and Project Files, 1918–1969; Papers of Samuel Flagg Bemis, Manuscript Group No. 74; Manuscripts and Archives, Yale University Library, 1–2; emphasis added.

3. Russell D. Buhite and David W. Levy, ed., *FDR's Fireside Chats* (Norman: University of Oklahoma Press, 1992), 179–180. See also President Roosevelt quoted in Carlton Savage, Assistant to the Assistant Secretary of State, to Secretary of State, September 19, 1941, 700.00112 Freedom of the Seas/102, Enclosure: The American Doctrine of Freedom of the Seas, Draft 1; 700.00112 Freedom of the Seas/100—700.00116/447; Box 1770, From: 700:00112 Freedom of the Seas, To: 700.00116 M.E./203; Decimal File, 1940–44; General Records of the Department of State, RG 59; NACP, 12. See also Carlton Savage, Assistant to the Assistant Secretary of State, to Secretary of State, September 19, 1941, 700.00112 Freedom of the Seas/102, Enclosure: The American Doctrine of Freedom of the Seas, Draft 2; 700.00112 Freedom of the Seas/100—700.00116/447; Box 1770, From: 700:00112 Freedom of the Seas, To: 700.00116 M.E./203; Decimal File, 1940–44; General Records of the Department of State, RG 59; NACP, 11.

4. Buhite and Levy, *FDR's Fireside Chats,* 180. See also President Roosevelt quoted in Carlton Savage, Assistant to the Assistant Secretary of State, to Secretary of State, September 19, 1941, 700.00112 Freedom of the Seas/102, Enclosure: The American Doctrine of Freedom of the Seas, Draft 1, 12. See also Carlton Savage, Assistant to the Assistant Secretary of State, to Secretary of State, September 19, 1941, 700.00112 Freedom of the Seas/102, Enclosure: The American Doctrine of Freedom of the Seas, Draft 2, 11.

5. Buhite and Levy, *FDR's Fireside Chats,* 181. See also President Roosevelt quoted in Carlton Savage, Assistant to the Assistant Secretary of State, to Secretary of State, September 19, 1941, 700.00112 Freedom of the Seas/102, Enclosure: The American Doctrine of Freedom of the Seas, Draft 1, 12. See also Carlton Savage, Assistant to the Assistant Secretary of State, to Secretary of State, September 19, 1941, 700.00112 Freedom of the Seas/102, Enclosure: The American Doctrine of Freedom of the Seas, Draft 2, 11.

6. Buhite and Levy, *FDR's Fireside Chats,* 184, 186. See also President Roosevelt quoted in Carlton Savage, Assistant to the Assistant Secretary of State, to Secretary of State, September 19, 1941, 700.00112 Freedom of the Seas/102, Enclosure: The American Doctrine of Freedom of the Seas, Draft 1, 12. See also Carlton Savage, Assistant to the Assistant Secretary of State, to Secretary of State, September 19, 1941, 700.00112 Freedom of the Seas/102, Enclosure: The American Doctrine of Freedom of the Seas, Draft 2, 11.

7. Secretary of State Cordell Hull, quoted in Carlton Savage, Assistant to the Assistant Secretary of State, to Secretary of State, September 19, 1941, 700.00112 Freedom of the Seas/102, Enclosure: The American Doctrine of Freedom of the Seas, Draft 1, 11. See also Carlton Savage, Assistant to the Assistant Secretary of State, to Secretary of State, September 19, 1941, 700.00112 Freedom of the Seas/102, Enclosure: The American Doctrine of Freedom of the Seas, Draft 2, 10.

8. Secretary of State Cordell Hull, quoted in Carlton Savage, Assistant to the Assistant Secretary of State, to Secretary of State, September 19, 1941, 700.00112 Freedom of the Seas/102, Enclosure: The American Doctrine of Freedom of the Seas, Draft 1, 11. See also Carlton Savage, Assistant to the Assistant Secretary of State, to Secretary of State, September 19, 1941, 700.00112 Freedom of the Seas/102, Enclosure: The American Doctrine of Freedom of the Seas, Draft 2, 10.

9. President Franklin Roosevelt's Message to Congress about SS *Robin Moor,* June 20, 1941; OF 4462, S.S. *Robin Moor* Incident, 1941; Box 1, OF 4454-OF 4484, OF 4485, Office of Strategic Services, 1940–October 1941; Official File; Franklin D. Roosevelt Presidential Library, Hyde Park, N.Y., 1.

10. Buhite and Levy, *FDR's Fireside Chats,* 191, 193–195. See also President Roosevelt quoted in Carlton Savage, Assistant to the Assistant Secretary of State, to Secretary of State, September 19, 1941, 700.00112 Freedom of the Seas/102, Enclosure: The American Doctrine of Freedom of the Seas, Draft 1, 13–14. See also Carlton Savage, Assistant to the Assistant Secretary of State, to Secretary of State, September 19, 1941, 700.00112 Freedom of the Seas/102, Enclosure: The American Doctrine of Freedom of the Seas, Draft 2, 12–13; emphasis added.

11. Carlton Savage, Assistant to the Assistant Secretary of State, to Secretary of State, September 19, 1941, 700.00112 Freedom of the Seas/102, Enclosure: The American Doctrine of Freedom of the Seas, Draft 1, 1–14.

12. Carlton Savage, Assistant to the Assistant Secretary of State, Memorandum for the Record, September 23, 1941, 700.00112 Freedom of the Seas/103; 700.00112 Freedom of the Seas/100—700.00116/447; Box 1770, From: 700:00112 Freedom of the Seas, To: 700.00116 M.E./203; Decimal File, 1940–44; General Records of the Department of State, RG 59; NACP. For the revised memorandum, see Carlton Savage, Assistant to the Assistant Secretary of State, to Secretary of State, September 19, 1941, 700.00112 Freedom of the Seas/102, Enclosure: The American Doctrine of Freedom of the Seas, Draft 2, 1–13. This draft is identical to the first draft, except for the excision of most of page 6, which described the difference between American attitudes before the First World War and American actions during the First World War.

13. Both Samuel Flagg Bemis and Janet Manson searched President Roosevelt's papers in the course of their research. In Bemis's case, the archivists at the time, particularly Herman Kahn and Elizabeth B. Drewry, searched for the documents as well. See Herman Kahn to Samuel Flagg Bemis, May 3, 1961; Folder 780, U.S. Navy—Naval War College—1961 Jan–Jun; Box 64, U.S. Navy, Naval War College, 1933–1962; Series II: Organization and Project Files, 1918–1969; Papers of Samuel Flagg Bemis, Manuscript Group No. 74; Manuscripts and Archives, Yale University Library, 1. See also Elizabeth B. Drewry, Director, Franklin D. Roosevelt Library, to Samuel Flagg Bemis, November 17,

1961; Folder 781, U.S. Navy—Naval War College—1961 Jul–Dec; Box 64, U.S. Navy, Naval War College, 1933–1962; Series II: Organization and Project Files, 1918–1969; Papers of Samuel Flagg Bemis, Manuscript Group No. 74; Manuscripts and Archives, Yale University Library.

In 2005, I also looked through the pertinent files at the Franklin D. Roosevelt Presidential Library in Hyde Park, N.Y., including the Official Files on the Navy Department (OF 18), the Chief of Naval Operations (OF 18r), the State Department (OF 20), the War Department (OF 25), the Joint Board (OF 25s), the Navy in World War II (OF 463c), Japan (OF 197), Sinking of American Ships, World War II, 1941–1942 (OF 463c), the American Merchant Marine (OF 99), the SS *Robin Moor* Incident, 1941 (OF 4462), and Neutrality (OF 1561); the President's Personal Files on Admiral Stark, Elihu Root, the Navy Department, and the chief of naval operations; the President's Secretary File for the Navy Department, State Department, and Neutrality files; and finally, documents in the President's Secretary File Safe File. Unfortunately, while there were a number of interesting documents, none was directly related to the decision to conduct unrestricted warfare in the Second World War.

14. For Hull, see G. Bernard Noble, Director, Historical Office, Bureau of Public Affairs, Department of State, to Samuel Flagg Bemis, October 31, 1961; Folder 781, U.S. Navy—Naval War College—1961 Jul–Dec; Box 64, U.S. Navy, Naval War College, 1933–1962; Series II: Organization and Project Files, 1918–1969; Papers of Samuel Flagg Bemis, Manuscript Group No. 74; Manuscripts and Archives, Yale University Library, 1–2. See also Mr. Nuermberger to George H. Dengler, Subject: Request from Professor Bemis of Yale University, November 9, 1961; Folder 781, U.S. Navy—Naval War College—1961 Jul–Dec; Box 64, U.S. Navy, Naval War College, 1933–1962; Series II: Organization and Project Files, 1918–1969; Papers of Samuel Flagg Bemis, Manuscript Group No. 74; Manuscripts and Archives, Yale University Library, 1–4.

For Stimson, see Samuel Flagg Bemis to Herman Kahn, June 3, 1961; Folder 780, U.S. Navy—Naval War College—1961 Jan–Jun; Box 64, U.S. Navy, Naval War College, 1933–1962; Series II: Organization and Project Files, 1918–1969; Papers of Samuel Flagg Bemis, Manuscript Group No. 74; Manuscripts and Archives, Yale University Library.

For Knox, see Elbert L. Huber, Archivist in Charge, Navy Branch, National Archives and Records Service, to Samuel Flagg Bemis, August 23, 1961; Folder 781, U.S. Navy—Naval War College—1961 Jul–Dec; Box 64, U.S. Navy, Naval War College, 1933–1962; Series II: Organization and Project Files, 1918–1969; Papers of Samuel Flagg Bemis, Manuscript Group No. 74; Manuscripts and Archives, Yale University Library.

15. Rear Admiral E. M. Eller to Samuel Flagg Bemis, February 2, 1962; Folder 782, U.S. Navy—Naval War College—1962; Box 64, U.S. Navy, Naval War College, 1933–1962; Series II: Organization and Project Files, 1918–1969; Papers of Samuel Flagg Bemis, Manuscript Group No. 74; Manuscripts and Archives, Yale University Library.

16. R. A. Winnacker, Historian, Office of the Secretary of Defense, to Samuel Flagg Bemis, June 29, 1961; Folder 780, U.S. Navy—Naval War College—1961 Jan–Jun; Box 64, U.S. Navy, Naval War College, 1933–1962; Series II: Organization and Project Files, 1918–1969; Papers of Samuel Flagg Bemis, Manuscript Group No. 74; Manuscripts and Archives, Yale University Library.

17. Rear Admiral E. M. Eller to Samuel Flagg Bemis, November 30, 1961; Folder 781, U.S. Navy—Naval War College—1961 Jul–Dec; Box 64, U.S. Navy, Naval War College, 1933–1962; Series II: Organization and Project Files, 1918–1969; Papers of Samuel Flagg Bemis, Manuscript Group No. 74; Manuscripts and Archives, Yale University Library.

18. Janet M. Manson, *Diplomatic Ramifications of Unrestricted Submarine Warfare, 1939–1941,* Contributions in Military Studies, No. 104 (New York: Greenwood Press, 1990), 174.

19. Ibid., 174.

20. Mr. Nuermberger to George H. Dengler, Subject: Request from Professor Bemis of Yale University, November 9, 1961, 1.

21. General Board Hearing on Proposed Amendment of Rules for Maritime Warfare, April 30, 1941; G.B. Study No. 425—May 15, 1941, Amendment of Rules for Maritime Warfare; Box 133; Subject File 425; General Board, Subject File 1900–1947; GR Navy, RG 80; NABW, 10–11, 19.

22. G. Bernard Noble, Director, Historical Office, Bureau of Public Affairs, Department of State, to Samuel Flagg Bemis, October 26, 1961; Folder 781, U.S. Navy—Naval War College—1961 Jul–Dec; Box 64, U.S. Navy, Naval War College, 1933–1962; Series II: Organization and Project Files, 1918–1969; Papers of Samuel Flagg Bemis, Manuscript Group No. 74; Manuscripts and Archives, Yale University Library.

In 2005, I looked through the pertinent files at the National Archives at College Park, Md. Except for documents filed under decimal number 700.00112 Freedom of Seas, which indicate that the State Department was intent upon defending freedom of the seas even if it meant war with Germany, there were no documents related to the decision to conduct unrestricted warfare. Among the pertinent files searched were the following: Naval vessels, rules, etc.; Navy Department; Navy advisers, affairs; Bombing of neutral merchant vessels; Legal Adviser; Naval Law; High seas, offenses committed on merchant vessels; Blockade, neutral commerce; Disarmament, 1930–1939; Disarmament Conference, 1930–1939; Convoying, merchant vessels; Convoying American merchant vessels; Commerce, neutral; and Prize money, naval. Under the decimal filing system, it is possible that some relevant documents might have been filed in a different place based on country codes. For this reason, I also attempted almost every possible permutation using the country codes of the time for the United States (11), Germany (62), and Japan (94).

23. Green H. Hackworth to Samuel Flagg Bemis, January 15, 1962; Folder 782, U.S. Navy—Naval War College—1962; Box 64, U.S. Navy, Naval War College, 1933–1962; Series II: Organization and Project Files, 1918–1969; Papers of Samuel Flagg Bemis, Manuscript Group No. 74; Manuscripts and Archives, Yale University Library.

24. Herman Kahn to Samuel Flagg Bemis, May 25, 1961; Folder 780, U.S. Navy—Naval War College—1961 Jan–Jun; Box 64, U.S. Navy, Naval War College, 1933–1962; Series II: Organization and Project Files, 1918–1969; Papers of Samuel Flagg Bemis, Manuscript Group No. 74; Manuscripts and Archives, Yale University Library, 1–2. See also Stetson Conn, Chief Historian, Office of the Chief of Military History, Department of the Army, to Samuel Flagg Bemis, June 27, 1961; Folder 780, U.S. Navy—Naval War College—1961 Jan–Jun; Box 64, U.S. Navy, Naval War College, 1933–1962; Series II: Organization and Project Files, 1918–1969; Papers of Samuel Flagg Bemis, Manuscript Group No. 74;

Manuscripts and Archives, Yale University Library. See also Edward S. Miller, *War Plan Orange: The U.S. Strategy to Defeat Japan, 1897–1945* (Annapolis: Naval Institute Press, 1991), 271, 314.

25. B. Mitchell Simpson, III, *Admiral Harold R. Stark: Architect of Victory, 1939–1945* (Columbia: University of South Carolina Press, 1989), 73.

26. Ibid., 74.

27. A fascinating example of how time shapes and modifies memory, particularly in war, can be found in John F. Guilmartin Jr., "Military Experience, the Military Historian, and the Reality of Battle," unpublished lecture/paper presented at the Shelby Cullom Davis Center for Historical Studies, Princeton University, October 8, 1982, unpublished TMs on file in the Center of Military History archive, 15–18. For a more extended discussion on the role of memory in history, see Jay Winter and Emmanuel Sivan, "Setting the Framework," in *War and Remembrance in the Twentieth Century*, ed. Jay Winter and Emmanuel Sivan (Cambridge: Cambridge University Press, 1999), 10–19.

28. Stetson Conn to Samuel Flagg Bemis, June 27, 1961.

29. Charles M. Barnes, Chief, Treaty Division, Proposal by the United States that all of the belligerent powers in the present war observe the terms of the 1907 Hague Convention respecting the laws and customs of war on land and other conventions regarding the conduct of land and naval warfare, May 20, 1942, FW700.00116/447, Cover Letter; 700.00112 Freedom of the Seas/100—700.00116/447; Box 1770, From: 700:00112 Freedom of the Seas, To: 700.00116 M.E./203; Decimal File, 1940–44; General Records of the Department of State, RG 59; NACP, 1–4.

30. Ibid., Enclosure: Memorandum on The Hague Conventions; 700.00112 Freedom of the Seas/100—700.00116/447; Box 1770, From: 700:00112 Freedom of the Seas, To: 700.00116 M.E./203; Decimal File, 1940–44; General Records of the Department of State, RG 59; NACP, 6.

31. Michael Nelson, ed., *Guide to the Presidency*, 2nd ed. (Washington, D.C.: Congressional Quarterly, 1996), 605–606. The Supreme Court in 1979 upheld the president's ability to unilaterally abrogate a ratified treaty, but legalists noted that this decision was based mainly upon the Supreme Court's belief that it had no jurisdiction in the matter, not on whether or not the president actually had such a right. The Constitution is unclear about which branch holds this authority, and both the executive and legislative branches have unilaterally terminated treaties upon occasion.

32. Louise Doswald-Beck, ed., *San Remo Manual on International Law Applicable to Armed Conflicts at Sea* (Cambridge: Cambridge University, 1995), 122. See also Stephen C. Neff, *The Rights and Duties of Neutrals: A General History* (Manchester: Manchester University Press, 2000), 184, 198–199, 204; Manson, *Diplomatic Ramifications of Unrestricted Submarine Warfare*, 182.

33. Samuel Flagg Bemis, Memorandum on Nimitz's Affidavit; Folder 778, U.S. Navy, Naval War College, 1958–1959; Box 64, U.S. Navy, Naval War College, 1933–1962; Series II: Organization and Project Files, 1918–1969; Papers of Samuel Flagg Bemis, Manuscript Group No. 74; Manuscripts and Archives, Yale University Library, 1–2.

34. Lieutenant Colonel Kenneth Keskel, U.S. Air Force, "The Oath of Office: A Historical Guide to Moral Leadership," *Air & Space Power Journal* 16, no. 4 (Winter 2002):

50. The exact oath, approved on July 11, 1868, is as follows: "I, A.B., do solemnly swear (or affirm) that I will support and defend the Constitution of the United States against all enemies, foreign and domestic; that I will bear true faith and allegiance to the same; that I take this obligation freely, without any mental reservation or purpose of evasion; and that I will well and faithfully discharge the duties of the office on which I am about to enter. So help me God."

35. U.S. Constitution, Art. VI; emphasis added.

36. Paul Roush, "Constitutional Ethics," in *Ethics for Military Leaders*, ed. George R. Lucas (Boston: Pearson Custom Publishing, 2000), 49; emphasis added.

37. William H. Rehnquist, *All the Laws But One: Civil Liberties in Wartime* (New York: Alfred A. Knopf, 1998), 38. Rehnquist's book is an excellent discussion of the conflict between military necessity and constitutional law.

38. Current Doctrine, Submarines, 1939, U.S.F. 25, Revised, prepared by Commander Submarine Force, April 1939; NRS 1977–86, Current Tactical Orders and Doctrine-Submarines, 1939–1944; Microfilm Reel; Operational Archives, NHC, Washington, D.C., 11.

39. "Submarine Operational History World War II, Prepared by Commander Submarine Force, U.S. Pacific Fleet, Volume 1 of 4"; Submarines Pacific Fleet, Operational History, Vol. 1 of 4; Box 357, Submarines, Pacific Flt-History—Bulletins, Submarine Vol. II, 1945; Type Commands; World War II Command File; Operational Archives Branch, NHC, Washington, D.C., 2, 7. As the source for his quotation Voge cited: "*Principles of International Law* by T. J. Lawrence—7th Edition. D.C. Heath and Co."

40. Clay Blair Jr., *Silent Victory: The U.S. Submarine War against Japan* (Philadelphia: J. B. Lippincott, 1975), 110. Blair wrote that Admiral Withers, commander, Submarine Force, Pacific Fleet, signed the authorization for unrestricted warfare, carried on board USS *Gudgeon* during the first war patrol from Pearl Harbor. According to Edward L. Beach, Admiral Nimitz signed the authorizations, but the practice eventually ended as unrestricted warfare became a fact of life in the Pacific War. See Edward L. Beach, *The United States Navy: 200 Years* (New York: Henry Holt, 1986), 485.

41. Beach, *The United States Navy*, 485.

42. Samuel F. Bemis, "Seminar and Panel Discussion—Prof. Bemis—Submarine Warfare," November 1, 1961, unpublished TMs; Box 65, U.S. Navy, Naval War College, 1961; Series II: Organization and Project Files, 1918–1969; Papers of Samuel Flagg Bemis, Manuscript Group No. 74; Manuscripts and Archives, Yale University Library. Also available in Box 3, Columbia University Oral Histories; Privileged Manuscript Collection; Operational Archives Branch, NHC, Washington, D.C., 16.

43. Memorandum on Annex D Major Situation, March 1, 1941; A16–3(28)(Jan–Apr); Box 59; 1940–1941—Confidential; Formerly Security-Classified General Correspondence of the CNO/Secretary of the Navy, 1940–1947; GR Navy, 1798–1947, RG 80; NACP, 1, 13.

CHAPTER II

1. Clay Blair, Jr., *Silent Victory: The U.S. Submarine War against Japan* (Philadelphia, J. B. Lippincott, 1975), 20, 84. See also Vice Admiral Charles A. Lockwood, *Sink 'Em All: Submarine Warfare in the Pacific* (New York: E. P. Dutton, 1951), 76.

2. Edward L. Beach, *Salt and Steel* (Annapolis: Naval Institute Press, 1999), 126–127. See also Blair, *Silent Victory,* 20, 61–62, 84; Lockwood, *Sink 'Em All,* 21, 75.

3. The story of American torpedo problems has been told in many studies. Undoubtedly, one of the best remains Clay Blair's *Silent Victory* (273–278, 429–431, 435–439). For Admiral Lockwood's discussion of his steady and prolonged fight to fix the faulty Mark XIV torpedo, see Lockwood, *Sink 'Em All,* 20–22, 75–76, 85–86, 88–89, 103–104, 111–114.

4. Beach, *Salt and Steel,* 127.

5. Blair, *Silent Victory,* 18–19.

6. Morton had concluded that the *Dolphin* was a "death trap" and should not be sent on any more war patrols. Consequently when he took *Dolphin* to sea, he failed to repair her deficiencies, and his squadron commander quickly relieved him of command. See Blair, *Silent Victory,* 251. See also James F. DeRose, *Unrestricted Warfare: How a New Breed of Officers Led the Submarine Force to Victory in World War II* (New York: John Wiley & Sons, 2000), 56.

7. Captain Brown was an experienced submariner, who himself had played football at the Naval Academy and later served as the football team's officer representative and manager during the early 1930s. Consequently, he either personally knew or had heard of numerous Academy football stars like Mush Morton and Slade Cutter, both of whom he fleeted up to command based in large measure upon their football achievements. In both cases, his unorthodox decisions were quite successful. Cutter and Morton tied as the second-top U.S. submarine aces of the war. One of the unsung heroes of the submarine force, Brown eventually earned flag rank and commanded the Submarine Force, U.S. Pacific Fleet, from 1949 to 1951. See Blair, *Silent Victory,* 251, 892, 984. See also Captain Slade D. Cutter, interviewed by Paul Stillwell, *The Reminiscences of Captain Slade D. Cutter, U.S. Navy (Retired),* vol. 1 (Annapolis: U.S. Naval Institute, 1985), 61, 152.

8. Although the legendary story of *Wahoo*'s third patrol has been told in virtually all books about the U.S. submarine force, the most complete version remains Dick O'Kane's first-person account. See Rear Admiral Richard H. O'Kane, *Wahoo! The Patrols of America's Most Famous World War II Submarine* (Novato: Presidio Press, 1987), 109–172.

9. Commander Edward L. Beach, *Submarine!* Bluejacket Books (Annapolis: Naval Institute Press, 1952), 36.

10. DeRose, *Unrestricted Warfare,* 4–6. DeRose focuses on five officers he called the "Wahoo Five," whom he credits with sparking the change that helped the submarine force succeed during the war. While his thesis is debatable, he certainly was correct to note the singular success of these officers, particularly Mush Morton, Dick O'Kane, and George Grider.

11. Keith Wheeler, *War under the Pacific* (Alexandria, Va.: Time-Life Books, 1980), 167.

12. Ibid., 70.

13. Blair, *Silent Victory,* 359–360.

14. Mark P. Parillo, *The Japanese Merchant Marine in World War II* (Annapolis: U.S. Naval Institute Press, 1993), 6–31, 63–83, 94–124. See also John Ellis, *Brute Force: Allied Strategy and Tactics in the Second World War* (New York: Viking, 1990), 468–476;

David C. Evans and Mark R. Peattie, *Kaigun: Strategy, Tactics, and Technology in the Imperial Japanese Navy, 1887–1941* (Annapolis: Naval Institute Press, 1997), 430–431.

15. Blair, *Silent Victory,* 551–552. See also Ellis, *Brute Force,* 470–471.

16. Oi Atsushi, "Why Japan's Antisubmarine Warfare Failed," in *The Japanese Navy in World War II: In the Words of Former Japanese Naval Officers,* 2nd ed., trans. and ed. David C. Evans, with introduction and commentary by Raymond O'Connor (Annapolis: Naval Institute Press, 1986), 397.

17. Ellis, *Brute Force,* 470–471.

18. Oi, "Why Japan's Antisubmarine Warfare Failed," 397–398. Oi actually specifies the date when the Japanese began to realize the Americans had solved their torpedo problems as August 20, 1943, about a month before the Americans officially considered their problems solved.

19. Blair, *Silent Victory,* 816–818. See also Ellis, *Brute Force,* 470–471, 474–475; Oi, "Why Japan's Antisubmarine Warfare Failed," 401–414; Parillo, *Japanese Merchant Marine,* 6–31, 63–73, 94–124.

20. Blair, *Silent Victory,* 844, 857–865. See also Ellis, *Brute Force,* 471–474.

21. Blair, *Silent Victory,* 877–879, 900. See also Oi, "Why Japan's Antisubmarine Warfare Failed," 392; Wheeler, *War under the Pacific,* 21–23; Parillo, *Japanese Merchant Marine,* 207, 243–244.

22. John W. Dower, *Embracing Defeat: Japan in the Wake of World War II* (New York: W. W. Norton/New Press, 1999), 91. See also *United States Strategic Bombing Survey, Summary Report (Pacific War)* (Washington, D.C.: U.S. Government Printing Office, 1946), 20–21; Parillo, *Japanese Merchant Marine,* 213–215.

23. Dower, *Embracing Defeat,* 90–93. See also Parillo, *Japanese Merchant Marine,* 215–221.

24. Oi, "Why Japan's Antisubmarine Warfare Failed," 414.

25. Blair, *Silent Victory,* 17–18.

26. Parillo, *Japanese Merchant Marine,* 225.

27. Blair, *Silent Victory,* 877–879. See also Wheeler, *War under the Pacific,* 21–23.

28. Masanori Ito, *The End of the Imperial Japanese Navy* (New York: Jove Books, 1956), 17.

29. "Submarine Operational History World War II, Prepared by Commander Submarine Force, U.S. Pacific Fleet, Volume 1 of 4"; Submarines Pacific Fleet, Operational History, Vol. 1 of 4; Box 357, Submarines, Pacific Flt-History—Bulletins, Submarine Vol. II, 1945; Type Commands; World War II Command File; Operational Archives Branch, NHC, Washington, D.C., 1–2; emphasis added.

30. Blair, *Silent Victory,* 106.

31. Ibid., 110. Blair wrote that Admiral Withers, commander, Submarine Force, U.S. Pacific Fleet, signed the authorization for unrestricted warfare, carried on board USS *Gudgeon* in the first war patrol from Pearl Harbor. According to Edward L. Beach, Admiral Nimitz signed the authorizations, but the practice eventually ended as unrestricted warfare became a fact of life in the Pacific War. See Edward L. Beach, *The United States Navy: 200 Years* (New York: Henry Holt, 1986), 485.

32. *Tentative Instructions for the Navy of the United States Governing Maritime and*

Aerial Warfare, May 1941, Reprinted April 1944, with changes issued to date (Washington, D.C.: U.S. Government Printing Office, 1944), 14–17. Compare to *Tentative Instructions for the Navy of the United States Governing Maritime and Aerial Warfare, May 1941* (Washington, D.C.: U.S. Government Printing Office, 1941), 14–17.

33. Cutter, *The Reminiscences of Captain Slade D. Cutter,* 1: 1, 72–73.

34. Ibid., 1:73. Perhaps the admiral had just seen *Pinocchio* (1940), inspiring his ambiguous answer.

35. Ibid., 1:74.

36. Ibid., 1:74–75.

37. Captain Slade D. Cutter, USN (Ret.), "Parks and the *Pompano,*" in *Submarine Stories: Recollections from the Diesel Boats,* ed. Paul Stillwell (Annapolis: Naval Institute Press, 2007), 6–7. See also Rear Admiral Julian T. Burke Jr., USN (Ret.), "Dodging Mines and Praying," in ibid., 189.

38. Blair, *Silent Victory,* 384–385.

39. O'Kane, *Wahoo!* 334.

40. Beach, *Submarine!* 36.

41. DeRose, *Unrestricted Warfare,* 81. The famous photograph of Morton and *Wahoo* sailing into Pearl Harbor, complete with broom and pennant, may be viewed at the photographic section of the NHC. See "Commander Dudley W. ("Mush") Morton," People—United States, Online Library of Selected Images, U.S. NHC Photographic Section, http://www.history.navy.mil/photos/pers-us/uspers-m/dw-mortn.htm (accessed August 29, 2005).

42. Some veteran submariners, like Wilfred Jay Holmes, even criticized Morton for risking his crew in the surface action against the *Buyo Maru*'s survivors. Holmes consistently criticized submarine commanders who risked their crews in unnecessary surface actions, and his opinion of Morton, while usually laudatory, was no different on this score: "There is no doubt that this remarkable man became intoxicated with battle, and when in that state of exhilaration he was capable of rash action difficult to justify under more sober circumstances." See W. J. Holmes, *Undersea Victory: The Influence of Submarine Operations on the War in the Pacific* (Garden City, N.Y.: Doubleday, 1966), 200.

43. O'Kane, *Wahoo!* 153–154.

44. Quartermaster Third Class David L. Johnston, USNR, Letter to the Editor about "Mush Morton and the *Buyo Maru* Massacre," by Ensign Joel I. Holwitt, U.S. Naval Institute *Proceedings* 129, no. 9 (September 2003): 24–26.

45. Lieutenant Commander David A. Adams, USN, prospective executive officer, USS *Honolulu* (SSN-718), Letter to the Editor about "Mush Morton and the *Buyo Maru* Massacre," by Ensign Joel I. Holwitt, U.S. Naval Institute *Proceedings* 129, no. 11 (November 2003): 24.

46. DeRose, *Unrestricted Warfare,* 65–66, 84.

47. Ibid., 287–288.

48. Blair, *Silent Victory,* 385.

49. Edwin P. Hoyt, *Submarines at War* (New York: Jove Books, 1983), 182–183.

50. DeRose, *Unrestricted Warfare,* 77, 94. The low percentage of fatalities arguably

supports Admiral Dick O'Kane's assertion that individual troops were not targeted, just their rafts and boats. See O'Kane, *Wahoo!* 153–154.

51. O'Kane, *Wahoo!* 175. See also Lockwood, *Sink 'Em All,* 69–71; Blair, *Silent Victory,* 365–368, 400.

52. Blair, *Silent Victory,* 386.

53. Ibid.

54. Ibid.

55. Adams, Letter to the Editor about "Mush Morton and the *Buyo Maru* Massacre," 24.

56. Samuel Flagg Bemis, Lecture Outline for History 32, Yale University, on Development of Belligerent Maritime Systems Affecting American Rights and Interests; Folder 778, U.S. Navy, Naval War College, 1958–1959; Box 64, U.S. Navy, Naval War College, 1933–1962; Series II: Organization and Project Files, 1918–1969; Papers of Samuel Flagg Bemis, Manuscript Group No. 74; Manuscripts and Archives, Yale University Library, 9.

57. Samuel F. Bemis, "Submarine Warfare in the Strategy of American Defense and Diplomacy, 1915–1945," December 15, 1961, unpublished TMs; Folder 785, U.S. Navy, Naval War College Paper, 1961; Box 65, U.S. Navy, Naval War College, 1961; Series II: Organization and Project Files, 1918–1969; Papers of Samuel Flagg Bemis, Manuscript Group No. 74; Manuscripts and Archives, Yale University Library, 4.

58. Emily O. Goldman, *Sunken Treaties: Naval Arms Control between the Wars* (University Park: Pennsylvania State University Press, 1994), 293–294, 317.

59. Clay Blair, *Hitler's U-Boat War: The Hunted, 1942–1945* (New York: Random House, 1998), 705.

60. This view is epitomized by a British staff letter to the U.S. Navy's senior naval leadership in the fall of 1941: Commander R. D. Coleridge, Royal Navy, and Major R. F. G. Jayne, Joint Secretaries, British Joint Staff Mission in Washington, to Commander L. R. McDowell, U.S. Secretary for Collaboration, Navy Department, Washington, D.C., Subject: Action by Submarines against Merchant Ships, 21st August, 1941; WPL-46 Letters (1939–1945); Box 147J, WPL-46—WPL-46-PC; Part III: OP-12B War Plans and Related Correspondence; Plans, Strategic Studies, and Related Correspondence (Series IX); Strategic Plans Division Records; Records of the Office of the Chief of Naval Operations, RG 38; NACP, 1.

61. The exact article is paragraph 45, in Part II, Section I, which states: "Surface ships, submarines and aircraft are bound by the same principles and rules." See Louise Doswald-Beck, ed., *San Remo Manual on International Law Applicable to Armed Conflicts at Sea* (Cambridge: Cambridge University, 1995), 15, 122. See also Stephen C. Neff, *The Rights and Duties of Neutrals: A General History* (Manchester: Manchester University Press, 2000), 184, 198–199, 204; Janet M. Manson, *Diplomatic Ramifications of Unrestricted Submarine Warfare, 1939–1941,* Contributions in Military Studies, No. 104 (New York: Greenwood Press, 1990), 182.

62. The exact article is paragraph 60, in Part III, Section IV. See Doswald-Beck, *San Remo Manual,* 20.

63. The exact article is paragraph 67, in Part III, Section V. See ibid., 21–22.

64. Ibid., 150–151.

65. Ibid., 151; emphasis added.

66. Ibid., 121–122.

67. Bemis, "Submarine Warfare in the Strategy of American Defense and Diplomacy," 54.

68. Manson, *Diplomatic Ramifications of Unrestricted Submarine Warfare,* 182.

69. Bemis, "Submarine Warfare in the Strategy of American Defense and Diplomacy," 55.

70. Ibid., 47.

71. Current Doctrine, Submarines, 1939, U.S.F. 25, Revised, prepared by Commander Submarine Force, April 1939; NRS 1977–86, Current Tactical Orders and Doctrine-Submarines, 1939–1944; Microfilm Reel; Operational Archives, NHC, Washington, D.C., 11.

72. The Japanese only "belatedly" began systematically convoying merchant ships after unrestricted warfare had taken a significant toll of the Japanese merchant marine. See Oi, "Why Japan's Antisubmarine Warfare Failed," 409. See also Evans and Peattie, *Kaigun,* 395–401, 434–441; *United States Strategic Bombing Survey,* 12.

CONCLUSION

1. Williamson Murray and Allan R. Millett, *A War to Be Won: Fighting the Second World War* (Cambridge: Belknap Press of Harvard University Press, 2000), 554–558.

2. Ibid., 224, 260, 554–558. See also Clay Blair Jr., *Silent Victory: The U.S. Submarine War against Japan* (Philadelphia, J. B. Lippincott, 1975), 852.

3. A detailed discussion explaining the German Navy's defeat in the Second World War is well beyond the scope of this study. Readers desiring an excellent and brief description of the flaws in German maritime strategy should read Holger H. Herwig, "Innovation Ignored: The Submarine Problem, Germany, Britain, and the United States, 1919–1939," in *Military Innovation in the Interwar Period,* ed. Williamson Murray and Allan R. Millett (Cambridge: Cambridge University Press, 1996), 239–241.

4. For a discussion of the role and history of the military and the civil authority, see Russell F. Weigley, "The American Military and the Principle of Civilian Control from McClellan to Powell," *Journal of Military History* 57, no. 5, Special Issue: Proceedings of the Symposium on "The History of War as Part of General History" at the Institute for Advanced Studies, Princeton, New Jersey (October 1993): 27–58.

5. Edward S. Miller, *War Plan Orange: The U.S. Strategy to Defeat Japan, 1897–1945* (Annapolis: Naval Institute Press, 1991), 352.

BIBLIOGRAPHY

PRIMARY SOURCES

Archival Sources

Archival Records, U.S. Naval War College, Newport, Rhode Island
Intelligence and Technical Archives, Record Group 8
Papers of Admiral Edward C. Kalbfus, Manuscript Group 50
Publications, Record Group 4
Franklin D. Roosevelt Presidential Library, Hyde Park, New York
Official File
President's Personal File
President's Secretary File
President's Secretary File Safe File
Manuscripts and Archives, Yale University Library, New Haven, Connecticut
Papers of Samuel Flagg Bemis, Manuscript Group No. 74
National Archives at College Park, Maryland
General Records of the Department of State, Record Group 59, Decimal File, 1940–44
General Records of the Department of the Navy, 1798–1947, Record Group 80, Formerly
    Security-Classified General Correspondence of the CNO/Secretary of the Navy,
    1940–1947
Records of the Office of the Chief of Naval Operations, Record Group 38, Records Relat-
    ing to Naval Activity during World War II
Strategic Plans Division Records
National Archives Building, Washington, D.C.
General Records of the Department of the Navy, 1798–1947, Record Group 80, General
    Board, Subject File, 1900–1947
Records of the Office of the Chief of Naval Operations, Record Group 38, Naval Histori-
    cal Center, Records Relating to the Asiatic Fleet and the Asiatic Defense Campaign,
    1933–1942
Operational Archives Branch, Naval Historical Center, Washington, D.C.
NRS 1977–86, Current Tactical Orders and Doctrine—Submarines, 1939–1944, micro-
    film reel
Office Files of Rear Admiral Samuel E. Morison, USNR

Papers of Admiral H. R. Stark
Personal Papers of Admiral Richmond Kelly Turner
Papers of Admiral Thomas C. Hart
World War II Command File, Type Commands

Unpublished Sources

Bemis, Samuel F. "Seminar and Panel Discussion—Prof. Bemis—Submarine Warfare," 1 November 1961. Unpublished TMs. Box 65, U.S. Navy, Naval War College, 1961. Series II: Organization and Project Files, 1918–1969. Papers of Samuel Flagg Bemis, Manuscript Group 74. Manuscripts and Archives, Yale University Library. Also available in Box 3, Columbia University Oral Histories, Privileged Manuscript Collection, Operational Archives Branch, Naval Historical Center, Washington, D.C.

———. "Submarine Warfare in the Strategy of American Defense and Diplomacy, 1915–1945," 15 December 1961. Unpublished TMs. Folder 785, U.S. Navy, Naval War College Paper, 1961. Box 65, U.S. Navy, Naval War College, 1961. Series II: Organization and Project Files, 1918–1969. Papers of Samuel Flagg Bemis, Manuscript Group No. 74. Manuscripts and Archives, Yale University Library.

Guilmartin, John F., Jr. "Military Experience, the Military Historian, and the Reality of Battle." Unpublished lecture/paper presented at the Shelby Cullom Davis Center for Historical Studies, Princeton University, October 8, 1982. Unpublished TMs, on file in the Center of Military History, Collins Hall, Fort Lesley J. McNair, Washington, D.C.

Papadopoulos, Randy. "Between Fleet Scouts and Commerce Raiders: Submarine Warfare Theories and Doctrines in the German and U.S. Navies, 1935–1945." Unpublished TMs. Possession of author.

Rindskopf, Rear Admiral Maurice. NS402: Junior Officer Submarine Practicum Distinguished Speaker Lecture. Presented to students at U.S. Naval Academy, January 28, 2003.

"Submarine Operational History World War II, Prepared by Commander Submarine Force, U.S. Pacific Fleet, Volume 1 of 4." Unpublished TMs. Submarines Pacific Fleet, Operational History, Vol. 1 of 4. Box 357, Submarines, Pacific Flt—History—Bulletins, Submarine Vol. 2, 1945. Type Commands. World War II Command File. Operational Archives Branch, Naval Historical Center, Washington, D.C.

"U.S. Naval Administration in World War II: Submarine Commands, Volume I." Unpublished TMs. Submarines, All Commands Administrative History, Vol. 1 of 3. Box 354, Service Squadrons S-12—Submarines—all commands Admin History Vol. 1 of 3. Type Commands. World War II Command File. Operational Archives Branch, Naval Historical Center, Washington, D.C.

Published Sources

Doswald-Beck, Louise, ed. *San Remo Manual on International Law Applicable to Armed Conflicts at Sea.* Prepared by International Lawyers and Naval Experts convened by the International Institute of Humanitarian Law. Cambridge: Cambridge University Press, 1995.

Foreign Relations of the United States: Diplomatic Papers, 1930. 3 vols. Vol. 1. Washington, D.C.: U.S. Government Printing Office, 1945.

Foreign Relations of the United States: Diplomatic Papers, 1936. 5 vols. Vol. 1: *General, The British Commonwealth.* Washington, D.C.: U.S. Government Printing Office, 1953.

Hazlett, Commander E. E., Jr. "Submarines and the London Treaty." U.S. Naval Institute *Proceedings* 62, no. 12 (December 1936): 1690–1694.

Hearings before the General Board of the Navy, 1917–1950. Available on microfilm.

Hubbard, Lieutenant J. C. "Future Uses of Submarines." U.S. Naval Institute *Proceedings* 62, no. 12 (December 1936): 1721–1726.

Map Room Army and Navy Messages, December 1941–May 1942. Map Room Files of President Roosevelt, 1939–1945. Available on microfilm.

Neutrality Laws. Ed. Elmer A. Lewis. Washington, D.C.: U.S. Government Printing Office, 1951.

Rickover, Lieutenant H. G. "International Law and the Submarine." U.S. Naval Institute *Proceedings* 61, no. 9 (September 1935): 1213–1227.

Strategic Plans Division Records. Records of the Office of the Chief of Naval Operations, Record Group 38. Available on microfilm.

Tentative Instructions for the Navy of the United States Governing Maritime and Aerial Warfare, May 1941. Washington, D.C.: U.S. Government Printing Office, 1941.

Tentative Instructions for the Navy of the United States Governing Maritime and Aerial Warfare, May 1941, Reprinted April 1944, with changes issued to date. Washington, D.C.: U.S. Government Printing Office, 1944.

Withers, Rear Admiral Thomas. "The Preparation of the Submarines Pacific for War." U.S. Naval Institute *Proceedings* 76, no. 1 (April 1950): 387–393.

SECONDARY SOURCES

Adams, Lieutenant Commander David A., USN. (Prospective executive officer, USS *Honolulu* [SSN-718].) Letter to the Editor about "Mush Morton and the *Buyo Maru* Massacre," by Ensign Joel I. Holwitt. U.S. Naval Institute *Proceedings* 129, no. 11 (November 2003): 24.

Adams, Henry H. *Witness to Power: The Life of Fleet Admiral William D. Leahy.* Annapolis: Naval Institute Press, 1985.

Adler, Selig. *The Isolationist Impulse: Its Twentieth-Century Reaction.* Westport, Conn.: Greenwood Press, 1957.

Alden, John. *The Fleet Submarine in the U.S. Navy: A Design and Construction History.* Annapolis: Naval Institute Press, 1979.

Arnold-Foster, W. *The New Freedom of the Seas.* London: Methuen, 1942.

Beach, Captain Edward L. *Run Silent, Run Deep.* Introduction by Edward P. Stafford. Classics of Naval Literature. Annapolis: Naval Institute Press, 1955.

———. *Salt and Steel: Reflections of a Submariner.* Annapolis: Naval Institute Press, 1999.

———. *Scapegoats: A Defense of Kimmel and Short at Pearl Harbor.* Annapolis: Naval Institute Press, 1995.

———. *Submarine!.* Bluejacket Books. Annapolis: Naval Institute Press, 1952.

———. *The United States Navy: 200 Years.* New York: Henry Holt, 1986.

Bemis, Samuel Flagg. *A Diplomatic History of the United States,* 4th ed. New York: Henry Holt, 1955.

Blair, Clay, Jr. *Hitler's U-Boat War: The Hunters, 1939–1942.* New York: Random House, 1996.

———. *Hitler's U-Boat War: The Hunted, 1942–1945.* New York: Random House, 1998.

———. *Silent Victory: The U.S. Submarine War against Japan.* Philadelphia: J. B. Lippincott, 1975.

Borchard, Edwin, and William Potter Lage. *Neutrality for the United States.* New Haven, Conn.: Yale University Press, 1937.

Buell, Thomas B. *Master of Sea Power: A Biography of Fleet Admiral Ernest J. King.* Boston: Little, Brown, 1980.

Buhite, Russell D., and David W. Levy, ed. *FDR's Fireside Chats.* Norman: University of Oklahoma Press, 1992.

Burke, Rear Admiral Julian T., Jr. "Dodging Mines and Praying." In *Submarine Stories: Recollections from the Diesel Boats,* ed. Paul Stillwell, 186–190. Annapolis: Naval Institute Press, 2007.

Churchill, Winston S. *The Second World War: The Gathering Storm.* Boston: Houghton Mifflin, 1948.

Cole, Wayne S. *Roosevelt and the Isolationists, 1932–1945.* Lincoln: University of Nebraska Press, 1983.

Corbett, Julian S. *The League of Nations and Freedom of the Seas.* London: Oxford University Press, 1918.

———. *Some Principles of Maritime Strategy.* London: Longmans, Green, 1911.

Cutter, Captain Slade D. Interviewed by Paul Stillwell. *The Reminiscences of Captain Slade D. Cutter, U.S. Navy (Retired).* 2 vols. Annapolis: U.S. Naval Institute, 1985.

———. "Parks and the *Pompano.*" In *Submarine Stories: Recollections from the Diesel Boats,* ed. Paul Stillwell, 1–9. Annapolis: Naval Institute Press, 2007.

DeRose, James F. *Unrestricted Warfare: How a New Breed of Officers Led the Submarine Force to Victory in World War II.* New York: John Wiley & Sons, 2000.

Devlin, Patrick. *Too Proud to Fight: Woodrow Wilson's Neutrality.* London: Oxford University Press, 1974.

Dingman, Roger. *Ghost of War: The Sinking of the* Awa Maru *and Japanese-American Relations, 1945–1995.* Annapolis: Naval Institute Press, 1997.

Divine, Robert A. *The Illusion of Neutrality.* Chicago: University of Chicago Press, 1962.

Dower, John W. *Embracing Defeat: Japan in the Wake of World War II.* New York: W. W. Norton/New Press, 1999.

Dyer, Vice Admiral George Carroll, USN (Ret.). *The Amphibians Came to Conquer: The Story of Admiral Richmond Kelly Turner.* 2 vols. Washington, D.C.: U.S. Department of the Navy, U.S. Government Printing Office, 1972.

Ellis, John. *Brute Force: Allied Strategy and Tactics in the Second World War.* New York: Viking Books, 1990.

Evans, David C., and Mark R. Peattie. *Kaigun: Strategy, Tactics, and Technology in the Imperial Japanese Navy, 1887–1941.* Annapolis: Naval Institute Press, 1997.

Felknor, Bruce L., ed. *The U.S. Merchant Marine at War, 1775–1945.* Annapolis: Naval Institute Press, 1998.

Friedman, Norman. *U.S. Submarines through 1945: An Illustrated Design History.* Annapolis: Naval Institute Press, 1995.

Gara, Larry. *The Presidency of Franklin Pierce.* American Presidency Series. Lawrence: University Press of Kansas, 1991.

Goldman, Emily O. *Sunken Treaties: Naval Arms Control between the Wars.* University Park: Pennsylvania State University Press, 1994.

Grotius, Hugo. *The Free Sea.* Translated by Richard Hakluyt. Edited and with an introduction by David Armitage. Natural Law and Enlightenment Classics. Indianapolis: Liberty Fund, 2004.

Güçlü, Yücel. "The Nyon Arrangement of 1937 and Turkey." *Middle Eastern Studies* 38, no. 1 (January 2002): 53–70.

Gugliotta, Bobette. *Pigboat 39: An American Sub Goes to War.* Lexington: University Press of Kentucky, 1984.

Halpern, Paul G. "World War I: The Blockade." In *Naval Blockades and Seapower: Strategies and Counter-Strategies, 1805–2005,* ed. Bruce A. Elleman and S. C. M. Paine, 91–103. Cass Series: Naval Policy and History. London: Routledge, 2006.

Herwig, Holger H. "Innovation Ignored: The Submarine Problem, Germany, Britain, and the United States, 1919–1939." In *Military Innovation in the Interwar Period,* ed. Williamson Murray and Allan R. Millett, 227–264. Cambridge: Cambridge University Press, 1996.

Holmes, W. J. *Double-Edged Secrets: U.S. Naval Intelligence Operations in the Pacific during World War II.* New York: Berkley Books, 1979.

———. *Undersea Victory: The Influence of Submarine Operations on the War in the Pacific.* Garden City: Doubleday, 1966.

Hoyt, Edwin P. *Submarines at War.* New York: Jove Books, 1983.

Ito, Masanori. *The End of the Imperial Japanese Navy.* New York: Jove Books, 1956.

Jessup, Philip C. *Elihu Root.* Vol. 2: *1905–1937.* New York: Dodd, Mead, 1938. Reprint. Hamden, Conn.: Archon Books, 1964.

Johnston, Quartermaster Third Class David L., USNR. Letter to the Editor about "Mush Morton and the *Buyo Maru* Massacre," by Ensign Joel I. Holwitt. U.S. Naval Institute *Proceedings* 129, no. 9 (September 2003): 24–26.

Jonas, Manfred. Review of *Diplomatic Ramifications of Unrestricted Submarine Warfare, 1939–1941,* by Janet Manson. *American Historical Review* 97, no. 2 (April 1992): 548–549.

Keskel, Kenneth. "The Oath of Office: A Historical Guide to Moral Leadership." *Air and Space Power Journal* 16, no. 4 (Winter 2002): 47–57.

LaVO, Carl. *Back from the Deep: The Strange Story of the Sister Subs Squalus and Sculpin.* Annapolis: Naval Institute Press, 1994.

Leutze, James. *A Different Kind of Victory: A Biography of Admiral Thomas C. Hart.* Annapolis: Naval Institute Press, 1981.

Link, Arthur S., ed. *The Papers of Woodrow Wilson.* Vol. 41: *January 24–April 6, 1917.* Princeton: Princeton University Press, 1983.

Lockwood, Vice Admiral Charles A. *Sink 'Em All: Submarine Warfare in the Pacific.* New York: E. P. Dutton, 1951.

MacMillan, Margaret. *Paris 1919: Six Months That Changed the World.* New York: Random House Trade Paperbacks, 2001.

McBride, William M. *Technological Change and the United States Navy, 1865–1945.* Baltimore: Johns Hopkins University Press, 2000.

Manson, Janet M. *Diplomatic Ramifications of Unrestricted Submarine Warfare, 1939–1941.* Contributions in Military Studies, No. 104. New York: Greenwood Press, 1990.

Mars, Alastair. *British Submarines at War: 1939–1945.* Annapolis: Naval Institute Press, 1971.

Miller, Edward S. *War Plan Orange: The U.S. Strategy to Defeat Japan, 1897–1945.* Annapolis: Naval Institute Press, 1991.

Miller, Nathan. *Star-Spangled Men: America's Ten Worst Presidents.* New York: Scribner, 1998.

Morison, Samuel Eliot. *History of United States Naval Operations in World War II.* Vol. 1: *The Battle of the Atlantic, September 1939–May 1943.* Boston: Little, Brown, 1947.

———. *History of United States Naval Operations in World War II.* Vol. 4: *Coral Sea, Midway, and Submarine Actions, May 1942–August 1942.* Boston: Little, Brown, 1949.

Murray, Williamson, and Allan R. Millett. *A War to Be Won: Fighting the Second World War.* Cambridge: Belknap Press of Harvard University Press, 2000.

Neff, Stephen C. *The Rights and Duties of Neutrals: A General History.* Manchester: Manchester University Press, 2000.

Nelson, Michael, ed. *Guide to the Presidency.* 2nd ed. Washington, D.C.: Congressional Quarterly, 1996.

O'Kane, Rear Admiral Richard H. *Wahoo! The Patrols of America's Most Famous World War II Submarine.* Novato: Presidio Press, 1987.

Oi Atsushi. "Why Japan's Antisubmarine Warfare Failed." In *The Japanese Navy in World War II: In the Words of Former Japanese Naval Officers.* 2nd ed. Trans. and ed. David C. Evans, 385–414. With an introduction and commentary by Raymond O'Connor. Annapolis: Naval Institute Press, 1986.

Padfield, Peter. *War beneath the Sea: Submarine Conflict during World War II.* New York: John Wiley & Sons, 1995.

Parillo, Mark P. *The Japanese Merchant Marine in World War II.* Annapolis: U.S. Naval Institute Press, 1993.

Polmar, Norman, and Thomas B. Allen. *Rickover: Controversy and Genius: A Biography.* New York: Simon & Schuster, 1982.

Prange, Gordon W., with Donald M. Goldstein and Katherine V. Dillon. *At Dawn We Slept: The Untold Story of Pearl Harbor.* New York: McGraw-Hill Book Co., 1981.

Rehnquist, William H. *All the Laws But One: Civil Liberties in Wartime.* New York: Alfred A. Knopf, 1998.

Richardson, Admiral James O., as told to Vice Admiral George C. Dyer. *On the Treadmill to Pearl Harbor: The Memoirs of Admiral James O. Richardson, USN (Retired).* Washington, D.C.: Naval History Division, Department of the Navy, 1973.

Rodgers, William Ledyard. *Greek and Roman Naval Warfare: A Study of Strategy, Tactics, and Ship Design from Salamis (480 B.C.) to Actium (31 B.C.).* Annapolis: Naval Institute Press, 1964.

Roscoe, Theodore. *United States Submarine Operations in World War II.* Written for the Bureau of Naval Personnel from material prepared by Rear Admiral R. G. Voge, USN, Captain W. J. Holmes, USN (Ret.), Commander W. H. Hazzard, USN, Lieutenant Commander D. S. Graham, USN, Lieutenant J. J. Kuehn, USNR. Designed and illustrated by Lieutenant Commander Fred Freeman, USNR. Annapolis: Naval Institute Press, 1949.

Ross, Steven T., ed. *American War Plans, 1919–1941.* Vol. 3: *Plans to Meet the Axis Threat, 1939–1940.* New York: Garland Publishing, 1992.

Roush, Paul. "Constitutional Ethics." In *Ethics for Military Leaders,* ed. George R. Lucas, 45–50. Boston: Pearson Custom Publishing, 2000.

Ryan, James W. *Freedom of the Seas and International Law.* New York: Court Press, 1941.

Shanks, Thomas G. *The American Atlas: Expanded Fifth Edition, U.S. Longitudes & Latitudes, Time Changes and Time Zones.* San Diego: ACS Publications, 1990.

———. *The International Atlas: Revised Third Edition, World Longitudes & Latitudes, Time Changes and Time Zones.* San Diego: ACS Publications, 1991.

Simpson, B. Mitchell III. *Admiral Harold R. Stark: Architect of Victory, 1939–1945.* Columbia: University of South Carolina Press, 1989.

Spector, Ronald H. *Eagle against the Sun: The American War with Japan.* New York: Free Press, 1985.

Sweetman, Jack. *The U.S. Naval Academy: The Illustrated History.* 2nd ed., revised by Thomas Cutler. Annapolis: Naval Institute Press, 1995.

Talbott, J. E. "Weapons Development, War Planning and Policy: The U.S. Navy and the Submarine, 1917–1941." *Naval War College Review* 37, no. 3 (May–June 1984): 53–71.

Till, Geoffrey. *Maritime Strategy and the Nuclear Age.* London: Macmillan, 1982.

Trimble, William F. "Admiral Hilary P. Jones and the 1927 Geneva Naval Conference." *Military Affairs* 43, no. 1. (February 1979): 1–4.

United States Strategic Bombing Survey, Summary Report (Pacific War). Washington, D.C.: U.S. Government Printing Office, 1946.

Vlahos, Michael. *The Blue Sword: The Naval War College and the American Mission, 1919–1941.* U.S. Naval War College Historical Monograph Series, No. 4. Newport: Naval War College Press, 1980.

Weintraub, Stanley. *Long Day's Journey into War: December 7, 1941.* New York: Truman Talley Books, Dutton, 1991.

Weir, Gary E. *Building American Submarines, 1914–1940.* Contributions to Naval History, No. 3. Washington, D.C.: Naval Historical Center, 1991.

———. "The Search for an American Submarine Strategy and Design, 1916–1936." *Naval War College Review* 44, no. 1 (Winter 1991): 34–48.

Wheeler, Gerald E. *Admiral William Veazie Pratt, U.S. Navy: A Sailor's Life.* Washington, D.C.: Naval History Division, Department of the Navy, 1974.

Wheeler, Keith, and the Editors of Time-Life Books. *War under the Pacific.* Time-Life World War II Series. Alexandria, Va.: Time-Life Books, 1980.

Wildenberg, Thomas. *All the Factors of Victory: Admiral Joseph Mason Reeves and the Origins of Carrier Airpower.* Washington, D.C.: Brassey's, 2003.

Wilson, John R. M. "The Quaker and the Sword: Herbert Hoover's Relations with the Military." *Military Affairs* 38, no. 2 (April 1974): 41–47.

Winter, Jay, and Emmanuel Sivan. "Setting the Framework." In *War and Remembrance in the Twentieth Century,* ed. Jay Winter and Emmanuel Sivan, 10–19. Cambridge: Cambridge University Press, 1999.

ELECTRONIC SOURCES

"Commander Dudley W. ("Mush") Morton." People—United States. Online Library of Selected Images. U.S. Naval Historical Center Photographic Section. http://www.history.navy.mil/photos/pers-us/uspers-m/dw-mortn.htm (accessed 29 August 2005).

Loebbaka, Charles. "Northwestern University Provost Emeritus Payson Wild Dies at Age 92." *Northwestern News,* 24 February 1998. http://www.northwestern.edu/univ-relations/media/news-releases/*archives97–98/*obits/wildb0-obit.html (accessed 9 February 2005).

INDEX

Entries referring to photographs in the gallery following p. 96 are designated by figure number.

Adams, John, 11

air conditioning in submarines, 74–75

aircraft as war weapons and need for sub-marines, 25–26

all-electric drives in submarines, 72

antisubmarine warfare, 78, 80, 166, 167

Arabic (British passenger ship), 14–15

armament, submarine: deck guns, 68–69, 73–74; and tactics, 82; torpedoes, 72–73, 162–63, 164, 165–66

Arma Mk 3 TDC, 74

armed merchant ships: abolition of, 27, 28, 40; assumption of all ships as, 90–91, 124–25, 131, 175; General Board on, 108, 114–15, 117; as impetus for unrestricted warfare, 15–16, 27, 178–79; international law's acknowledgement of, 177; interwar failure to deal with, 30, 45–47; legislation to allow U.S., 132; limitation of commerce raiding to, 76–77; Naval War College on, 103–4, 105; as source of conflict in submarine's role, 24, 35, 38, 41; War Plans Division on, 106–7

Armed Neutrality (1780), 9–10

arms reduction efforts, 22–23, 32

Astral, 59, 60, 198n47

Aube, Adm. Théophile, 20

Baralong (British Q-ship), 15

Barb, USS, *fig. 4 gallery*

Barnes, Lt. Cdr. William H., 178

BARNEY, Operation, 166

Battle of the Atlantic, U.S. Navy's planning priority for, 85–86, 88

Bauer, Adm. Hermann, 62

Beach, Edward L., 160, 164, 171

Bemis, Samuel Flagg: on end of freedom of the seas, 175; on First Armed Neutrality, 9; on General Board's rejection of Naval War College, 109; on ineffectiveness of international law, 161; on ineffectiveness of Submarine Protocol, 178; on merchant ships as noncombatants, 2; on Navy's unilateral decision on unrestricted warfare, 155; on neutrality legislation, 59; and timing of unrestricted warfare order, 142, 144; on unilateral decision for unrestricted warfare, 136, 150; and U.S. support for freedom of the seas, 5

Bethmann Hollweg, Theobald von, 15

Blair, Clay, 167–68, 169, 174, 175

Bloch, Rear Adm. Claude C., 49–50, 70

blockades: British support for long-range, 31; close blockade, 9, 14, 62, 94–95, 102; First Armed Neutrality, 9; General Board on, 117; JAG view of, 94–95, 113–14; Naval War College on, 102–3; submarine's role in, 14, 62; in war plan against Japan, 65–66, 86; WWI blockade of Germany, 13

Borchard, Edwin, 45, 62

Britain, Great: abolition of submarines mis-sion, 20, 25–26, 43; and armed merchant

Britain, Great (*continued*)
ship problem, 16; civilian mariner casualties, 181–82; and free ships, free goods concept, 7–8; and London Naval Treaty, 44; opposition to absolute freedom of the seas, 12, 17–18; protection of merchant shipping in Mediterranean, 30; support for long-range blockades, 31; and unrestricted warfare, 61, 101, 121–27, 129–32, 198n50; U.S. commitment to support, 85; WWI threat from unrestricted warfare, 14–15

Brown, Capt. John H. "Babe," 164, 173–74, 224n7

Bryden, Maj. Gen. William, 85

bubble eliminator device, 74

Bureau of Ordnance, 162–63

Buyo Maru, 171–74, 226n42

Cachalot (V-8), USS, 71–72

capital ships: fleet submarine role as attacker of, 23–24, 63–64, 66–75, 77–78, 204n99; proposed reductions for London Naval Treaty, 32; submarine as cheap alternative, 19. *See also* cruiser rules of warfare

casualties, WWII: civilian mariners, 167, 181–82; Japanese civilian starvation/malnutrition, 1, 3, 167; from Morton's shooting of prisoners of war, 173

Catherine the Great of Russia, 9, 10

Christie, Ralph W., 67

Churchill, Winston S., 15, 30, 113

civilian leadership: Navy's lack of consultation prior to WWII hostilities, 144, 150–51, 154–58, 183–84; Stark's failure to inform on Navy's doctrine changes, 132, 135, 137–38

civilians. *See* casualties, WWII; merchant shipping

civil-military relationship, unrestricted warfare decision's strains on, 159–60, 183–84

Civil War, U.S., 12

Clark, Bennett Champ, 58

Clement, Lt. Col. William T., 139–40

close blockade, 9, 14, 62, 94–95, 102

coastal defense submarines, 70, 76

Coe, James, 146

Coleridge, Cdr. R. D., 122

combat areas/zones: British, 101, 121–22, 198n50; Germany's respect for, 59–60; Roosevelt's establishment of, 58–59. *See also* strategical areas

command leadership on submarines, problems with, 163–64

commerce raider, submarine as: command-level appreciation of, 121; effectiveness of, 164–68; French support for, 19–20; lack of training for role, 78; vs. naval combatant role, 63–64, 67–69; Navy's expectations for, 75–76; Root's attempt to deny, 33–34; and threat to freedom of the seas, 17, 18; U.S. acknowledgment of usefulness, 24. *See also* unrestricted submarine warfare

Conn, Steven, 132

Consolato del Mare, 7

contraband supplies and cruiser rules of warfare, 8, 9–10, 12, 95, 107

Control Force Conference, 67–69, 73

Corbett, Julian S., 17–18

Covington, USS, *fig. 1 gallery*

Crimean War, 10

criminal sanctions on submarine commanders, 33, 40

cruiser rules of warfare: and armed merchant ship problem, 24; contraband handling, 8, 9–10, 12, 95, 107; erosion of, 62; German observing of, 59–60; historical precedent, 6–7; impracticality for submarines, 14–15, 27, 46, 104, 108, 114–15, 125–26; interwar application to submarines, 42, 43–44; Naval War College's analysis of, 101; Navy's peacetime attachment to, 27–28, 66, 90, 118; and neutrality rights, 7–8; private property concept for merchant cargo, 6–7, 8; reinstatement of after WWII, 177–78; and revision to *Instructions*, 95; Root's attempt to apply to submarines, 33; as traditional treatment of merchant shipping, 14

Cutter, Capt. Slade D., 79, 81, 170

Cuttlefish (V-9), USS, 71–72, 73

Cynthia Olson (U.S. merchant ship), 139, 178, 215n1

Dana, Lt. Marshall M., 74
Daniels, Josephus, 27
deck guns for submarines, 68–69, 73–74
Declaration of London, 12–13
De Djure Praedae Commentaris (Grotius), 6–7
deep-diving approach, 80
DeRose, James F., 173
deterrent function of submarine, 26
diesel technology for submarines, 71–72
displacement, submarine, 71
Divine, Robert A., 53
Dolphin, USS, 73, 74, 224*n*6
Doyle, Capt. Walter, 129

economic considerations in U.S.'s loss of neutral rights, 49, 54–55, 56–57
economic warfare: cruiser warfare rules restrictions on, 104; effectiveness of, 21, 164–68, 179–80; legitimacy of, 38; as naval goal, 65–66; plan against Japanese, 1–4, 65–66, 86–87, 88–89, 125. *See also* commerce raider, submarine as
end-around tactic, 82
engines for pre-WWII U.S. submarines, 71–72
English, Rear Adm. Robert H., 67, 173
escorted convoys, rules on attacking, 114–15
Estimate of the Situation, 97–98
ethical issues. *See* moral issues
European Theater, U.S. Navy's planning priority for, 85–86, 88
Evans, Capt. W., 23

Fairfield, Adm. A. P., 107–8, 113, 115
Fife, Rear Adm. James, Jr., 128–29, 145, *fig. 8 gallery*
fire control computer developments, 74
First Armed Neutrality (1780), 9–10
Fiske, Cdr. L. S., 106, 110
Five-Power Naval Limitation Treaty (1922), 32
Five-Power Supplemental Treaty, 32–42
fleet submarine role, U.S. development of, 23–24, 63–64, 66–75, 77–78, 204*n*99
Fourteen Points, Wilson's, 17
France and submarine warfare, 19–20, 30, 31, 43–44
Franco, Francisco, 29

Franco-American Treaty (1778), 9
freedom of the seas: and abolition of submarines effort, 21–23; impracticality in submarine era, 37–38; interwar legislative loss of, 48–62; interwar violations in Mediterranean, 29–30; loss to unrestricted submarine warfare, 3, 171–76; Naval War College on, 104, 107; Navy's compromise on, 27–28; overview of U.S. position, 1–2; post-WWI debate on, 31–32; practical erosion vs. political illusion of, 116–17, 151–54; pre-WWI changes in, 5–13; U.S. commitment to, 5, 8–12, 14, 151–54, 181; WWI's effect on, 13–18
Freeman, Rear Adm. C. S., 70, 75, 76
free ships, free goods concept, 7–8, 9, 10
Furlong, Adm. W. R., 73

Gatch, Capt. Thomas, 110
General Board of the Navy: and fleet submarine development, 67, 73–74; on interwar debate over submarine warfare, 26–28; on Naval War College's analysis, 107–19; on neutral rights protection, 50, 55–58; photo, *fig. 2 gallery;* and revisions to *Instructions*, 92, 109–19; on Root's restrictions on submarines, 34–42
General Motors Winton diesel engine, 72
Geneva Naval Conference (1927), 42
Germany: military failure of unrestricted warfare for, 183; respect for U.S. combat area borders, 59–60; Roosevelt's condemnation of unrestricted warfare by, 151–53; U-boat casualties, 182; U-boats vs. U.S. fleet submarines, 204*n*99; and U.S. allowance for unrestricted warfare, 48, 49, 112, 114, 132–33; WWII submarine warfare, 61; WWI submarine warfare, 13, 14–16, 190*n*15
Gerow, Brig. Gen. Leonard H., 85
Great Britain. *See* Britain, Great
Greer, USS, 152–53
Grotius, Hugo, 5–7
Gugliotta, Bobette, 145–46

Habana Convention on Maritime Neutrality of American States, 42
Hackworth, Green H., 49, 157

Harding, Warren G., 31–32, 72
Hart, Adm. Thomas C.: and Fife, 128; on folly of abolishing submarines, 23–24; move toward unrestricted warfare doctrine, 90–91; photo, *fig. 9 gallery;* on size of submarines, 200*n*23; and SOC role in submarine development, 66–67, 69; and strategical areas as unrestricted war zones, 122; timing of orders for unrestricted warfare in WWII, 135, 140–49, 155
Hazlett, Cdr. Edward E., 77
Hendrix, "Monk," 146
Holland and free ships, free goods concept, 7–8
Holmes, Capt. Wilfred Jay, 78, 79, 147–48, 226*n*42
Holtzendorff, Adm. Henning von, 15–16
Hopkins, Harry, 141
Horne, Rear Adm. Frederick J., 110, 114
Hoyt, Edwin, 173
Hubbard, Lt. Joseph C., 77
Hughes, Charles Evans, 32
Hull, Cordell, 127, 136, 137, 152, 156
Hyde, Charles Cheney, 125

Ingersoll, Rear Adm. Royal, 85, 107, 118
Instructions for the Navy of the United States Governing Maritime Warfare, 24, 89, 91–96, 114, 174. *See also Tentative Instructions*
interdiction of enemy supplies vs. freedom of the seas, 7–8. *See also* economic warfare
international law: and abolition of submarines effort, 25; and constraints on building submarines, 70–71, 73; Declaration of London, 12–13; Declaration of Paris (1856), 10–12; First Armed Neutrality (1780), 9–10; Five-Power Supplemental Treaty, 32–42; ineffectiveness of, 29–47, 61, 161, 182; and legality vs. morality, 124, 126–27, 159–61, 169; London Naval Treaty (1930), 32, 42–47, 70–71, 73; vs. military necessity, 161, 178–80, 182–83; Nyon Agreement, 30, 45; and protection of unarmed merchant shipping, 16; and revision to *Instructions,* 91–96, 105–19; *San Remo Manual,* 176–78; Second London

Naval Treaty (1936), 2, 45; and strategical areas designation, 89. *See also* freedom of the seas; U.S. Naval War College "International Law and the Submarine" (Rickover), 45–47
isolationism, U.S. interwar, 51–53, 58, 85
Italy and submarine warfare, 29–30, 31, 45
Ito, Masanori, 168

JAG (judge advocate general), Navy: on Neutrality Acts, 55; and revisions to *Instructions,* 92–93, 94–95, 108, 110; Stark's lack of consultation with, 155
Japan: attack on *Cynthia Olson,* 139, 178, 215*n*1; attack on Pearl Harbor, 139–49, *fig. 10 gallery;* civilian casualties in, 1, 3, 167, 182; economic warfare plan against, 1–4, 65–66, 86–87, 88–89, 125; interwar acknowledgment of threat from, 23–24; and London Naval Treaty, 44–45; military control assumption for merchant vessels, 102, 131; moral justification for unrestricted warfare against, 124, 126–27, 159–61; neglect of merchant marine, 165–66; support for submarine warfare, 20–21
Jayne, Maj. R. F. G., 122
Jefferson, Thomas, 11
Jessup, Philip C., 41–42
Jeune Ecole, 19–20
Joint Board, 84–85
judge advocate general (JAG), Navy. *See* JAG (judge advocate general), Navy

Kalbfus, Rear Adm. Edward: on Neutrality Acts, 50–51, 55; and offer of comments on new *Instructions,* 105–6; photo, *fig. 7 gallery;* strategic analysis role, 97–105, 101
Kimmel, Rear Adm. Husband, 90, 92
King, Adm. Ernest J., 121
Knox, Frank, 107, 127, 141, *fig. 12 gallery*
Lage, William Potter, 62
Land, Cdr. Emory S., 25, 26
LaVO, Carl, 146–47
Layton, Vice Adm. Geoffrey, 121–22
League of Nations, 31, 192*n*10
The League of Nations and Freedom of the Seas (Corbett), 17–18
legal issues. *See* international law

Lehigh (U.S. merchant ship), 59, 60
"Letter of Information Concerning Maritime Warfare," 118–19
Leutze, James, 90
Lippman, Walter, 51–53
Lockwood, Vice Adm. Charles A., 73, 163, 170, 173
London Naval Treaty (1930), 32, 42–47, 70–71, 73
London Planning Section memorandum, 20–24
London Submarine Protocol (1936): currency of, 176; establishment of, 45; failure of in WWII, 62, 152, 159, 160; signatories, 195n61; and U.S. support for freedom of the seas, 2
Long Day's Journey into War (Weintraub), 147
long-range blockade: British support for, 31; Naval War College on, 102–3; submarine's role in, 14, 62; as type, 95; WWI, 13
Lowe, Capt. F. L., 106, 109, 110, 111–12
Lucas, Lt. Col. L. C., 92
Lurline, SS, 139
Lusitania (British passenger ship), 14–15

magnetic exploders for torpedoes, 162–63
Mahan, Alfred Thayer, 34–35
M.A.N. engine for pre-WWII U.S. submarines, 71–72
Manson, Janet M., 3, 127, 144, 155
Marcy, William L., 11
Mare Liberum (Grotius), 5–7
marine control stations, 131, 134
Mark XIV torpedo, 162–63
Marshall, Gen. George C., 84–85, 131
Masters, Ruth, 46
McNarney, Col. Joseph T., 84, 85
McNemar, Leslie C., 110, 111, 112, 114, 134
merchant shipping: deck guns as weapon of choice against, 74; early U.S. protection of neutral, 11–13; Italy's interwar attacks on, 29–30; Japan's, 102, 131, 165–66; and neutrality legislation, 9, 54–55, 103–4; noncombatant status of, 2, 5, 16, 18, 171–77; private property concept for cargo, 6–7, 8; Root's efforts to protect, 32–42; shipping lanes for neutral, 125, 131, 134; U.S. plan to attack Japanese, 1–4, 65–66,

86–87, 88–89, 125; WWI issues for, 13–18. *See also* armed merchant ships; cruiser rules of warfare; unrestricted submarine warfare
military necessity vs. international law, 161, 178–80, 182–83
Miller, Edward S., 65, 87, 184
minelaying role for submarines, 63, 64
Minnesota, USS, 64
moral issues: and conduct of unrestricted warfare, 16, 27–28, 168–75; freedom of the seas as moral right, 16, 56–57; justification for unrestricted warfare against Japan, 124, 126–27, 159–61; U.S. legitimizing of unrestricted submarine warfare, 60
Morison, Samuel Eliot, 142
Morton, Dudley W. "Mush," 163–64, 171–74, 224n6, 226n42
Mussolini, Benito, 29–30, 111

Napoleonic Wars, 10
Narwhal, USS, 74
Nautilus-class submarines, 73
naval combatant role for submarines, 63–64, 66, 75–76, 78, 82–83
naval forces. *See* Royal Navy; U.S. Navy
naval skirmisher role for submarines, 76
Naval War College. *See* U.S. Naval War College
The Netherlands and free ships, free goods concept, 7–8
Neutrality Act (1935), 49–51, 59–61
Neutrality Act (1939), 53–61, 112
Neutrality for the United States (Borchard and Lage), 62
neutrality legislation revision (1941), 132–33
neutral rights: early U.S. protection of, 8, 11–13; economic cost of loss of, 49, 54–55, 56–57; and exemption from search and seizure, 7–8; First Armed Neutrality, 9–10; and freedom of the seas, 6, 8; German violation of, 151–53; lanes for neutral shipping, 125, 131, 134; Naval War College's questioning of, 103–4; and nonbelligerent vs. neutral status, 103–4, 107, 108, 111, 116; responsibility not to carry contraband, 47; U.S. interwar giveaway of, 48–62

night surface attacks, 79–80, 82

Nimitz, Adm. Chester W., 105, 178

Nittsu Maru (Japanese merchantman), *fig. 14 gallery*

non-belligerent vs. neutral status, 103–4, 107, 108, 111, 116

noncombatants, merchant ship sailors as: Bemis on, 2; and moral problem of unrestricted warfare, 16; pre-WWI erosion of concept, 5; renewal of status in *San Remo Manual*, 176–77; vs. submarine as commerce raider, 18; U.S. role in abrogating protection, 171–76

Nuremberg tribunal, 176

Nye, Gerald, 58

Nyon Agreement, 30, 45

oath of office, naval officers' violation of, 159–60

offensive nature of submarines, 70, 73

O'Kane, Dick, 164, 171, 172

Operation BARNEY, 166

ORANGE, War Plan, 64–66, 70, 86

Pacific Theater. *See* Japan

Pan-American Maritime Law Treaty (1929), 42

Papadopoulos, Randy, 82

Parillo, Mark, 168

Paris Peace Conference (1919), 31

Parks, Lewis, 79, 81

passive sonar-only attack tactics, 78–79, 80

Pearl Harbor, Japanese attack on, 139–49, *fig. 10 gallery*

Pennell, James, 146

periscope observations, U.S. Navy's discouragement of, 78–79

Pierce, Franklin, 11, 187n20

piracy and privateering, 11

Plan Dog, 84–87, 88, 205n9

Plan of 1776, 8–9, 10–11

Pompano, USS, 79, 81

Porpoise-class submarine, 74

Pratt, Adm. William V., 43, 67

privateering, abolition of, 10–12

private property, merchant cargo as, 6–7, 8, 11

prizes, taking of, 120

qualified neutrality vs. non-belligerency, 111, 116

RAINBOW 1 war plan, 89

RAINBOW 3 war plan (WPL 44), 87–91, 104, 106

RAINBOW 5 war plan (WPL 46), 120–23, 125, 142

Reeves, Adm. Joseph M., 75, 202n59

retaliation justification for unrestricted warfare, 122, 126, 178, 198n50

Reuben James, USS, 60

Richardson, Adm. James O., 90, 92

Rickover, Lt. Hyman G., 41, 44, 45–47, 77

Robin Moor, SS, 59–60, 152

Robinson, Joseph T., 43, 194n54

Rodgers, Rear Adm. William Ledyard, 33–38, 65, 92, *fig. 2 gallery*

Roosevelt, Franklin D.: armed merchant ships permission, 132; avoidance of documentation for controversial decisions, 157–58; combat area designations, 58–59; on freedom of the seas, 2, 151–54; photo, *fig. 11 gallery*; on Plan Dog, 85; Stark's discussions with (1941), 137, 141–42

Root, Elihu, 32–33, 35, 41–42

Root treaty, 31–42

Roush, Paul, 159–60

Rowcliff, Adm., 110, 111, 115

Royal Navy, 25–26, 121–23

Russia and freedom of the seas, 9, 10

S-44, USS, *fig. 3 gallery*

Sagadahoc (U.S. merchant ship), 59–60, 198n47

Sailfish, USS, 146–47

Salmon-class submarines, 72, 73

sampans, ethics of sinking, 170–71

San Diego, USS, 64

San Remo Manual, 176–78

Savage, Carlton, 153–54

S-boat design, U.S., *fig. 3 gallery*, *fig. 4 gallery*

scouting role for submarines, 63, 76

Sculpin, USS, 146–47

Seadragon-class submarines, 72

Seahorse, USS, 170

Sealion, USS, 82, 147

search and seizure rules of naval warfare.
  See cruiser rules of warfare
Seawolf, USS, 74
Second Hague Conference (1907), 12
Second London Naval Treaty (1936), 2, 45
Sexton, Adm. Walton R., 112, 115, 116
shipping lanes for neutral merchants, 125,
  131, 134
Sieglaff, Barney, 169
Sims, Adm. William Sowden, 22–23
Snyder, Adm., 110
SOC (Submarine Officers Conference),
  66–70, 72–73
Some Principles of Maritime Strategy (Corbett), 17
Sound Military Decision (Kalbfus), 97–98,
  101
sound-only attack tactics, 78–79, 80
Soviet Union and protection of merchant
  shipping, 30
Spanish Civil War, 29–30
speed and submarine's role, 67, 69–70, 72, 82
Stark, Adm. Harold R.: on all Japanese
  merchants as armed, 90, 131; civilian
  authorization problem for unrestricted
  warfare orders, 132, 135, 137–38, 156, 157–
  58; and neutrality legislation, 54; photo,
  fig. 5 gallery, fig. 11 gallery; and Plan Dog,
  84–85; pre-Pearl Harbor instructions,
  133–38; reluctance to openly commit
  to unrestricted warfare, 105–7, 127; and
  revision to *Instructions,* 93, 118–19; and
  Roosevelt's public opposition to unrestricted warfare, 154; on strategical areas,
  120–21; and theater priorities for WWII,
  88; and unrestricted warfare orders timing, 140–49
State Department: as barrier to unrestricted
  warfare approval, 109, 111, 114, 125–26,
  129, 156–57; efforts to abolish submarines, 43; post-Pearl Harbor attitude on
  unrestricted warfare, 158; and revisions to
  Instructions, 93, 95–96, 109
Steele, Cdr. James M., 104
Stimson, Henry, 43, 136–37
stone blockade type, 95
strategical areas: as de facto war zones, 106,
  108, 119, 122, 125, 127, 130, 134; as defensive

war zones, 113; in RAINBOW war plans,
  87–91, 120–21
strategic blockade type, 94
strategic war zone type, 113
Sturgeon, USS, 147
Styer, Charles W., 67
Submarine Force doctrine, 75–78, 81–83
Submarine Officers Conference (SOC),
  66–70, 72–73
submarine patrols, definition, 76
submarine warfare: armament for submarines, 68–69, 72–73, 82, 162–63, 164,
  165–66; casualties for submariners,
  182; coastal defense role, 70, 76; efforts
  to abolish, 20–23, 25, 27, 31, 32; fleet
  submarine development, 23–24, 63–64,
  66–75, 77–78, 204*n*99; interwar attempts
  to limit, 29–30, 32–47; interwar Navy
  doctrine, 20–28, 75–78; military advantages of, 61–62, 86–87; pre-WWI Navy
  attitude, 19–20; submarine specifications
  and design, 66–67, 68–70, 71–72, *fig. 3
  gallery, fig. 4 gallery;* training for pre-
  WWII submariners, 78–81. *See also* commerce raider, submarine as; cruiser rules
  of warfare; Germany; international law
Sussex, 15
Swanson, Claude, 49

Talbott, J. E., 144, 148–49
Tambor-class submarines, 72, 73, 74
tankers, difficulty in taking out Japanese,
  165–66
Target Bearing Transmitter (TBT), 80
TDC (torpedo data computer), 74
technological advances in submarines,
  73–75
Tentative Instructions: vs. actuality of war
  plans, 114; debate on purpose of, 110;
  General Board's refusal to add to, 109–19;
  issuing of, 96; Naval War College's recommendations, 97, 104–5, 108
territorial waters, 6, 112–13
time zones and confusion over unrestricted
  warfare orders, 145, 148–49, 185*n*2
torpedo armament, 72–73, 162–63, 164,
  165–66
torpedo data computer (TDC), 74

trade, maritime. *See* economic warfare; merchant shipping

training for pre-WWII submariners, 78–81, 82

Treaties of Utrecht, 8

Treaty of Ghent (1812), 11

Treaty of Versailles (1919), 31

troop transports as enemy combat vessels, 77

Turner, Rear Adm. Richmond Kelly: character of, 87; and General Board's letter of information, 118; photo, *fig. 6 gallery;* and Plan Dog, 84, 85; and RAINBOW 3 war plan, 88; and reluctance to go public with unrestricted warfare, 129; on retaliation justification for unrestricted warfare, 150

two-ocean war, preparing for, 85–86, 121

U-boats, German, 13, 182, 183, 204*n*99

Undersea Victory (Holmes), 147–48

United States: as agent in loss of freedom of the seas, 48–62, 112, 114, 132–33, 171–76; armed merchant ships legislation, 132; commitment to freedom of the seas, 5, 8–12, 14, 151–54, 181; economic considerations in loss of neutral rights, 49, 54–55, 56–57; fleet submarines vs. German U-boats, 204*n*99; interwar view of submarine warfare, 21–23, 43; isolationism of, 51–53, 58, 85; restrictions on submarines as danger to, 38–39; submarine casualties, 182; U.S. commitment to Britain, 85. *See also* U.S. Navy

unrestricted submarine warfare: armed merchant ships as impetus for, 15–16, 27, 178–79; and Britain, 14–15, 61, 101, 121–27, 129–32, 198*n*50; civilian casualty cost of, 181–82; and civil-military relationship in U.S., 159–60, 183–84; decisive victory for U.S., 164–68, 184; by Germany, 48, 49, 112, 114, 132–33, 151–53, 183; Japanese use of, 139; as military necessity, 87, 178–80; moral issues in, 27–28, 124, 126–27, 159–61, 168–75; Naval War College's analysis of, 61–62, 99–105; neutrality legislation's legitimizing of, 50, 57, 58–59, 60, 132–33; passing on of expectation to commanders, 128–29; Pearl Harbor attack

as signal for use of, 139–49; post-WWII reapplication of restrictions, 176–78; in RAINBOW war planning, 89–90, 120–23; retaliation justification for, 122, 126, 178, 198*n*50; Rickover's argument for legitimacy of, 47; Root's proposal to outlaw, 34; Stark's orders concerning, 118, 132, 133–38, 140–49, 156, 157–58; as threat to freedom of the seas, 3, 171–76; U.S. commitment to start at outbreak of hostilities, 126–27, 129, 131–32, 139–49; U.S. opposition to, 23, 181; U.S. reluctance to commit until hostilities, 129–32; in WWI, 15. *See also* U.S. Navy

U.S. Naval Forces in Europe Planning Section, 21–24

U.S. Naval War College: General Board's reaction to analysis of, 107–19; on Neutrality Acts, 50–51, 55; and revision of *Instructions,* 92–93, 97, 104–5, 108; strategic analysis curriculum, 97–104; ultimate influence over Navy doctrine, 127; on unrestricted warfare, 61–62, 99–105; War Plans Division reaction to analysis of, 105–7

U.S. Navy: and appeal of unrestricted warfare, 2; avoidance of unrestricted warfare, 39, 76–77; and fight against Neutrality Acts, 48–62; fleet submarine development, 23–24, 63–64, 66–75, 77–78, 204*n*99; on inevitability of unrestricted warfare, 61–62, 123–27, 183; *Instructions,* 24, 89, 91–96, 114, 174; interwar submarine doctrine, 20–28, 75–78; lack of guidance on unrestricted warfare limits, 169–71, 173–74; Plan Dog, 84–87, 88, 205*n*9; pre-WWI debate on submarine's role, 19–20; RAINBOW war planning, 87–91, 104, 106, 120–23, 125, 142; rejection of abolition of submarines idea, 22–24; training for pre-WWII submariners, 78–81; transition to unrestricted warfare, 81–83; unilateral decision on unrestricted warfare, 132, 135, 137–38, 144, 150–51, 154–61, 183–84; War Plan ORANGE, 64–66. *See also* General Board of the Navy; JAG (judge advocate general), Navy; *Tentative Instructions*

V-7, USS, 71
V-8, USS, 71–72
V-9, USS, 71–72
Vlahos, Michael, 65
Voge, Rear Adm. Richard, 82, 168–69, 174–75
V-submarines, 71–72

Wahoo (SS-238), USS, 164, 171–74, fig. 13
  gallery
War of 1812, 11
War of Spanish Succession, 8
War Plan ORANGE, 64–66, 70, 86
War Plans Division: and British pressure
  for unrestricted warfare, 123–27; and
  fight against Neutrality Acts, 54–55;
  on Naval War College on unrestricted
  warfare, 105–7; Plan Dog, 84–87, 88,
  205n9; RAINBOW war planning, 87–91,
  104, 106, 120–23, 125, 142; and revision of
  Instructions, 93, 108, 110, 111–12. See also
  Stark, Adm. Harold R.
war warning message from Stark, 136
war zones for unrestricted submarine warfare: British, 101, 121–22, 198n50; General
  Board on, 108, 111–13, 116–17; Germany
  in WWI, 13; Germany's respect for U.S.,
  59–60; JAG on, 94; Naval War College
  on, 50–51, 62, 101–2, 103, 104; Navy's
  process toward accepting, 125, 130–31;
  Roosevelt's pre-WWII establishment of,
  58–59; War Plans Division on, 106. See
  also strategical areas

Washington Naval Treaty (1922), 32
Washington Submarine Treaty, 32–42
Weintraub, Stanley, 147
Wild, Payson S., Jr., 98–99, 101–2, 103–4,
  161, 208n4
Wilkins, Weary, 169
Wilson, George Grafton, 24, 92–93, 98–99
Wilson, Woodrow: and armed merchant
  ship problem, 16; vs. Britain on freedom
  of the seas, 13–14, 17–18; compromise
  on freedom of the seas, 17, 31; condemnation of unrestricted submarine warfare,
  16; freedom of the seas support from,
  2; vs. Germany on freedom of the seas,
  13–14
Winton diesel engine, 72
Withers, Rear Adm. Thomas, 80
World War I, 13–18, 63–64, 181, 190n15
World War II: London Submarine Protocol's
  failure in, 62, 152, 159, 160; Pearl Harbor
  attack and decision to go to war, 139–49,
  fig. 10 gallery; timing of orders for
  unrestricted warfare, 135, 140–49, 155;
  unrestricted warfare and victory for U.S.,
  164–68. See also Britain, Great; casualties,
  WWII; Germany

Yarnell, Rear Adm. Harry E., 23, 67, 200n17

zones dangerous to navigation, British, 101,
  121–22, 198n50